# THE SHELL GAME

# THE
# SHELL
# GAME

WRITERS PLAY WITH BORROWED FORMS

Edited and with an introduction by Kim Adrian

Foreword by Brenda Miller | Postscript by Cheyenne Nimes

UNIVERSITY OF NEBRASKA PRESS | LINCOLN AND LONDON

Acknowledgments for the use of copyrighted
material appear on pages 245–46, which
constitute an extension of the copyright page.

Library of Congress Control Number: 2017043654

Designed and set in Minion by N. Putens.

# Contents

# Foreword

Discovering the Hermit Crab Essay

BRENDA MILLER

In the summer of 2001, Suzanne Paola and I were hard at work writing *Tell It Slant: Writing and Shaping Creative Nonfiction*. We divvied up the chapters according to our interests, each of us bringing different perspectives to the many aspects we could cover under the umbrella of "creative nonfiction." I wrote most of my chapters at my desk in the two-room house I'd rented when I first moved to Bellingham, Washington: a blue shack above the railroad tracks with a view of the industrial shoreline of Bellingham Bay. My cat, Madrona, kept me company, sitting on the wide windowsill and twitching her tail.

It was a beautiful summer, as summers often are in the Pacific Northwest. So as I was wrestling with the chapter called "The Lyric Essay," I abandoned my desk and my cat, heading out to my favorite place on the planet: Deception Pass State Park. This park is named for the treacherous currents that eddy and flow under two immensely high bridges spanning Fidalgo and Whidbey Islands. As you cross those bridges, you feel neither here nor there, suspended in air with views of water blaring from every side. You are blessedly out of your element, dangerously so—in a state the romantics called *sublime*.

I had been immersed in a lyric mindset for days, so Deception Pass seemed, itself, to be a lyric essay: a place where beauty juts up against danger, where the contrasting parts come together to make new, unexpected sense. At Deception Pass, you can be surprised at every turn: by a clutch of madrones precipitously leaning out across the water or a mermaid totem that narrates, through images, an ancient Salish legend of transformation. Tide pools appear at low tide, exposing creatures who are usually hidden.

I'd been pondering a particular form of lyric essay that "borrows" other forms to tell its story: essays in the forms of recipes, for example, or field guides, or indexes. But this form demanded something more imagistic, more metaphoric, more, well, *lyric* to describe it. In these essays—which I'd been writing for a few years—my narrative voice had been transformed; I was able to express things I'd never been able to do in any other way (or that I didn't even know I wanted to express). Though my narrative self was vulnerable, it also felt powerful, protected. For example, I wrote an essay called "How to Meditate" that, under cover of the instructional form, was able to distill years of intensive meditative practice into one ten-day writing retreat. Along the way this essay divulged the humor, the pain, and the complexity of this practice for a young woman just finding her way as an adult.

As I crouched down in the tide pools, I saw a whelk shell scuttling about, seemingly on its own. It settled, moved a few inches, and then settled again. I realized I was seeing a hermit crab, a creature who forages for abandoned shells in order to survive. I eventually described them this way in *Tell It Slant*:

> A hermit crab is a strange animal, born without the armor to protect its soft, exposed abdomen. And so it spends its life occupying the empty, often beautiful, shells left by snails or other mollusks. It reanimates these shells, making of them a strange new hybrid creature that has its own particular beauty, its own way of moving through the tide pools and among the rocks. Each one will be slightly different, depending on the type of shell it decides to inhabit.

I continued my walk around the windswept headlands of Deception Pass, noting with enhanced pleasure the view out to the Olympics, layered with islands dotting the horizon. I mused on the chapter I'd been writing, and by the time I returned home to my humble shack, I understood that the hermit crab—a creature who would die without finding its borrowed shell—provided the perfect metaphor for the essays I'd been writing and reading: essays that have their own "soft, exposed" abdomens. The form acts as a cover, a protection, for this material to move into the world.

So I anointed this type of creative nonfiction the "hermit crab essay" as a way to explain, through metaphor, how a writer can play with form to deal with difficult material that might not be able to live in the world without its own borrowed "shell."

Suzanne and I are delighted that, years after the publication of the first edition of *Tell It Slant*, the term "hermit crab essay" has become an integral and accepted part of the creative nonfiction lexicon. With every iteration, both the hermit crab creature and the hermit crab essay become more deeply understood, and the possibilities for the form grow by the day. We've always thought there should be an anthology devoted to these inventive forms, and we're so glad that this one, *The Shell Game*, now exists. This book will be a fascinating read for all those who love writing that propels us beyond the edges of the known world.

# Introduction

A Natural History of the North American Hermit Crab Essay

KIM ADRIAN

**TAXONOMY**

DOMAIN: Anima

   KINGDOM: Homo Sentio

      PHYLUM: Ars

         CLASS: Litterae

            ORDER: Exagium

               FAMILY: Lyrica

                  GENUS: *Paguridae*

**COMMON NAME**

Hermit crab essay[*]

**ALTERNATE NAMES**

Borrowed form; appropriated form; received form; hybrid; false document; readymade; curio.

**NUMBER OF SPECIES**

Theoretically infinite, realistically somewhere in the thousands. Maybe tens of. Some of the more conspicuous include: grocery lists; how-to instructions; job applications; syllabi and other academic outlines; recipes; obituaries; liner

---

[*] Since 2003 (with the publication of Suzanne Paola and Brenda Miller's field guide, *Tell It Slant*, in which the term first appeared).

notes; contributors' notes; chronologies of all orders; abecedarians of all types; hierarchies of every description; want ads; game instructions; mind maps; organizational flow charts; questionnaires; playing cards; tarot cards; horoscopes; tables/charts/spreadsheets; medical advice and warnings; blog entries; Twitter feeds; Facebook posts; email exchanges; police blotters; newsletters; hotel registers; log books; care and use instructions; time cards; catalogue copy; to-do lists; play-by-play commentaries; theatrical programs; maps and their legends; architectural renderings; computer codes; other codes; fill-in-the-blank forms; tests/exams/evaluations; directions (as for travel); directions (as for assembly); paint color fans; Rolodexes; little black books; white pages; yellow pages; illustrated guides; letters of resignation; wedding vows; divorce papers; manifestos; diaries; notes to self; menus; grant applications; award ceremonies; morphologies; ingredient lists; nutritional values; pricing options; photo captions; indexes; tables of content; etymological histories; theoretical abstracts; knitting patterns; sewing patterns; other patterns; packing lists; travel itineraries; and so on; and so forth.

## FIELD MARKS

As a rule, hermit crab essays look funny. Not quite right. There's either too much going on in the visual field (see Caitlin Horrocks's "The Six Answers on the Back of a Trivia Card") or not nearly enough (see Jenny Boully's "The Body [an Excerpt]"). Often, the titles are ungainly (e.g., Ander Monson's "Outline toward a Theory of the Mine versus the Mind and the Harvard Outline"). But such imperfections are part of the charm, since, like its namesake, the hermit crab essay insists on approaching its own existence at a tilt—not quite sideways, but a little bit lopsided and, at the same time, weirdly bullheaded. The shells themselves may (as indicated by the species listed above) take almost any form. Indeed, in terms of shells, there is only one serious requirement worth mentioning: the form should be formal. Established. Recognizable. Traditional. Brave in its mulish adherence to common conventions. Otherwise, what's the point? Only when such a form is in place can the hermit crab essay exert its full magic, tempting one's inner aesthete with its very oddness, forcing upon its readers a private debate: Is this a thing of beauty? An ingenious expression of the human imagination? Or a cop-out? A cheap grotesquerie?

Although perhaps the more thoughtful question is rooted in a much simpler requirement: does it work?

## SIZE (WITH AND WITHOUT SHELL)

Without its shell, the contents of a hermit crab essay are often absurdly diffuse and in this sense can be considered large, even enormous, as their authors frequently attempt to cram complex love affairs, whole childhoods, decades-long mourning processes, devastating war stories, endlessly involute parent-child relationships, entire lifetimes, and stubbornly thorny existential and/or political and/or anatomical and/or cultural and/or spiritual investigations into a single shell. And yet the form permits such hijinks, even encourages them. The shell gives shape—sturdy structure—where otherwise there would be nothing but the boundless overflowings of human thought, memory, and emotion. Its remarkable ability to contain emotional, spiritual, and intellectual sprawl is due in large part to intrashell divisions, which neatly sidestep the need for conventional "transitions." Wild digressions, within such a structure, appear perfectly natural, so that even terribly rambling trains of thought are able to achieve not only coherence, but, on occasion, astonishing elegance as well (see, for example, Karen Hays's "The Clockwise Detorsion of Snails: A Love Essay in Sectors").

On the other hand, it should be noted that the occasional hermit crab essay is so incredibly tiny without its shell that it is hardly worth mentioning. In these cases, the donning of an extra-literary structure manages not only to illuminate but to greatly amplify what might otherwise be lost to the oblivion that is personal, unspeakable pain. (Randon Billings Noble's "The Heart as a Torn Muscle," which details a love affair that never happened, is an excellent example of this miniature variety.)

## ANATOMY

Like its biological cousin, the hermit crab essay is extremely vulnerable without its hijacked home. Asymmetrical, unguarded, scattered, the subject of such an essay is right to seek haven in the safety of a readymade form. However, the hermetic conditions that arise with the use of an appropriated structure can quickly become problematic. The most reliable sign that an essay lacks adequate air is a tendency toward the *meta* end of the literary spectrum. As soon as a hermit crab essay starts talking about itself *as* a hermit crab essay, things usually start to stink. Unfortunately this is a fairly common problem, perhaps because writers of this particular genre seem, for some reason, to have read too much Borges and Barthes, or perhaps because, as a rule, they are so in love with the act of writing that writing about the act of writing has, for them, an irresistible draw. And yet, as far as the common reader is concerned, this sort of thing quickly becomes a snore. Just as the biological hermit crab is periodically obliged to hop out of its shell in order to sweep it clean of its own droppings, so the author of a hermit crab essay would be well advised to trim away all unnecessary meta-narrative gestures, which can become so tiresome so quickly, especially in a form that practically screams its postmodern heritage from the top of its tiny, self-reflexive lungs.

### RELATIVES AND ANCESTORS

This taxon's most ancient ancestor can be found in the mimetic impulse—although of course, the same is true of every species falling under the phylum Ars. That said, the hermit crab essay is a kind of mimesis on steroids, which might explain why its closest relatives reside almost exclusively on the remote sidelines of literature—at least outside of fiction (where borrowed forms enjoy a long and varied history, particularly in the order Novellus, beginning, at the beginning, with *Don Quixote*: a false document without rival). In nonfictional realms, we find kissing cousins in the constrained writings of Oulipo, whose literary lipograms, reverse-lipograms, acrostics, palindromes, anagrams, and word substitution games, such as the famous N+7, all exhibit a decidedly impish approach to the question of form. Abecedarians are also clear antecedents, and we find traces of *Paguridae*, as well, in some Symbolist literature.[†] Book-length examples are hard to come by, but, when done well, hint at the miraculous. One notably beautiful specimen of this size is Primo Levi's *The Periodic Table* (1975).[‡]

---

[†]  See especially "The Passion Considered as an Uphill Bicycle Race," by Alfred Jarry.

[‡]  Of this all serious students of the genre should make a careful study.

Popular contemporary cousins include six-word memoirs, twiction, and the blog-born listicle. Nonliterary ancestors can be traced primarily to mid-century visual artists whose works explore themes of appropriation (e.g., Duchamp, Kruger) and that type of music sometimes called *programme* (e.g., Vivaldi's *The Four Seasons*).

### DIET
Omnivorous.

### PREY
Love; history; grief; mystery; disappointment; abandonment; confusion; apathy; longing; nostalgia; anxiety; desire; anger; despair; memory; fantasy; fear; loss; wonder; curiosity; et cetera.

### PREDATORS
In some areas of the world, hermit crab essays—like all essays (not to mention stories, novels, memoirs, poems, and plays)—are threatened nearly to the point of extinction by the repression of free speech. Other predators include reactionary critics, timid publishers, and prudish editors. And, needless to say, writer's block and lack of daring gobble many a *Pagurid* whole while still in the embryonic stage.

### HABITAT
In recent years, hermit crab essays have colonized the pages of literary magazines (both digital and paper) in greater and greater numbers; anecdotal reports also indicate that they have begun appearing regularly in private journals, on café napkins, and in creative writing workshops across the country.

### DEVELOPMENT AND REPRODUCTION
The best essays of this type are usually conceived in a moment of bright insight. An explosion of possibility. A *Hey!-You-put-chocolate-in-my-peanut-butter-You-got-peanut-butter-on-my-chocolate!* kind of thing. An unexpected juxtaposition that is somehow just right. Things tend to flow from there.

## PROJECTED EVOLUTION

Due to the current fascination with all things mixed and morphed—a fascination spurred, perhaps, by globalization, or, perhaps, by shifting gender lines,
and likely triggered, in either case, by the vast and generally baffling changes to
our economic infrastructures that continue to emerge during this, our relentless age of information, with its sexless, borderless currency of code—it seems
likely that hermit crab essays, and indeed, hybrids of every description, will
continue to grow in number and influence over the coming decade at least.
In addition, *Paguridae* is well positioned to avoid the ravages so mercilessly
visited upon other creative nonfiction forms, such as straight-up memoir
or literary journalism, by the apparently never-ending debate regarding the
precise divide between fact and fiction, as the hermit crab essay stakes a claim
neither to fact nor to fiction, but only to honesty and a certain playfulness.

## FURTHER NOTES

Yes indeed, the future looks rosy for the hermit crab essay. That said, there is the
matter of *shells* to consider, and shells—while hypothetically infinite—seem to
lose their novelty rather quickly. The more inventive writers in particular often
reject out of hand previously used shells, preferring instead to seek out new
and untried forms. For this reason, the hermit crab essay would seem to be a
self-limiting phenomenon: a somewhat charming blip of literary trendiness.
Only time will tell, of course, but it is also possible that these types of essays
are just the tip of the iceberg, so to speak—harbingers of a new kind of literary
drag. And instead of disappearing like a spent trend, the hermit crab essay may
yet spawn an entire new breed of essays—essays we can't even imagine from
here, essays that refuse to draw a line between fact and fiction, that refuse even
to acknowledge such a line, and that throw on disguises of every description—
spangled stilettos, hair shirts, false beards, nylon eyelashes—in order to more
fully inhabit some internal truth and in this way do what the best specimens
of the noble order Exagium have always done: get to something real.

THE SHELL GAME

# Grand Theft Auto

JOEY FRANKLIN

Shortly after midnight
Putnam neighborhood
Athens, Ohio

In the silent-street hours of morning on Friday, May 8, 2009, a wanted felon named Craig M. steals a wallet from an unlocked car parked on Lorene Avenue, just a few blocks from my apartment. Lorene runs north and south, skirting the eastern edge of a stately neighborhood with flower-potted porches and brick-paved streets—streets accustomed to the clang of bicycle wheels and the chain song of dog-walkers; streets sheltered by a canopy of oaks and birches, guarded by the glow of street lamps and the promise of small-town neighborliness—streets completely unprepared for this man Craig, now skulking up the sidewalk, his head down, fingers pawing through a wallet, heart humming with the thrill of the score.

Two blocks west of Lorene, Craig makes a small purchase using a credit card from the stolen wallet. He buys doughnuts, perhaps, or maybe a cup of coffee or a pack of cigarettes. I know he was there because police tell me a security camera trained on the front entrance recorded a grainy image of Craig leaving the store on foot. That's the important detail—"on foot." I can imagine him standing there at the curb, holding a steaming cup of coffee to his lips or perhaps tapping a pack of cigarettes against his palm as he stares out into the darkness. The night is young, and Craig is feeling good, but wherever he goes next, he's going on foot. At this point, he has yet to steal my car.

12:10 a.m.

Putnam Square Apartments #1203

Athens, Ohio

I turn out the light in my living room and lock the dead bolt on the front door.
I look briefly out the front window at the cars in the parking lot before twisting the blinds closed and heading upstairs to bed where my wife, Melissa, lies
asleep under the covers. I'm the on-site manager here, and it's my job each
night to put the apartment complex to bed. I patrol the sidewalks checking
for trash, burned-out lights, and at least theoretically, any suspicious activity.
But I've been making rounds each night for nearly a year now, and I've never
seen anything even remotely troubling. This is Athens, Ohio, a small, earnest
Appalachian college town with an enthusiastic Little League, a teeming farmers'
market, and a fifteen-mile bike trail dotted with joggers, dog-walkers, and the
occasional recumbent bicyclist. Sure, it's a party town on the weekends, but
people here leave their doors open, offer rides to strangers, and never give a
second thought to long walks in the evening shade of all those oaks and birches.
One hears about the occasional assault or robbery, but Athens has no real
crime rate to speak of. The prison isn't much larger than the elementary school.

I climb into bed beside Melissa and pull the covers up to my chin. Our two
boys sleep in the room down the hall, and outside their window, the glow of
a street lamp illuminates the parking lot like a stage.

1:30 a.m.

Putnam Square Apartments

Athens, Ohio

Craig makes his way east from Lorene Avenue and enters the quiet parking
lot of the Putnam Square complex not long after I fall asleep. He's from out of
state, somewhere in Pennsylvania according to police, and perhaps he's just
looking for stuff to pawn—CDs, clothing, maybe an iPod or a cell phone, a
wallet if he's lucky. Then again, maybe he's looking for a quick ride home, his
ticket out of town. Or maybe he's heading west, running from Philadelphia or
Pittsburgh and whatever trouble he left behind—petty theft, drugs, something
more sinister? A part of me wants the man who's about to steal my car to be
more than a strung-out addict looking for a fix: a writer of bad checks, maybe,

a passer of fake IDs, a wooer of women in every town he comes to. I want him, when he steps through the lamplight of my complex, to feel as though the world is crooked and that he is pulling a straight line through it. I hope, for his sake, that our town feels ripe for the taking and that he feels like more than a just a blip on the quiet calm of this Appalachian spring night.

At the very least, I hope he really needs a ride.

And I hope he has higher standards than to go after my car first. Certainly he tries the handle of the black Explorer parked in front of #708, the one with the wax job and chrome rims. Then the tricked-out Jetta outside #905, then maybe the blue Pathfinder in front of #1202. The Lexus in front of #1204.

Locked. All of them.

It must be desperation, then, that leads Craig to my maroon Ford Escort with the dented quarter panel and dangling bumper. When he lifts the handle, he not only finds the doors unlocked, but by the street lamp's glow I'm sure he notices a camping chair, a folding bike rack, and two car seats. Never mind the interior smells of rotten milk and stale Cheerios; never mind the diapers and fast-food wrappers covering the floor; never mind the cracker crumbs smashed into the upholstery. This car is open, and hey, look there, in the tray beneath the emergency brake—a set of keys.

I imagine Craig turns to the Lexus behind him, and then to the Pathfinder across the way, and then back to my beat-up old wagon, the smudged peanut-butter-and-jelly fingerprints on the back window just now coming into focus.

Does he shrug before he climbs in?

Does he adjust my seat? Put on the belt?

At that moment, asleep in our bedroom, Melissa and I do not hear Craig close our car door. We do not hear the engine start, nor do we hear the fading sound of that engine as our car turns the corner out of the complex, driven away by a determined, if slightly disappointed, car thief who must feel, on the one hand, like the luckiest man in Athens, and on the other, like the butt of some cruel joke.

7:00 a.m.

Putnam Square Apartments #1203

Athens, Ohio

In the morning, before Melissa or the children are out of bed, I descend the stairs and put on my sandals to take out the trash. The dumpsters are out my front door, but when I step out onto my porch, I stop, confused by the empty space where my car should be. I look around for an explanation.

I take the garbage to the dumpster and peer down into the grassy ditch that runs along the back of the parking lot, thinking that I may have left the car in neutral, that it may have simply rolled out of sight. But there are no tire marks in the grass, no car sitting idly in a stream of ditch water. I go back inside.

Upstairs, I wake Melissa to tell her our car has been stolen, and she doesn't believe me. She gets out of bed and repeats my search. When she cannot find the car, she pauses in the living room, realization dawning over her, and then she says, "Do you think someone's playing a joke?"

Midmorning

Unknown location

Athens, Ohio

Where Craig takes our car first is unclear. We can extrapolate about Friday's events using clues he leaves behind in the car after it is recovered by the police:

One O'bleness Hospital discharge bag,

One O'bleness Hospital water jug,

Several items of clothing, including a gray sweatshirt and a white tank
   top,

One hairbrush,

One bottle of lotion,

Two cigarette lighters,

A gas can containing three gallons of gasoline,

One iPod charger,

One Ford factory alloy wheel, originally attached to the car, but
   apparently removed by Craig and replaced with the spare,

Approximately one hundred small white tablets of Oxycodone in a
    prescription bottle, written for a woman named Colleen, and
One empty can of Coors Light.

Here's my hypothesis: sometime Friday morning, while I'm busy on the phone with the police and my insurance company, Craig uses our car to pick up a woman named Colleen from the local hospital. She has apparently been in long enough to need a change of clothes, a hairbrush, and, as soon as she gets out, a cold beer.

9:15 a.m.

Putnam Square Apartments #1203

Athens, Ohio

Standing in my living room, dialing my insurance company's phone number, I do not feel as though my single-most-valuable possession has been stolen. Nor do I recognize the irony that this beat-up Ford sits atop my "most valuable possessions" list. Frankly, I don't feel much of anything. I should be frantic. Furious. I'm a graduate student working three jobs to support my family, and some freewheeling opportunist just drove off with our only vehicle. But I don't feel any of those things. If I feel anything at all, it's a mixture of curiosity and pity.

Who would steal our car?

Our Ford has been through three engines and two major accidents. We've replaced the timing belt, the alternator, and another thousand dollars' worth of miscellaneous engine parts. We've even joked about leaving it on a street corner somewhere overnight with the keys in the ignition. Of course, we'd never really do that, but now we don't have to.

The insurance agent on the phone tells me the car will have to be gone for a month before they'll pay out on a claim. I tell her we're hopeful the car will turn up. I tell her we feel stupid for leaving the keys inside it, that it's just not like us, that we can't believe our luck. Then I hang up and explain the situation to Melissa, who is looking out the window at the empty space in front of our apartment.

"Well," she says. "I guess it's time to go car shopping."

Midday
cvs Pharmacy
Athens, Ohio

Craig and Colleen stop by a cvs Pharmacy sometime on Friday to fill the prescription for the Oxycodone. Then they head north on State Highway 33 toward Columbus. I am surprised at the sheer quantity of pills in the prescription when I later find them in my car. The bottle gives off a satisfying rattle when I pick it up.

At some point that day, Craig removes our bike rack from the back of the Escort. It is never recovered. Also unaccounted for when we retake the vehicle are the fold-up camping chair and a few dollars' worth of McDonald's gift certificates that we'd been saving in our glove box for the occasional drifter holding a sign on the highway.

I like to think that Craig and Colleen stop at the McDonald's on Highway 33 just outside Columbus and use our coupons to order double cheeseburger meals with large Cokes. I want them to ask for extra tomato and to go back for refills. I hope that Colleen doesn't, in the silence of waiting for their order, ask Craig about the car he's driving but instead tells him how glad she is to finally be out of the hospital.

They probably talk about hospital food as they eat, making jokes about green Jell-O and tapioca pudding, and Colleen laughs as she places a french fry in her mouth, savoring the salt, distracted momentarily from whatever part of her still hurts.

Perhaps Craig came to Athens to meet Colleen—an old friend from Pennsylvania? A cousin? A lover? Maybe he found out her discharge date and came to surprise her. Certainly the car had been a surprise—child seats in the back, a sippy cup rattling around the floorboards.

Maybe after lunch, Craig tells Colleen the car belongs to a friend, and maybe Colleen believes him. Or, more likely, she tries to ignore what she has already figured out: this is not some friend's car, and they're going to be in trouble. Real trouble. She wants to say something, but instead, she stands out on the curb in the McDonald's parking lot, smoking a cigarette while Craig pulls the jack from the back of the car.

4:00 p.m.

Ohio University

Athens, Ohio

At school, the car theft makes a great story. My students laugh for five minutes. They know what my car looks like, and they accuse me of orchestrating the whole thing. Friends pat me on the back and offer rides. Melissa sends me a text with links to minivans on eBay. We chat online about car loans and insurance payouts and resale values and down payments. I allow myself to imagine driving a new Mazda5 or a Honda Odyssey. We chat off and on for an hour about new cars, and then I remember our old one has been gone less than a full day.

"Maybe the car will turn up," I write. It seems like the right thing to say. The honest thing. But even as I type it, I don't want to believe it.

"Yeah," Melissa writes back after a long pause. And then she changes the subject.

Early evening

City limits

Columbus, Ohio

Sometime Friday evening, Colleen and Craig pick up a woman named Brenda, and to make room for three, Craig must do something about the car seats. I imagine that after driving all day in my car, Craig has adjusted to his unfamiliar surroundings. He's figured out the sticky brake, the unresponsive accelerator, and the buttons and knobs for the air-conditioning. He definitely changed the radio presets to all the local rock stations, and his cell phone is charging on the floor. But maybe what he can't get used to are the car seats in the rearview mirror. Sure, I can believe Craig is okay with the idea of me standing on my porch in my pajamas and scratching my head—the sucker who left his keys in his car—but I want to think it's harder to laugh off those car seats and the kids who will no longer use them.

And maybe Colleen finally speaks up. She is glad to see him, and she is glad for the ride, but frankly, she can't believe what he's done.

"What if we get pulled over," I imagine her saying, her elbow propped up on the armrest, her forehead in her palm. "You'll go to jail. We'll go to jail."

I see Craig shrinking in his seat, in my seat, feeling stupid for not thinking all this through. I can see Colleen ripping into him about rash decisions, about putting himself first, about the car seats in the back of the car. Craig hollers something about picking her up, wanting to see her, something about ditching the car as soon they can. Colleen takes off her gray sweatshirt and throws it in the back. I see her reaching around one of the car seats to her hospital bag and pulling out a large white bottle of pills. She unscrews the cap, pulls out a few tablets, and pops them in her mouth, downing them with a drag of melted ice from the bottom of her Coke cup still sitting in the holder. Colleen tosses the bottle of pills toward the back of the car and curses. She pulls a cigarette from a pack tucked in the console beneath the emergency brake and lights it. She inhales deeply, holds in the smoke, and then rolls down the window to exhale. The air around them fills with the whoosh of the open window, and then they are quiet.

Perhaps picking up Brenda creates a welcome shift in the mood inside the car. Perhaps Craig is grateful for an excuse to take one of those seats out and put it in the way back, glad to unbuckle the other one and push it over onto its side, out of sight.

9:00 p.m.
Putnam Square Apartments #1203
Athens, Ohio

We're not even through our first day as victims of grand theft auto, and we've already stopped using "if" in our car-shopping discussions. The police have told us that 90 percent of stolen cars are recovered in the first seventy-two hours or they're not recovered at all. And if they do recover the vehicle, they're pretty sure they'll find it in a ditch somewhere out in the country, abandoned after some alcohol-induced joyride. Of course, someone could sell the car piece by piece, but considering its condition, my money is on the joyride theory—the car thief tearing up the highway toward some wild deep of West Virginia or disappearing down some Kentucky dirt-road hollow, leaving nothing but a trail of cigarette butts and empty beer cans behind him.

Yes. I'm sure of it. The car is gone, already buried hood-deep in some backwoods bog at the end of a long, rutted road to nowhere, and we'll never see her again.

We put the kids to bed and spend the rest of the evening looking up cars online. One particular van, a red Mazda5, has caught our attention—low miles, straight body, and clean interior. But what really gets us is the price—nearly $3,000 less than every other comparable model. Then Melissa notices why. At the bottom of the page, in small print, are the words, "Salvage title: theft recovery."

11:55 p.m.

Downtown

Columbus, Ohio

Just before midnight, Brenda is driving our car with Colleen in the passenger seat and Craig in the back when she makes a right turn without signaling and nearly hits a patrol car. I don't know why Craig has invited Brenda to drive—perhaps Colleen didn't want to sit by him anymore; perhaps Craig has been thinking about his fight with Colleen and about rash decisions and jail, and maybe he thinks he knows a little about the laws governing grand theft auto, and so he intentionally puts someone else in the driver's seat. Maybe he's been drinking—maybe they've all been drinking—but I imagine the moment he sees the red and blue lights reflecting off the dark interior of the car, he regrets letting Brenda get behind the wheel. Either way, during the routine traffic stop, the officers run the car's plate, discover it has been stolen, and, as they say, the game is up. For all of us.

When questioned about the car, Brenda points to Craig in the backseat and says something about the car belonging to one of his friends. Brenda is arrested for possession of a stolen vehicle. Craig is arrested for his implication in Brenda's story. Colleen is not arrested, but the car is impounded, and she has to find her own way home without the prescription drugs, hairbrush, sweatshirt, and everything else in the back of the car.

Our Escort sits on the side of the road, leaning slightly on one spare tire as it waits for a tow truck, its only passengers the two upturned car seats in the back.

Shortly after midnight
Phone call
Athens, Ohio

A few minutes after the arrest, a Columbus police officer sends a text message to the Athens City Police Department. The officer on duty calls to give us the good news. My wife and I are in bed when the phone rings.

The officer informs us that our car has been found and tells us to call the station in the morning for instructions. I hang up the phone. We both sit up in bed and laugh. Losing our Escort was like losing the family pet—if the family pet were an incontinent mutt with fleas and a penchant for vomiting on the carpet.

We were sad to see it go.

But not really.

And now we were happy to get it back.

But not really.

Midmorning Saturday
Police impound lot
Columbus, Ohio

Saturday morning I call Officer Filar of the Athens City Police Department, and he gives me the address to the Columbus impound lot where my car has been towed. In this conversation, I first learn about Craig, Colleen, and Brenda and the circumstances of their arrest. I'm surprised to get names and brief histories from the officer, surprised at how quickly my mind gives imaginary faces to these people who've been driving my car around, and surprised at how giving them faces makes them suddenly unsavory.

A little after nine, I catch a ride with friends to the impound lot and spend two hours standing in lines, filling out forms, and talking over the phone with a representative from my insurance company who is very glad to hear that our luck has changed. I end up paying fifty-five dollars to get my own car out of impound.

From the bizarre collection of personal items I find inside the car, it appears that Brenda, Colleen, and Craig had assumed possession of the vehicle and, in essence, moved in. I clean out the car and leave everything that doesn't belong to me with an officer at the impound lot. I climb in the driver's seat and turn the key and, for the first time, begin to feel something akin to loss. It's a weary, disheveled confusion, like someone has been in my bed without my knowing it.

1:45 p.m.

AutoZone

Canal Winchester, Ohio

I stop at an AutoZone on my way back to Athens so I can replace the spare tire with the wheel in the back of the car. At this point, I still can't figure out why Craig removed it, and I'm here to buy an air pressure gauge to see if it's flat. I've gone from feeling violated to feeling annoyed.

Standing at the AutoZone counter, I share the events of the day with the cashier, a short, curly-haired woman with the chapped hands of a mechanic. She thinks Craig probably removed the wheel to sell it. She tells me this as if it's the most obvious explanation in the world, as if any other explanation is ridiculous, as if she can tell that I'm one of those guys who probably deserves to get his car stolen.

She's right. The tire isn't flat.

Craig must have wanted to sell the wheels but didn't want to drive up to a pawn shop in a stolen car. If he'd found a buyer, would he have removed all four wheels and left my car cut off at the knees in some back alley, resting on its own knobby axles?

As I jack up the car out in front of the AutoZone, I imagine Craig doing the same thing with this same jack less than twenty-four hours earlier. Maybe someone even stopped to help, or at least offered him a "tough break, man," as they walked past. Craig would have nodded and smiled, maybe said something offhanded about the car always giving him trouble.

"But hey," he might have said. "At least she runs." Kneeling against the car in a parking lot or on the side of the road, arms twisting the long, awkward crank of the jack, Craig would have looked like any other person replacing a flat tire. He would have looked just like me.

2:00 p.m.

Captain Car Wash

Canal Winchester, Ohio

My last stop before driving home is a car wash down the street from AutoZone. I know it's probably just in my head, but I feel as if I can taste other people in my car. The air smells of cigarette smoke, and the press of strange bodies seems to linger in the upholstery. My son's peanut-butter-and-jelly fingerprints are still on the window, but those prints are covered by the prints of strangers now sitting in jail somewhere in Columbus.

I throw away garbage and vacuum the floorboards. I reprogram the channel presets on the radio. Under the backseat, I find a large, gray sweatshirt that stinks of tobacco. I don't want to know who it belongs to. I set the shirt in the way back and return to cleaning. I wash the outside of the car and then look at the wheels. Their spiral grooves are always dirty, stained brown with road grime. I hate these wheels because they're so hard to clean. I laugh at the idea of Craig trying to sell them. No matter how much I scrub them with the foam brush, they're still dirty.

After a final rinse, I wipe down my Escort with clean towels from the car wash and look at the wheels one more time. If Brenda had remembered to use her turn signal, I might not be standing here staring at my car like it's some kind of infected sore. Craig, Colleen, and Brenda might have gotten to wherever it was they were going, and my wife and I might still be car shopping. Later, when this is all over, I will want to imagine the rest of their histories I didn't get from Officer Filar—I'll want to get inside their heads, to taste their motives, to play out how all this went down, to pass out the benefit of the doubt like candy.

In this moment, though, I just want a clean car.

I reach inside the back of the car and pull out the abandoned, gray sweatshirt. Carefully, I roll one sleeve around my hand and crouch down next to a wheel. The brown grime comes off easily on the cotton knit, leaving behind silver metal. When all four wheels are clean, I wad up the sweatshirt and throw it into a garbage can. And when I do, I think about the people who spent an entire day in my car, and I feel a little guilty, as if I've just stolen someone's shirt.

# Ok, Cupid

SARAH MCCOLL

## My self-summary

In the Rider-Waite tarot deck, the Empress sits on a throne surrounded by wheat that sways like congregants at her feet. Beneath a shapeless cotton gown printed with pomegranates, a secret slammin' bod. She wears a crown of stars. Empresses do not fuck around with online dating.

## What I'm doing with my life

The other evening I walked home from the gym in my crazy-print leggings. Cold December black rain and the wet sidewalks like mirrors for streetlights. A man who had lost both his legs came zooming up behind me in a wheelchair. He was singing, to no one in particular. *You're just too good to be true, can't take my eyes off of you.* His cigarette spiraled smoke like a genie escaping from a brass lamp. *You'd be like heaven to touch, I want to fuck you so much.* He really spit his improvised line, as if he would enter a woman like a poison.

The Syrian men who work at the bodega on the corner still mention my ex-husband, what a nice guy. He has not stepped across their threshold for a pack of Marlboro Lights in some twenty-one months, but *I like that Sebastian*, they offer unprompted. They chide me in my crazy-print leggings—*Stop losing weight!*—and then shame me when I arrive late at night unbalanced after too many drinks. *Got the munchies?* they ask, ringing up kettle chips and a chocolate bar. When I want to rebel against something I've yet to identify, I buy a pack of American Spirits. Those receive no comment, since the Syrians all smoke in the neon light of the Shiner Bock sign out front. Sometimes, on the way home, I have a date in tow. We need toilet paper or a six-pack. They survey the unfamiliar faces with narrowed eyes, open the cash register brusquely, and a gray cat weaves between my calves.

Sunday I walked to the ATM on the corner of Sixth Avenue and Ninth Street. It's between my gym and the farmers' market, and the very same trans woman is there each noon, saving all in need of cash from having to unlock the door with a card swipe; she swings it open from inside. All she asks in return is *whatever you can do to help, baby*. I needed to endorse checks. No pen in my purse or on the vestibule table. *You need a pen, baby? I always keep one on hand, case I meet a guy.* I signed my name on the back of the check, withdrew cash, and this time, pressed a dollar into her hand on my way out. We all want the same things.

I'm really good at

Beginnings. Falling in love with unavailable men because my willful heart expects to win. This, despite all counsel and popular belief to the contrary. First, an affair with a man about to slip a diamond ring on the finger of a woman he loved, and a year later, with one who is already married. He turned the water on in the hotel bathroom sink, and I heard his ring clang onto the white enamel. Only then did I realize which hand he'd had inside me. Built-in constraints have interesting effects, my friend tells me.

Favorite books, movies, shows, music, and food

We've reached the pretension-laid-bare portion of the program. Interpretations get muddy fast. Pedal steel means a man who is steady and has soul, but the one who mentioned Judith Butler was a dick. You never can tell. When you say you like Charles Bukowski, is that code for something? My list shows a wholesome enthusiasm for aesthetic and corporeal pleasure (see self-summary above), and big, life-changing ideas presented by way of understatement. Marilynne Robinson is my acknowledgment of the sublime. Three mentions of feminism to ward off the scaries, but it's hopeless since the scaries haven't read a word. If humility is out of fashion, I am drawn to it like a wasp-waisted secretary dress. Tacos. Everyone says tacos.

Six things I could never do without
It's as if you do not know what a thing is. Not people like your family, not concepts like compassion. Clogs. Frying pans, coffee beans, a library card. Joni Mitchell's *Blue*. I still wake up in the morning, with the sun at half-mast and the windshields wet, wanting to put the key in the ignition and go.

I spend a lot of time thinking about
At a reading, I saw an author defend the cover of her book on which her slim legs are crossed in a tight dress and her hair falls around her face like stage curtains. *Your book is so intelligent,* the host volunteered, *but the cover looks like chick lit.* I felt resistant to the cover, too, but it was a memoir. How, I wondered, could her form misrepresent its contents?

When I was engaged to the man I would marry, I visited my father. He knocked on my bedroom door one morning with a cup of coffee, placed it on the bedside table, and then stepped out of the room again. I leaned against the pillows in a pale blue vintage slip that my stepmother, at bedtime, had said made me look like Elizabeth Taylor in *BUtterfield 8*. When my father returned to my bedroom, he had a robe in his hand, which he laid across my lap before sitting in a pink rocking chair by the window. I understood I was to slip my arms through the robe's sleeves. He was a man, but he was also my father. *Your fiancé is very handsome,* my father began, leaning back with careful authority. *It's important that you take good care of yourself,* he said.

When I visited my father at his law office when I was young, I sat on the green rug and pulled open the deep file drawers of his desk, filled with stacked *Playboys*. In hot Texas summers, we ran laps together at the track in the relative cool of the early morning. He drove me to Weight Watchers and bought a microwave for the school cafeteria so I could bring my Lean Cuisines. Here we are again. A man has pledged his love, and my father is on hand with helpful advice about how the world really works: other women, slim and hairless with polished shoes and high, tight asses, will be ready to take my place should I not safeguard as much beauty as I can maintain or manufacture.

On a typical Friday night I am
I did not feel lonely until surprise love enveloped me like the sweep of a magician's cape and then was snapped away. Was there ever a rabbit in that hat? A woman was certainly sawed in two.

You should message me if
Should it feel like a runaway train or a magic carpet ride or a pair of bedroom slippers? If we find it, or make it, how do you preserve what begins as holy? Can we keep it alive like a bed of moss under glass, creating its own weather system? Once, a man told me I was a weather system all on my own.

Aries, ENFJ.

# Rubik's Cube, Six Twisted Paragraphs

KATHRYN A. KOPPLE

The architect and sculptor Ernö Rubik once said, "The fact that it can do this without falling apart is part of its magic." He was referring to the world's most famous puzzle: Rubik's Cube. The Cube consists of twenty-seven miniature cubes held together by a hidden mechanism. An expert Cubist can solve the puzzle in under a minute. According to Rubik, there are "forty-three quintillion permutations." I would exclaim, "How incredible is that!" but he lost me at "quintillion." Solved or not, the Cube will always be an object of magic to me. The secret of the Cube is that it wouldn't exist without math. Where is the magic in math? I wish I had an answer. There have been times when I couldn't figure out how to use a calculator. Weren't calculators made for people like me? People who, for no obvious reason, are incapable of doing math. It is a horrible way to live. Always, this yearning to be able to add and subtract, multiply and divide. Always, this excruciating sense of inferiority. Algebra is a gate-keeper subject. Once you achieve an understanding of algebra, you can advance to higher and higher levels of math. I have this persistent sense that geometry, calculus, physics—each one sounding like a Greek god—look down on me. In fact, I know it. Regardless of his invention's mathematical complexities, Rubik has always regarded it as a work of art. Cubists from Picasso to Raymond Duchamp-Villon have been fascinated with perspective, motion, and formal innovation. Cubism was thus born out of mystery and provocation; it challenges the viewer to experiment with new modes of thinking about art. To quote Arthur Jerome Eddy, "The extravagances of the Cubists may serve to open our eyes to beauties we have always felt without quite understanding."

The architect and sculptor Ernö Rubik once said, "The fact that it can do this without falling apart is part of its magic." Rubik was born on July 14, 1944, in Hungary. His mother was a poet. His father manufactured military gliders. Individuals close to Rubik describe him as withdrawn and lonely. He may have very likely suffered from bouts of depression. My father died on the 23rd of December in 2003. He left Albany, Georgia—his birthplace—at sixteen to study painting in Manhattan. He produced dozens of oils and sculptures. By the time things fell apart for him, I was in my twenties. I was aware of his eccentricities but hadn't fully comprehended his mental state. Art had long since failed to hold his imagination. He'd moved on to purer forms of mysticism, and there were many mornings I'd wake to find he hadn't slept. He talked about meditation, visions, avatars, and something called "the breathless state." A magical thinker, my father found all the answers to the universe he needed in visits to the library. The library housed more than information alone: it held secrets, codes, messages, proof of who he'd been in past lives and who he would be in the future. I learned to humor him, especially when he could talk of nothing else but the Red Baron, or some other off-key topic. He could be wonderful company until he wasn't. My father spent nine years in a state mental institution. Underground tunnels provided passages for the transport of patients from one building to another. The tunnels were also used to take patients to the asylum morgue. Some never made it out of the tunnels alive. Much has changed since my father was committed. Many of the old asylums have been shut down. Treatments have improved. Psychiatry has discovered that Rubik's Cube can be therapeutic. It seems perfectly logical. Every diagnosis represents a complex matrix. One has to fall apart many times to understand precisely what this means.

The architect and sculptor Ernö Rubik once said, "The fact that it can do this without falling apart is part of its magic." Rubik invented the Cube to demonstrate the complexity of spatial movement. It is one thing to create a three-dimensional object and quite another to invent a three-dimensional object with moving parts. People are like the Cube: they are three-dimensional objects with moving parts. Hands grasp, toes curl, knees bend, eyelids flutter—a ballet of reflexes and gestures. My mother's reflex when I was sick was to flip out. She couldn't bear being around me when I was sick because my father was sick, and that was all she could take. When I was a teenager, I had a seizure. I had the seizure at the hospital. My mother blamed Kathy F. She blamed me for being friends with Kathy F. She considered Kathy F. typically middle class; anything typically middle class induced revulsion in my beautiful, educated, high-strung mother. I was with Kathy F. visiting her brother in the hospital. Her brother's appendix had ruptured. Poor kid. He nearly died. I noticed how white the bedsheets were and then how bright they became. It was the onset of the seizure. My brain going through an electrical storm. I'm not sure my brain has ever fully calmed down, but I have not had another seizure. Rubik's Cube has been known to trigger epileptic episodes. In a notable journal of neurology, a physician explains that seizures may occur due to damage in the area of the brain responsible for spatial processing and calculation. Looking at the Cube or holding it will not trigger a seizure. The danger lies in twisting and moving the Cube.

The architect and sculptor Ernö Rubik once said, "The fact that it can do this without falling apart is part of its magic." Where did the idea for the Cube come from? Rubik is elusive on this point although he does mention toying around with 15-puzzle as a child. 15-puzzle is an exceptionally tricky sliding tile puzzle. In *Metamagical Themas*, Douglas Hofstadter tells us that 15-puzzle caused "mass insanity" when it came out in the late nineteenth century. Who knew? Not I. There weren't a lot of puzzles in my house when I was growing up. Just the one. My father was full of ideas you might describe as borderline. He specialized in the marginal, the uncertain, the equivocal, and the unclassifiable. He was determined to see what other people couldn't. Once when we were in a bookstore, I asked him how to recognize a great painting. He scowled. He'd been looking through one of those coffee table editions of master works and began to turn page after page, saying, *You see that? That's a great painting. Here, another great painting. This is a great painting.* They were all great paintings, every single one. Except what made them great wasn't visible to me, and he was letting me know it never would be. After that, I wouldn't talk to my father about art. Who needed the humiliation? Life was hard enough. He could go chase the invisible without me. And he did until no one could make sense of what he was talking about. He became isolated, untethered, delusional. My mother had him committed. Later I would learn he believed we were dead. Or was it that he believed he had murdered his family? Either way, being his daughter, it is horrible to think about. Hofstadter describes Rubik's Cube and 15-puzzle as "kin." "There is no route," writes Hofstadter, "that does not call for the partial but temporary destruction of the visible order achieved up to a given point." Shiny, colorful—and delightful to the eye—the Cube has a dark side.

The architect and sculptor Ernö Rubik once said, "The fact that it can do this without falling apart is part of its magic." In Hungarian, the Cube was originally called Bűvös Kocka or magic cube. Now, the puzzle is known in hundreds of languages. It has become part of the lexicon in countries around the world. I always wonder about people trying to solve the Cube in a foreign language. How do the instructions to the puzzle translate from one idiom to another? Does any part of the puzzle get lost in translation? Sound, syntax, sense. I obsess about what is lost or gained in the transit from one idiom to another because I am a translator. But with the passing of years, I have found that a second language can provide a refuge. There is the past, with its persistent memories of failure and disappointment. The past is always less present in a second language; it is put away in a drawer or some other dark place as hundreds of windows open up. The routine present becomes instantly vivid by switching out of the ho-hum of everyday parlance into the lexical carnival of a foreign language. Speaking of the future no longer brings a sense of living on borrowed time. There is always more time in a foreign language. Rubik speaks of puzzles as providing clear solutions to life's messy problems. He would rather focus on what can, as opposed to what can't, be solved. As for the Cube, it is still known as Bűvös Kocka in Hungarian.

The architect and sculptor Ernö Rubik once said, "The fact that it can do this without falling apart is part of its magic." Many practitioners describe the Cube as an awakening—life changing, religious. Epiphanies involving the Cube are everywhere. "That night, I dreamed three monks showed me a puzzle. The monk in the middle held out his hands and showed me something that looked like a Rubik's Cube. All three said in one voice, *This piece is here, and that piece is there* . . . They showed me the puzzle pieces fit together." The dreamer is Dr. Randolph Pinch, author of *From God's House to You*. The Cube as talisman, juju, fetish, amulet, rabbit's foot, lucky charm. As cult object. At this point, I am in a classic Cube bind. The Cube is so messed up that it has begun to mess with me. So I turn to one of many solution guides. Step one: Fear. Do not be afraid to live. Do not let your anxieties overwhelm you. Keep your appointments with your psychiatrist. Step Two: Shame. Remember to honor as well as mourn your father. Who else would read "Air and Angels" to you at bedtime? Step Three: Understanding. Your mother can't help who she is. She will not change. Step Four: Objectivity. Remember that you are a small part of a much larger equation. If this makes you feel insignificant, do not fret. You may be no more than a morsel in the banquet of life, but you are lucky to be alive. Step Five: Awareness. Don't let tragedy cause you to turn a deaf ear to joy. Joy speaks in many tongues; it takes many forms. Step Six: Faith. You're still working on it.

# Solving My Way to Grandma

LAURIE EASTER

ACROSS

1   "Mom, I have something to tell you. You might want to sit down." When my daughter said this, my first thought was *Uh-oh, who died?* Not *Oh my god, she's pregnant.*

   (Expect the _____)

2   The first words out of my mouth were: "You know, I've had an abortion." She did not in fact know this because I had never spoken of it. I said it because I wanted Lily to know that abortion was an acceptable option.

Afterwards she told my secret to her younger sister, who implored me via text message: *When did you have an abortion?!* I conveniently avoided responding.

(Two words: a term for when only part of a story is told)

3   When we had this conversation, Lily was a few weeks shy of turning twenty-six years old and one month into the massage therapy school her father and I paid for by going into debt on our credit card while she lived with us and we supported her. Her boyfriend was twenty-one, jobless, without a driver's license, and lived with his mother.

I got pregnant with Lily when I was twenty-two. My job was delivering pizzas for Domino's. Her dad worked as an auto mechanic. By the time she was born, I had turned twenty-three and her father thirty-six. I had been on my own since I was sixteen. Together, we had little money, but we were independent.

(A history of a character or person that tells what led up to the main story and promotes better understanding)

4   I suggested Lily have an abortion even though she was older than I was when I'd had her. "You can always have a baby later when it's the right time," I said. Yet when I became a mother, I didn't know what I was getting into and was wholly unprepared. Is there ever a right time for landmark decisions?

(Behaving in a manner where one's words and actions are contradictory)

5   My younger daughter got defensive in her sister's honor. "It's *her* decision," she said accusingly. She thought my mentioning abortion was an attempt to sway her sister's decision. She was right. But I realized being pro-choice does not mean the outcome will always be abortion. Being pro-choice implies just what it says: a choice. And sometimes that choice is to have the baby.

("The first step toward change is awareness. The second step is _____." —Nathaniel Branden)

6   I know we don't have control over much in life, not really. We can try our damnedest to control things, especially as parents.

Sometimes we are successful and other times not. But a simple idea I had never considered before struck me deeply: as a parent, there is one thing we have absolutely no control over whatsoever—if or when we become a grandparent.

(A "lightning bolt" moment)

7  The mainstream, socially accepted, ideal American trajectory is you go to college, get a job, save money, get engaged, get married, save more money, build your nest, then have children. We did everything backward—her father and I: we had a baby; bought land on credit; built a makeshift, illegal dwelling; had another baby; and then after nineteen years as a couple got married and accrued student loan debt by going to college in our forties and fifties.

(Not conforming to type)

8  Throughout my daughter's pregnancy I worried constantly. Would she finish massage school? If not, had we just gone into debt for nothing? Where would they live? How would they support themselves? Who would pay her car payment and insurance? Would her boyfriend get a job? Would the stress of having a child end their relationship? Would my daughter end up as a single mother? How much would I be called upon to help?

(High _____)

9  *I'm too young to be a grand-mother,* I thought. I clung to the stereotype that grandmothers are old and white haired and wrinkled. I wasn't done being hip and cool and rebellious. At forty-eight years old, I wasn't done being young. When I thought Grandmother, I thought Crone. Elder. Wise Woman. The last stage in the archetypal trinity of the Goddess, preceded by Maiden and Mother. One step closer to death. These were not the terms in which I viewed myself.

(Two words: Often happens in midlife)

10  Talk to nearly anyone and you will hear a story about a grandma who was a towering presence and influential force. I revered my own Grandma June: artist, painter, quilt maker, woodblock carver and printer. She baked chocolate chip cookies and stocked full the cookie jar on her kitchen counter whenever

we'd visit. She read me *Eloise in Paris*, *The Jungle Book*, and *The Little Prince*. She taught me how to sew, crochet, and play piano. She took my brothers and me to Pescadero Beach, where we built elaborate sand castles, and she made gingerbread houses with us at Christmas. She traveled the world: China, Greece, Kenya, Turkey. You name it, she went there. Of all people, she was my favorite.

(Dearly _____)

11  In comparison to the ideal grandmother, I was off to a poor start—and the baby hadn't even been born yet! I often wondered how I would ever live up to my own expectations for the role. I dubbed myself The Worst Grandma Ever.

("The only thing we have to _____ is _____ itself."
—Franklin D. Roosevelt)

DOWN

12  My daughter grew frustrated at my urging her to not have the baby. Everything in her body raged *Yes* to the future child, only the size of a pea. I knew this sensation. I had felt it on more than one occasion.

(My own heart's _____)

13  When I was nineteen, I had my first serious love affair. He was a thirty-one-year-old charismatic, obscure man, bordering on cuckoo, with a tendency toward anger and domination. From the beginning, he convinced me to get off the pill, citing how "unhealthy" it was. Like an impressionable fool, I acquiesced. Two pregnancies and subsequent abortions later, I learned there are worse things than taking birth control pills.

(Susceptible to physical or emotional attack or harm)

14  The first time I got pregnant, the decision to have an abortion was a no-brainer. The second time, though, my body wanted the baby and my spirit wanted it, too. Still, my head said *No*. My boyfriend already had a toddler with a woman in another state. He never saw his child and did not accept responsibility for him. I knew I could not be bound to this man for life. I knew a child deserved better. I knew a superior father existed elsewhere.

(Opposite of simple, aka it's _____)

15  Usually, the first thing people say when you tell them you are going to be a grandmother is

*Congratulations!* Without hesitation. Despite the circumstances. It's an automatic response, like stopping at a red light and going at a green one. In our culture, it's expected that everyone is happy about becoming a grandparent.

(To assume is to make an ass out of u and me)

16 My friend, Liz, who became a grandmother in her mid-forties, understood my turmoil. She had huge resistance to becoming "Grandma." But she said, with a knowing smile, "You're going to love it."

("_____ is the daughter of experience." —Leonardo da Vinci, *Thoughts on Art and Life*)

17 When my daughter was six or seven months along, I bent down and said to her belly in a high-pitched, sing-song voice: "Hello, baby, this is your Auntie Laurie."

(The path of least _____)

18 "What are you going to be called?" people asked. I thought hard about this. I searched the Internet for alternatives to the traditional "Grandma." *Savta* in Hebrew. *Mémé* in French. *Abuela* in Spanish. *Nonna* in Italian. *Yiayia* in Greek. *Oma* in German. *Amma* in Icelandic. *Bubbe* in Yiddish. *Bibi* in Swahili. *Babcia*

in Polish. Nana, Gram, Grammy, Grandmother. I realized this would be the first and only time in my life I would choose my own name. The decision was overwhelming.

(In regards to 19-down)

19 I settled on "Bunny," a throwback to high school when I was called "Bun" because my last name is Easter, just like the holiday. Now I'm called "Grandma Bunny."

(Synonym for name)

20 Lily labored through the night, strong and resilient. I watched as a baby emerged from her—my own firstborn—the cord wrapped around his neck three times. He arrived unresponsive. The midwife put an Ambu bag over his face to stimulate breathing. "Talk to the baby," we instructed the new parents. It was two minutes before breath lit up his little body. But once he inhaled and his skin bloomed pink from oxygen, his eyelids opened in the most deliberate and graceful manner, like a ballerina's swooping *port de bras*, and he gazed about the room, fully present.

(To bear _____)

21 I held my grandson for the first time the day after he was born, swaddled in receiving blankets,

dark eyes alert. He sucked hard on my index finger. People who are grandparents will say there is nothing else like it, that from the moment your grandchild is born, you feel instantaneous love.

("Beauty is _____, _____ beauty" —John Keats, "Ode on a Grecian Urn")

22 When you become a grandparent, the dynamic shifts. You don't have any actual say in matters concerning your grandchild. You can express your views or offer advice (if and when it is requested), but your kid doesn't have to listen. She's the parent now, not you. She makes the decisions, and she decides how much of an influence you have with her child. In a certain way, you have to relinquish your identity as a parent.

(Sweet _____)

23 I don't know how it happened, but Tristan is the epitome of the Happy Baby, so good natured and adaptable to his ever-changing environment. I often wonder if Lily realizes how lucky she is. Whenever he comes to visit, I play the *Ghostbusters* theme song and dance ridiculously in front of him, singing, "I ain't afraid of no ghosts!" He jumps up and down on his mother's lap, mouth wide open in a smile revealing his first two bottom front teeth, laughter erupting like the clattering of coins from a slot machine.

(When you win big, you hit the _____)

# Genome Tome

PRISCILLA LONG

Suddenly all my ancestors are behind me. Be still, they say. Watch and listen. You are the result of the love of thousands.
—Linda Hogan

## 1. Grandmother

Six million years before we were born (before any of us were born) there lived in Africa a great ape, which our species has named *Pan prior*.[1] Out of *Pan prior* both the chimpanzees and our own line evolved. This grandmother ape, how shall we think of her? Shall we despise her as if she were a massive piece of crud in our shiny kitchen? Shall we deny that we have inherited her genes? Shall we strut about as if we ourselves were made of computer wire and light?

## 2. Corps of Discovery

The Human Genome Project is the Lewis and Clark Expedition of the twenty-first century. In 1804 Meriwether Lewis and William Clark and thirty-one other souls (the Corps of Volunteers for Northwest Discovery) traveled into a country that was to them entirely unknown. They traversed rivers, mountains, prairies, swamps, rapids, cataracts. They took specimens and made notes and drew maps. To map the human genome, twenty thousand to twenty-five thousand genes strung along twenty-three pairs of chromosomes, is also to journey into the unknown. Lewis and Clark meant to befriend the Indians,

---

[1] There are two versions of this essay; this is the original, first published in 2005.

but in the end, they cleared the way for the destruction of indigenous ways of life thousands of years old. As human genomes are mapped, as the genomes of mice and flowers and fleas are recorded, much will be revealed—the secrets of life itself. And make no mistake about it: much will also be destroyed.

### 3. Alba

Take the gene that produces florescence in the Northwest jellyfish. Inject the green gene into the fertilized egg of an albino rabbit. Get Alba. Alba, the green-glowing bunny. Alba, designed by an artist in Chicago, created by a lab in France. Alba, a work of art, a work of science. Alba, the white bunny with one strange gene. Alba's jellyfish gene makes Alba glow green. Oh, Alba. Oh, funny bunny. Oh, unique creature, foundling, sentient being without fellow being. Oh, freak without circus, star without sky, tree without ground. Alba the ur-orphan among the creatures of the earth, not a jellyfish, not hardly, but not entirely a bunny either.

### 4. Recombinant Recipe: Milk-Silk

The spider web is the strongest natural fiber in existence. But for centuries attempts to raise spiders in the manner of raising silkworms have failed due to the spiderly taste for other spiders. Spiders eat spiders eating spiders.

The genomic solution: introduce a spider gene into the goat genome. Spider-goats in their spider-goat barns are renewing the economy of rural Quebec. Spider-goats look like goats—curious eyes, heads cocked to one side, perky ears. Their milk, strained like cheese, spun like silk, produces a filmy fabric, lightweight, stronger than steel, softer than silk. So strong is milk-silk that a bullet fired at point-blank range bounces off, unable to penetrate. And beautiful it is.

Milk-silk is a natural fabric. It is as natural as daffodils or baby crows or maggots creeping in a cow pie. It is as natural as a spring breeze or a drop of spring rain. And, too, milk-silk is an unnatural fabric. It is as unnatural as a robot or a tack or an airplane taking off for Peru. Milk-silk is both natural and unnatural. Still, it is more natural than Nylon.

5. Next of Kin

Chimps have long arms for climbing and for swinging in trees, and they have opposable thumbs and opposable big toes. They knuckle walk—walk on all fours with their hands folded into fists. They are born with pale faces that gradually turn brown or black.

Chimps live in large, sociable communities that have an alpha male and several (less dominant) alpha females. They express affection by grooming each other with obvious pleasure and elaborate precision (they can remove a speck from an eye or a splinter from a toe). They can be quite aggressive; communities have been known to go to war. Chimps are territorial, and when they happen upon an isolated foreign individual on their border, they kill. Like humans, they are capable of cannibalism, of infanticide. But chimps also laugh and kiss and hug. They dine on a diet that varies from plants to ants, using stick-utensils to work the ants out of the ant cupboard. During the day they spread out in small groups to forage for food. While they are thus scattered, the males drum, stamp, and hoot: the chimpanzee Global Positioning System. At night they gather and make nests high in the trees.

When a chimp is born, the other chimps come around offering to groom the mother for a chance to inspect her baby. Mother chimps are fiercely attached to their infants. Baby chimps suckle for three to five years. Adolescents stick with the family and help to babysit the little squirt. The baby requires a long time, five to seven years, to learn all the ways of chimpanzees, from chimp talk (so to speak) to tickling to hunting food to building the nightly nest. A chimpanzee becomes an adult between eleven and thirteen years of age, and can live to age sixty.

In December 2003, a chimpanzee genome was read for the first time. Chimps are so genetically similar to humans that some scientists want to reclassify them to the *Homo* (hominin) genus. Others disagree, arguing that language and culture may have a minuscule genetic basis but major species consequences.


6. Lament for Ham and Enos

In the late 1950s, the United States Air Force acquired sixty-five juvenile chimpanzees. Among them were Ham and Enos. No doubt Ham and Enos and the others had witnessed the slaughter of their mothers.

Let the new life begin. The Air Force used the chimps to gauge the effects of space travel on humans. The small chimps were spun in giant centrifuges. They were placed in decompression chambers to see how long it took them to lose consciousness. They were exposed to powerful g-forces—forces due to acceleration felt by pilots or by riders on roller coasters.

Three-year-old Ham was the first chimpanzee to be rocketed into space. This occurred on January 31, 1961. NASA archives record "a series of harrowing mischances," but Ham returned alive. The results pleased astronauts and capsule engineers, and three months later Alan Shepard became the first American to be shot into space.

Enos, age five, was launched on November 29, 1961. Enos had undergone a meticulous year of training to perform certain operations upon receiving certain prompts. Upon launch, however, the capsule malfunctioned, and Enos received an electric shock each time he acted correctly. Nevertheless, he continued to make the moves he knew to be right, shock after shock after shock. He orbited Earth two times and returned alive.

The following year John Glenn orbited Earth three times. On March 1, 1962, in lower Manhattan, four million people gathered to greet Glenn and two fellow astronauts with a huge ticker-tape parade, confetti falling like snow at Christmas. On November 4 of that same year Enos died of dysentery.

Ham was transferred to the National Zoo in Washington DC. The other chimps, the chimps captured with Ham and Enos, were transferred to "hazardous environments" duty. To test the new technology of seatbelts, they were strapped into sleds, whizzed along at 30, 50, 100 mph, slammed into walls.

By the 1970s the Air Force, done with the chimps, leased them out for biomedical research. These highly sociable primates, now adults in their twenties, were stored in concrete-block cells with bars in front but no windows between cells to provide contact with fellow chimps.

Chimpanzees are our nearest relatives in the primate world. But there are differences between us. On a chimp's face, a grin is an expression of fear (a "fear grimace"). There were films taken of Ham during his flight and upon his recovery from the ocean after his capsule plunged into the Atlantic. When primatologist Jane Goodall saw this footage, she said, "I have never seen such terror on a chimp's face."

## 7. Lucy in the Sky with Diamonds

The fossilized skeleton of Lucy, discovered in 1974 in Hadar, Ethiopia, was the oldest of hominin remains then known. Lucy died 3.2 million years ago. While her discoverers, Donald Johanson and his team, were looking at her bones in amazement, a Beatles tape played in the background. They named Lucy after the Beatles' song "Lucy in the Sky with Diamonds." Lucy was short, about four feet high, with long arms for climbing. She stood upright. That's the important thing. Her proper species name is *Australopithecus afarensis*. From her group, several species of hominins evolved. *Homo erectus* evolved. We evolved. That's the old story. It's a nice story. It has a nice beginning, middle, and end.

But it's probably not true. Bones speak, but they do not enunciate. Skulls and femurs and molars are measured and compared and recompared, and theories replace theories. Thighbones and skulls "from the same species" placed side by side look different, and fossilized bones, alas, do not produce DNA.

In 2000 the creation story got a new beginning. About six million years ago, our human ancestor split off from *Pan prior*. This missing link, this half-ape half-hominin has been the longed-for find, the physical anthropologist's Holy Grail. In Kenya, in 2000, scientists Martin Pickford and Brigette Senut discovered a very few very old bones. *Orrorin tugenensis* lived six million years ago, the time our oldest human ancestor split off from *Pan prior*. These scientists claim that Lucy was not our direct ancestor but an offshoot that died out. That *Orrorin tugenensis* were our true ancestor hominids. These beings stood upright, but also displayed the attributes of knuckle-walking, tree-climbing apes. Donald Johanson thinks Pickford and Senut might be right.

After that (if that really was that), perhaps fifteen different species of humans evolved. Between one million to three million years ago (before *Homo sapiens*), perhaps ten different human species lived simultaneously. There were side branches and extinctions. *Homo neanderthalensis* was one of the side branches, and these beings shared the earth with *Homo sapiens*, our people, who evolved in Africa probably 200,000 years ago. Not so very long ago.


## 8. Mother

Our ancient mother, the mother of us all, lived in Africa some 200,000 years ago. She was one individual in a world population of *Homo sapiens*—recently evolved out of *Homo erectus*—amounting to two thousand individuals at most. There were other females of course, but their lines died out long before historical times. Everyone alive today descends from this one woman, from one of her two daughters. This is the astonishing news revealed by the book of the human genome, the book whose pages we are just beginning to turn.

## 9. History and Geography

We are apes evolved into *Homo erectus*. We are Africans, *Homo sapiens* evolved from a group of *Homo erectus* who lived in Africa 200,000 years ago. Not so very long ago. Twelve thousand generations ago.

We are *Homo sapiens*, alone knowing. We know, and we don't know. We wonder. We wonder where we came from. We wonder who we are. We wonder where we are going. We pose questions.

## 10. Questions

1. Are we, then, the greatest of the great apes?
2. Is human kindness more human than "inhuman" cruelty?
3. What makes a cell divide? Am I dividing against myself?
4. If we were once single-celled creatures, was I once a single-celled creature?
5. Identical twins: aren't we the pioneer clones?
6. How does Earth's age, 4.5 billion years, relate to our age?
7. If grammar is innate, is iambic pentameter innate?
8. If you could read the book of your genes, would anything there surprise you?
9. Would it surprise you to learn that you were mixed race?
10. Can humans and chimpanzees mate?
11. What will life look like after five hundred years of genetic experiments?
12. Is human selection less natural than natural selection?
13. Where did we come from? Where are we going?
14. If a twin is not the same person, why would a clone be the same person?
15. Should art include the creation of life?
16. Is there a gene for creativity, and if so what protein does it express?
17. If a scientist creates a new species, is the scientist the parent? Who gets custody?

18. Do I belong to myself, in the cellular sense?

19. Who wrote the book of life?

20. Is my cell line mine? Is my genome mine?

21. Considering that more genetic variation exists within racial groups than between racial groups, what is race?

22. Was our first mother happy?

23. How can you say that?


## 11. The Grammar Gene

Linguist Noam Chomsky argues that grammar is not learned, that it somehow comes with our DNA. People in any language recognize grammatical structures, apart from the sounds or meanings of words. Grammar is innate, whereas diction and meanings are cultural and, over the slow centuries, in flux. Others argue that what is inherited isn't grammar, it's a propensity to search for patterns in speech. We move from "Mama!" to "Mama get ball!" to "I think Johnny went to the store to get milk, at least that's what he said he was going to do before he found out he won the lottery"—a construction that will forever elude the most brilliant chimps taught to "speak."

Did language evolve out of primate vocalizations? Or did it evolve out of an entirely different part of the brain, the part that can practice throwing to improve one's aim, the part that can plan to marry off one's unborn daughter to the as-yet-unconceived son of the future king.

There is something about language that we inherit. Perhaps our mother taught us to speak, but she could never teach a chimp to speak, except in the most rudimentary way after years of work. We are born with something structural about language in our DNA.

The structure of language lurks below the meaning of words. Chomsky wrote, "Colorless green ideas sleep furiously." This grammatical sentence illustrates that grammar and meaning have about as much relationship to one another as strangers on a blind date. Grammar is the towny. This dude, this thug, knows the ins and outs of the place by heart. He runs the show, and he practically owns the territory. His date just blew into town. She's all fluttery in this gaudy multipart outfit she copped at various exotic bazaars and flea markets. Half the time she's got no idea what she's saying, but she's easy, in actual fact a slut willing to go along with just about anything.

Oh my.

## 12. Grammar Gene Mutation

Courtly cows dispense with diphthongs. Chocolate-covered theories crouch in corners. Corners rot uproariously. Refrigerators frig the worms. Catastrophe kisses the count of five. A statement digests its over-rehearsed rhinoceros. Bookworms excrete monogamous bunnies. Blue crud excites red ecstasy. All this during the furious sleeping of colorless green ideas.

## 13. The Ghazal Gene

The ghazal is an old poetic form, very old, very stringent, very strange. It is older than the sonnet. Or so writes the poet Agha Shahid Ali. According to Ali, *ghazal* is pronounced to rhyme with *muzzle* and the initial *gh* sound comes from deep in the throat like a French rolled *r*. Like a smoker quietly clearing his throat.

The ghazal goes back to seventh-century Arabia, perhaps earlier, in contrast to the sonnet, which goes back to thirteenth-century Italy. If grammar is genomic, could the ghazal be genomic?

A ghazal performs itself in couplets, five or more. The couplets have nothing to do with one another, except for a formal unity derived from a strict rhyme and repetition pattern. In the last couplet it is customary for the poet to mention him or herself by name, by pseudonym, or as "I." In all other couplets this is strictly illegal.

The ghazal is the form of choice for the incorrigible narcissist because it always returns to the subject of the poet, rather like a bore at a cocktail party.

The ghazal has been tortured and butchered in English, which pained Agha Shahid Ali and moved him to write a rant. This humorous but headstrong harangue precedes an anthology of good ghazals in English, *Ravishing DisUnities*.

Or maybe they're not so good. Some are exquisite. Others stand in complete violation of Ali's ground rules. What does it matter?

If you construct a ghazal on a subject so that each couplet chews on the theme announced in the title like a meat chopper, or if you violate the form by using slant rhyme—say, *white/what* instead of *white/fight*—or if you violate the rule of no enjambment between couplets, the form disintegrates. The eerie magic of the ghazal, its ravishing disunity, its weird indirection, falls to pieces. The thing becomes awkward, stiff, forced like a too-fancy, out-of-date party dress purchased at a thrift shop, which, besides missing a button, is too tight and unsightly.

I have committed God-awful ghazals. At first, I missed the point about autonomy of the couplets. Then one day I was visited by the muse, Keeper of Classical Forms. Perhaps she was sent by Agha Shahid Ali, who died of a brain tumor on December 8, 2001. He was fifty-two years old.

I gutted my ghazals and began again.

## 14. Genome Ghazal

One Earth, one ur-gene, in the beginning.
Mountain air. No green, in the beginning.

Black towers. Steel and glass. Blue dawn
downtown. Pristine in the beginning.

Old friend, did you slip into not-being,
or was death like a dream, in the beginning?

Dirt-obliterated bones, bits of bowls,
stone tools—unseen in the beginning.

Sibilant hiss, susurrous sigh—Priscilla—
What did it mean, in the beginning?

## 15. In the Beginning

When I was twelve, I took up bird-watching. On the first day of my new hobby, I set out down the dirt road of our dairy farm noting in my tablet any bird I saw. Crow. Red-winged blackbird. Sparrow—I had no idea what kind. Turkey buzzards spiraling down. A cardinal flashing red in a black locust tree. That evening over supper, I read my list to my brother and sisters, and to my rather worn-down parents.

The next day my twin sister Pammy took up bird-watching. She returned with a list twice as long. Besides my birds, she had recorded a wood thrush, a black-capped chickadee, and a yellow finch. Our mother put an immediate stop to Pammy's bird-watching hobby. She forbade Pammy to watch for birds or to put down the names of birds. Pammy was not even to speak of birds. Bird-watching was my hobby, not Pammy's hobby.

Pamela is my identical twin. We each, like everybody else, have three trillion cells, give or take a few. Most of these cells have at their center a copy of our genome. My genome is identical to Pamela's genome. Therefore, Pamela and I feel we have something to interject into the debate on cloning. But here I speak for myself.

I speak for myself because I am looking out of my own eyes. I live in the Puget Sound region—a land of clouds, salmon, Orca whales, congested traffic, and double-leaved bascule bridges. Like many Seattleites, I grumble at the excessive sunshine in mid-July. I like foghorns and ducks and snowcapped mountains. Rainy Seattle with its cafés and bookstores is a perfect reading-and-writing city, and I am happy here, happy as a coot bobbing on Green Lake. My place, the Pacific Northwest, affects who I am.

Genes don't even determine all physical characteristics. I have curly hair; Pamela has straight hair. That could be because of the weather, or maybe I have more kinky thoughts.

Once an old friend of mine, long out of contact, saw Pamela in Washington DC, jogging in Rock Creek Park.

"Priscilla!" she screamed.

"I'm not Priscilla!" Pamela called back. She waved but did not bother to stop.

Years later I reunited with my friend, and she informed me of my mental lapse, my rudeness, my inexplicable behavior. I reminded her that I have a twin sister who may or may not have identical fingerprints. In any case, I'm not responsible—for anything.

In my memory, our childhood is fused. For years I told the story of how our mother taught us to read at the age of three. Once I told the story in the presence of my mother, who informed me that Pamela had learned to read at the age of three. I had exhibited zero interest in reading until I was six or seven. I must have thought, as Pammy was learning to read: Oh! Look! We can read!

Twins share the same genome, but they do not share the same environment. One twin dominates; the other carves a niche out of whatever space the dominant twin—in our case Pamela—leaves available. One may be more conservative, the other more deviant.

Our desires send us out on our various paths; they color the persons we become. Pamela grew up wanting to be a scientist, and at eight or nine this moved her to collect white mice and to experiment with questionable liquid mixtures in her chemistry laboratory. When she was sixteen (in the bad old days of 1959), she wrote to medical schools asking how she should prepare herself to be admitted. Each and every school wrote back: girls need not apply. We are formed by our generation, our era, as much as by our genes.

But times changed. After Pamela graduated from college and worked for a decade as a social worker, she came to her senses and got a PhD. She is now a brilliant historian of Renaissance science and technology.

I wanted to be a poet, and that sent me down a different road.

If a twin is not the same person, why would a clone be the same person? How could you replace one twin with another? Each looks at the world through his or her own eyes. Place, choice, chance—all affect who a person is. Who could imagine that one person—that ineffable, multivarious, complicated, constantly changing complexity that is a single human being—could be the same as another?

Today Pamela and I are the best of friends, a mutual aid society, career consultants, fashion consultants. I live by myself; she lives with her husband and receives visits from her college-age daughter. We both write books—utterly different sorts of books.

I'm not a bird-watcher, but I like watching widgeons paddling about on Green Lake squeaking like a flock of bathtub toys. They look identical to me, probably because I do not take the time to distinguish their particulars. Pamela would do better. I think she has a life list, and I think widgeons are on it.

## 16. Dolly

Dolly, cloned from an udder cell of a six-year-old sheep, was born on July 5, 1996. She looked very lamblike, with her white wool and curious eyes. Dolly the newborn had six-year-old cells. She soon went stiff with arthritis. She soon came down with lung disease. Sheep live for eleven or twelve years and in old age typically suffer arthritis and lung disease. Dolly's caretakers, considering her progressive lung disease, put her to sleep in February 2003. She was not yet seven years old.

Dolly illustrates the difficulties of reproductive cloning. She was just a lamb, like any other lamb, soft and woolly and frisky. But she was one cloning success out of hundreds of failed tries, and even then, she had complications and died young, if you count her age from the time she was born. Since Dolly, other large mammals have been cloned. One calf's hind end is fused into one back leg. Extreme abnormalities in cloned animals are routine. Life is not easy to create in the lab.

The idea of using reproductive cloning to clone human babies is fraught with the nightmare of tragic "successes"—infants with severe abnormalities. Any cloned infant would enter a life of many problems and early death. The most heartwarming argument used in favor of reproductive cloning is that human cloning could provide the grief-stricken parents of terminally ill babies a copy of their lost child. It could give them their baby back.

I am here to speak as one of nature's clones. A genetically identical being is not the same being. A cloned baby would not return a dying baby to its parents. It would not erase the grief of losing a child. A cloned baby is a different baby. It is an identical twin, not the same little boy, not the same little girl. A cloned baby would start life in the wake of grief and death—already a radically different life beginning. It would delete neither the death nor the grief over the death of the child that lived for only a short while. Imagining that a cloned baby could replace a lost child is as insensitive as the idiot persons who say to grieving parents, "You can always have another child!"

### 17. Stem-Cell Research

But stem-cell research is a different thing. Stem cells are fetal cells; no born child is involved. Stem cells are the body's ur-cells, the first to grow after the sperm and egg join. Stem cells are poised to become any body tissue, from liver to brain to skin. Stem-cell research holds the promise of curing paralysis, Alzheimer's, multiple sclerosis, Parkinson's . . .

To my way of thinking, stem cells are not a human being but a potential human being. I do not disrespect the right-to-lifers, but I've always wondered why they don't go on a campaign to save the world's eighteen million infants and toddlers who die every year, mostly from diarrhea—preventable deaths of born children.

## 18. The Ancient One

Looking into this petri dish, into this dish of our own cells, we can see, after a fashion, our ancestors. We can unravel their journeys. It is as if DNA were a telescope with multiple lenses pointed at the deep past, each lens revealing a different scene. The Human Genome Project, added to the archeological breakthrough of carbon dating, added to new archeological digs, added to the study of languages living and dead, added to the study of blood types, added to sonar sweeps of ocean floors that were once dry land, will rewrite the story of who we are and who our ancestors were.

We know now that *Homo sapiens* spread out from Africa. That is a long story. We know the species spread to Asia and to Europe. Another long story. Then some of them came to America.

The old story is that peoples out of some sort of Asian gene pool walked to the North American continent over the Bering land bridge when the Bering Strait was iced over, some twelve thousand to thirteen thousand years ago. These people, these ancient ones, evolved into American Indians, into South American Indians, into Cherokees and Crows and Sioux and Mayans. That's the old story. A newer old story is that they came earlier, in waves, and that some may have come by boat.

Kennewick Man threatened to rewrite the old story. Teenagers found a man's bones half-buried in a bank of the Columbia River in eastern Washington on July 28, 1996, during Kennewick's annual unlimited hydroplane races. The bones were determined to be 8,400 years old, one of the oldest complete skeletons ever found in the Americas. Controversy flared when an archeologist working for the Benton County coroner's office declared that they were Caucasoid bones (a white man's bones). The skeleton had a narrow, elongated skull, like Europeans, unlike Native Americans. This would suggest that the ancestors of Europeans arrived in the Americas before the ancestors of Native Americans did.

However, genetic research has uncovered that Native Americans have a common ancestor with native peoples who now occupy south-central Asia.

Several of these peoples have narrow, elongated skulls. The scientist who breez-
ily declared in the first week of the find that the Kennewick Man's bones were
white man's bones spoke in haste.

In the case between Native Americans who want to bury the Ancient One's
old bones and certain scientists who want to examine them, the courts have
ruled that Kennewick Man's bones may be studied. Although DNA has yet to
be extracted (it's difficult and sometimes impossible to extract DNA from old
bones), it is now considered quite far-fetched to think of Kennewick Man as
European.[2]

## 19. My Ancient Ones

My ancestors are European. They came out of Africa, just as all of our ancestors
did. They lived for many generations in the cold steppes of Russia and in the
cold steppes of eastern Europe. During these many generations, groups that
would become Asian were moving east, probably along the seacoast. Eventually
some arrived in North America. At the same time, groups that would become
Caucasian were moving into what were then the steppes of Germany. The earth
was becoming colder. *Homo sapiens* were hunting with more social coopera-
tion than before. Neanderthal bones show that the Neanderthals were having a
hard time. They were starving. This was about twenty thousand years ago. The
last ice age lasted a long time. Then it got warm again. Germany grew trees.
Germany grew the Black Forest. Children played in the woods, got lost in the
woods. The woodcutter's children, Hansel and Gretel, found their witch . . .

## 20. The Courage of the Ancestors

Back in the forested hills and hollows of Old Germany, the Brothers Grimm
went about collecting fairy tales, legends, riddles, ridiculous superstitions.
This was in the early 1800s, but the stories they collected were of course much
older, handed down from previous generations. Grimm's fairy tales are known

---

2   Since 2005, the science has evolved, sometimes with startling speed: scientists have
    learned to extract DNA from old bones; Kennewick Man has been determined to in
    fact be related to Native Americans, not Caucasians; the human origins story has
    undergone dramatic twists and turns. Transgenic spider-goat research has moved to
    Utah, and a commercially viable spider-milk silk has yet to be achieved.

the world over and can be compared to analogous fairy tales from just about every culture.

Their legends are less well known. One of them, Number 328 in the Brothers Grimm published collection, is titled "The Dead from the Graves Repel the Enemy." According to this legend, the town Wehrstadt got its name—related to the verb *wehren*, to repel—after the town suffered an attack by "foreign heathens" of vastly superior force. At the moment of defeat, the dead rose from their graves "and courageously repulsed the enemy, thus saving their descendants."

## 21. Grandma Henry's Love Story

My mother's father, whom I called Granddaddy, was hard working and rather taciturn. He spoke little, except when he was laughing and talking in Pennsylvania Dutch with his insurance customers. My mother's mother, whom I called Grandma, talked in a constant stream in English, considering herself to be emancipated from Pennsylvania Dutch. My grandparents did not speak overly much to each other.

One day Grandma told me the following story. Decades after their wedding day, their three children grown, grandchildren already born, Granddaddy told Grandma, "You were the most beautiful girl in the whole town!" At this point, Grandma paused in her telling of the story. Then she said, "Why didn't he ever tell me that before? I never knew I was beautiful!"

## 22. Mother's Love Story

My mother once told me, "I was the adored first child."

My mother wrote to her mother, my Grandma Henry, every single week from the time she went away to Bucknell College to the time (that same year) she married my father and they had their first three children before they turned twenty. She continued writing to her mother every week, regular as clockwork, for decades, until her mother, my Grandma Henry, died on August 29, 1987.

My mother's own dying was long and painful, involving diabetes and strokes. During the years of her extreme disablement, my father was her caretaker. Dr. Barbara Henry Long died on May 29, 2003, at 11:45 at night. A couple of weeks after she died, in the midst of all the turmoil and arrangements, my father took out a framed photograph of my mother, taken when she was eighteen. "She gave me this picture after our first date," he told us. In the photograph, Barbara Jane Henry is young with a long and thinner face. Her brown hair curls softly. Her eyes are shining with happiness.

## 23. Naming Names

The crime of Christoph Tanger, a German innkeeper, was stealing horses. He was tempted by the devil to associate with thieves. These are the facts reported in the printed account of his hanging, which took place on March 13, 1749, in Gemersheim, a town on the Rhine River in what is now southern Germany. The "leading out" of Christoph Tanger occupied four hours. The procession cheering him on to his execution sang "more than 20 of the finest Evangelical Lutheran hymns." Upon "entering the circle" it was intoned, "Now we are praying to the Holy Spirit." Christoph Tanger himself thanked the Lord and, according to his pastor, "repeatedly recommended to me his wife and children, that the latter should be raised in his religion, which is so much a consolation to him. Whereupon under constant cheering up he died without much pain!"

Two years later Christoph's widow, Anna, and their children arrived in Pennsylvania. Their German became Pennsylvania German, their Dutch became Pennsylvania Dutch. I am here because of the broken love between Christoph and Anna. I am here because of their son Andreas, witness at age six to his father's broken neck. I am here because of the love between Andreas Tanger and Catherine Lottman, married in 1768. I am here because of their children and their children's children, ending with my mother. They are the vessel from which my genes were poured. They are the ancestors who gave me this world. They are the lovers who put me into this blue dawn, watching and listening . . .

# As Is

BRIAN OLIU

1 item found for BRIAN OLIU

| ITEM TITLE | BIDS | PRICE | TIME LEFT |
| --- | --- | --- | --- |
| AUTHENTIC brian oliu **AS IS** | 0 | $9.95 | 11h 22m |

Meet the seller

Seller: beoliu (8)

Feedback: 91.6% Positive

Member: since Nov-22-82 in United States

**Item #45192910201 AUTHENTIC BRIAN OLIU torso **AS IS****

You are bidding on one (1) authentic BRIAN OLIU. The item has some damage or imperfections, as noted here, and is sold AS IS. The item is sold under the impression that it will be used for parts because the item is beyond repair. This item DOES NOT WORK and is being sold as NOT WORKING.

**From the Manufacturer:** There came a point in BRIAN OLIU's life that he felt he deserved more space in the world. Those who chose not to gain mass were giving in, giving in to nothing; the air presses against them, creeping up and eating away space in between thighs and underneath chins. Everyone is allocated a certain amount of characters, and to use any less than the allocated amount would be going against our creator and doing ourselves a disservice. As a result, everyone wants to touch BRIAN OLIU, to be a part of something so large, if only for a moment. They wish to wrap their arms around his body. They want to jump on top of him and ride him like a greased pig. They punch him in the chest. They want to feel "safe." BRIAN OLIU has never felt safe. BRIAN OLIU is the freak show, the tilt-a-whirl, the moon bounce, the prize with the button eyes, the funnel cake, the carnival.

The seller acknowledges that the item being sold is defective. The seller acknowledges outright mistreatment of the item. The torso currently measures 1.5′ × 2.5′ × 1.5′. At one point, the measurements were much smaller, and the torso took up a significantly smaller amount of space in the world. The original size of the item, sans defections, is completely uncertain. Bloated like this listing. The item is *special* because of said defects. Appraisers have stressed this *special* quality multiple times since BRIAN OLIU's birth. BRIAN OLIU is a temple and a gift from God, and the seller has breached this contract.

**Shipping:** The buyer agrees to pay for shipping, which may or may not cost more than the item itself. There is nothing passive about the gravitational mass of this item. The seller's first-grade science fair project, made of foam core (which floats), illustrated how much the seller, as a first grader (already > 60 lb.) would weigh on the various bodies in the solar system. This, even today, reminds the seller of chocolate and nougat: the wrapper picked clean of caramel pus and disposed of in a twelve-gallon cafeteria trash can. The solitary dollar crumpled in item's pocket since five minutes before the school bus came was FOR LUNCH and was not used FOR LUNCH. This is a typical memory for the seller, one among those of deadlines and diets and sweatpants shopping. BRIAN OLIU is so fat that when he walks he breaks Three Bridges Elementary School's all-purpose room tile. The seller would dream about the day when he would board a rocket ship, fly to the moon (he weighed the least there), and see a red digital 16.6 blinking back at him. Jupiter was the seller's favorite, until he realized he would weigh 253.3 pounds on Jupiter, a horrifying number then, a goal now. His project would be on display along the walls of the cafeteria for a week, until someone dumped ketchup on his popcorn moon. The seller won honorable mention for his project, beating out countless baking soda volcanoes and slingshots; the reward was an ice cream social.

The average adult human male has approximately five liters of blood in his system at one time. BRIAN OLIU has almost 50 percent more than most humans.

One can ascertain that BRIAN OLIU is 50 percent more alive than everyone else. One liter of blood weighs approximately one kilogram, or 2.2 pounds. On days he would get kicked in the stomach in sterile high school hallways, or days he looked in the mirror a little too long, the seller would imagine punching down on the crest of his nose and letting pounds of plasma and tissue gush from his nostrils. As he felt the gravitational pull to the earth loosen, he would open a bottle of aspirin (with his eyes closed) and take three. Aspirin helps with circulation. Other days, it would be the stripping of fat with a piano wire, the makeshift soup skimmer cutting through hardened lipids like NO FOOD METAPHORS hot paperclips through Styrofoam.

**Item Defects:** In between the sixth and seventh rib lies the item's heart, which will not be functional at the point of sale. The result of this is likely to be congestive heart failure (Medical Code ICD-10: 150.0) occurring because of the inability to produce enough blood to cause the seller to function correctly. Multiple times a day, the seller will feel as if his heart is about to cease pumping blood and that his veins and aortas are filling up with air, forming a carbon dioxide spider. These moments come and go and happen often in stale bars with sticky floors and while sitting alone at his desk. The seller will clutch at his chest, say the first nine words "Our Father, who art in heaven, hallowed be thy . . ." and collapse. *It was so strange, one minute he was standing/sitting at the bar/at his desk/and the next second/moment he was on the floor/floor and he was gone/dead.* BRIAN OLIU is so fat that he's going to contract heart disease and die from the complications of obesity. The morning after, everyone will gather at his former house, and someone will bring Dunkin' Donuts Munchkins (the official food of mourning), and another person will laugh and say "Brian always said that Munchkins were the official food of mourning," and there will be some wince-smiles, and people will no longer feel guilty about eating fried dough and powdered sugar in the wake of such a tremendous fall. Well, I can't say I was *shocked*.

**Buyer's Contract:** Upon the winning of the item, the buyer agrees to follow the regulations set by the seller in regards to the distribution of parts, as laid out in the list below:

Heart: Eight-year-old boy with juvenile onset diabetes

Intestines: forty-eight-year-old father of three with celiac disease, who
   just wants to participate in the transubstantiation on Sundays

Kidneys: fifty-five-year-old first-time grandmother with chronic renal
   failure

Lungs: thirty-three-year-old prisoner suffering from pneumothorax after
   taking a plastic spoon shiv to the left pectoral

Liver: twenty-two-year-old first-round draft choice of the Indianapolis
   Colts on injured reserve because of haemochromatosis

Pancreas: twenty-four-year-old supermodel with cystic fibrosis

Regrettably, there is some fear by the seller that the intended usage of parts is
not possible; severe obesity renders otherwise good organs useless. Not only is
the torso not aesthetically pleasing, but also the fattened liver and the swollen
heart have been rendered inoperable by the seller's ineptitude and disregard
for his product. In fact the only plausible use for the parts encased within
BRIAN OLIU is as a delicacy. BRIAN OLIU is so fat that upon his death, even
people who have spent years on organ transplant waiting lists will be unable
to use his slop.

Therefore, upon the conclusion of the bidding the item is to be desiccated
and mummified. The buyer agrees to cut open the item and begin packing
the insides with crystallized sugar. The buyer then agrees to pour molasses
onto the item, filling in pores and stretch marks with high fructose syrup. The
buyer will then use red licorice rope to sew the chest cavity shut and spackle
the lacerations shut with cake frosting. BRIAN OLIU will never spoil.

This would be a perfect item for collectors.

# Falling in Love with a Glass House

Twenty-Four Views of Ludwig Mies van
der Rohe's Farnsworth House

JENNIFER METSKER

### Figure 1: Preliminary Plan of the Glass House

Sugar maples shade the barest of floor plans. Every line is glass. Every pause is structure. The house is like a body as perfect as a pure idea. I can see why Dr. Edith Farnsworth, specialist in kidneys, with her estimable intelligence and her "equine features," consented to this plan, thereby commissioning a bitter love story between her and Ludwig Mies van der Rohe, a story which took place along a river bank fifty miles from Chicago over three or so years of questionable picnics. It's a story that begins with shared ideals and ends with eight steel beams, four sheets of glass, two steel slabs, and a limestone deck.

### Figure 2: Edith Farnsworth, Photograph Taken in 1973

In a book that tells the story of the house, a quote accompanying a photograph of Edith states: "Witnesses agree, rather equine in features." With additional descriptors like "six-feet tall, ungainly of carriage," Edith isn't a natural beauty. But I admire the woman who lived in the world's first glass house, so I won't throw stones. She does not smile in the photograph. Having sold her glass house ten years before the picture was taken, she has managed to erase her disappointment from her face. But I can see in her eyes every square foot of those 9.6 wooded acres and the glint of the swift Fox River that ran through them. I can see spring times (three or so), a variety of wildflowers, and exchanges of considerable wit. I can see picnics spread on a red checkered grid. I can hear her laugh, buck toothed and lively.

### Figure 3: Philip Johnson Glass House, 1949

Though the Farnsworth House was the first glass house ever designed, it was not the first glass house ever built. Mies designed the house for Edith immediately upon commission in 1946, but he took his time breaking ground. The task required wine and sandwiches, flirtation and patronage. Architect and client often drove to the site together and saw each other frequently in the city. Edith's sister recalls, "She was mesmerized by him, and she probably had an affair with him." During their three-year dalliance, Philip Johnson designed and built his own glass house. Years later, after a visit to the Johnson house that ended abruptly in an enraged departure, Mies expressed with disdain that Johnson "made too many mistakes in the details."

"God is in the details," he is known for saying, though no one claims having ever heard him say it.

### Figure 4: View of the Farnsworth House from the North, Watercolor

This view of the Farnsworth House provides a looser, more colorful perspective of the site in pastel washes of watercolor. This image was painted during the picnic years, after Edith commissioned the design in 1946 but before the house cast its shadow on the land. Given what is known about Mies and his affairs with women, I gather there was less lightness and ease between him and Edith than this watercolor suggests. In the 1940s the architect's life was excessive. He was obsessed with work and was known for drinking heavily. Surely he was fulfilling other commissions at the time.

And then there was Lora Marx, the woman he met at a New Year's Eve party a year before he designed the house for Edith. He and Lora were drawn to each other "suddenly and electrically," and they began a relationship that night that lasted until his death. Did Edith not see this relationship already forming when she arrived on the scene? Was it hidden by the gestural trees?

### Figure 5: 330 North Wabash

330 North Wabash is a thirty-six-floor black glass skyscraper that looks down on the Chicago River and the city center, two blocks from Lake Michigan. Though Mies died before its construction began in 1969, this building is considered to

be one of his major achievements, and it was the first of his buildings that I ever saw in person. In 1999 I was living in Chicago with my boyfriend, Scott, who worked in this building. Though I visited him at work a couple of times, this is really his view. This photograph is taken from the plaza below, which Scott crossed on his way to work. From this angle, the building is a monolith of black glass cutting into the blue sky with an unforgiving geometry; it doesn't so much reflect the nearby buildings as swallow them in its surface. The building's sleek sides and placement exacerbate the wind that whips up the Chicago River from the lake, especially in winter. The wind tunnel created by the building is so strong that on gusty days it can almost knock a person over. Scott used to tell a story about this view. He once watched a woman step out of the revolving doors, and whoosh, the wind whisked her across the icy plaza toward the river. To save herself, she threw her body at a cement planter and landed face first in the dirt. The attention this brought to the building's precarious placement caused the management to install ropes from the planter to the door. On windy days, employees were instructed to cling to these ropes and pull themselves toward the building. My boyfriend liked to end his story by saying that he refused to grab these ropes, that he would rather let the wind take him.

Over time, Scott would eventually become my husband and then my ex-husband, and even after he is gone, this story will stick with me. It's like a metaphor for something that I can't quite grasp—just as I'm about to understand what it means, the wind carries it away.

### Figure 6: Sketch of the Site of the Farnsworth House

This is Mies at his most pure. No maple trees, no grassy meadow, no Edith, no horizon. Just a rectangle placed beside the bank of a river. With a rapt and affluent woman as his patron, Mies could project his ideal form. Later, when reporters asked him about this house, he would say, "When one looks at Nature through the glass walls of the Farnsworth House it takes on a deeper significance than when one stands outside." He also believed that "a total union of the architectural space and its natural setting cannot be achieved unless that space loses its identity."

### Figure 7: Mies and Lora Marx at a New Year's Eve Party, 1940

Lora Marx described her encounter with Mies as "love at first sight" though in this photograph, she isn't looking at Mies at all. The photograph shows him studying her face while she looks away, oblivious to the white paper rose he has plucked from the party decorations and gallantly extends toward her. The black cat Lora clasps in her arms makes her seem childlike, distracted. She is as oblivious to the cat's struggle to get away from her as she is to Mies's desire to gain her attention. The cat squirms and extends its claws; very soon she will need to let go of it. But for the moment, Lora holds the cat to her chest and stares off gleefully at something or someone other than the architect, and in doing so, she successfully holds his attention. When the time comes to let the cat go, she will let it go. If it comes back, she will pet it, cradle it. No hard feelings. She is a woman of such self-possession that she doesn't seem to need to possess anything at all.

### Figure 8: View of the Fireplace and Core

This sketch is overconfident, as if dashed off quickly, too quickly, considering how much depends on it. The Farnsworth House was meant to be the highlight of Mies's American career. He had distinguished himself in Germany, but in the States his minimalism wasn't considered minimal enough to set him apart. Thus the Farnsworth house and its almost frightening austerity was born. Because the house's outer walls are made of clear glass, it needed a solid interior core to contain the less attractive electrical wires and plumbing and to provide enough privacy for a bathroom. This part of the house had to be more than an idea; it needed to function for the house to be considered a success. In 1949, the construction crew poured the first concrete footings and the concrete revealed the large and unforgiving mistakes in Mies's design; in order for the house to support his ideal of "less is more," more work had to be done. He had to redesign the core of the house and start again. By 1950 construction difficulties had caused the cost of the house to run over into the tens of thousands. Even before the completion of the house in 1951, Edith Farnsworth had filed suit against him for the damages she incurred from his poor planning. He summed up the situation differently: "The lady expected the architect to go along with the house."

*Figure 9: Mies in His Office at 37 South Wabash*

For a number of years, Mies van der Rohe's office was located in the same building where I attended school in Chicago. This is a view of him at his desk in that office. He's staring out the window, his desk clear of clutter: no papers or writing utensils. The sunlight against the window obscures his view, obliterating the cityscape in a brilliant white glare—this room could be anywhere. This is not the way this building looks now. Today, the building houses art studios and classrooms. The materials of making are everywhere. Scott would sometimes meet me in front of this building when my classes ended, and we would walk to the El and ride home together. During this time, I was more interested in my work than in people. I have very few memories of spending time with Scott while I was in school. One night as we walked to the El, he claims that he told me he wanted to break up with me. I have no memory of this conversation. All I know about our exchange is what he told me later: "You told me we couldn't break up because it would take too much time and you needed to focus on your painting." And so we stayed together.

Looking back, I believe it was our shared belief that our work came first that kept us together. He must have agreed with me on some level that we didn't need romance as much as a supportive partnership. Or maybe he didn't agree. Either way, this agreement became the core of our relationship, a core that functioned for a time, despite its poor design.

*Figure 10: The Farnsworth House during Construction*

The site during winter reveals patches of snow, bare trees, construction scraps and barrels. Steel beams jut from the frozen ground. Mies stands on the site, and his silhouette, from behind, in trench coat and hat, is in perfect alignment with one of the girders. Squint and he's an I-beam. If Edith could have seen this view of him before commissioning the house, she might have known he wasn't suited for daily habitation.

*Figure 11: Sketch of the Interior for the Farnsworth House*

The interior of the finished house consists of a single room surrounded by glass with separate living spaces "suggested" rather than defined. The only private spaces are two small bathrooms, one for Edith and one for her "suggested" guest. The I-beams are positioned closer to the center of the structure, away from the corners so that the roof and floor slabs extend out beyond the house seemingly without support, like two long magnets in a state of active resistance. Though few and far between, the linear beams lift the house up from the river's flood cycle but do not protect it. Eventually water seeped through the door to strand the tiny bathrooms. Then the visitors arrived. The tourists who came to see the house were as common as weeds in the landscape. Edith complained they caused the herons to seek their "lost seclusion" upstream. But I imagine that when she stood on the terrace of the finished house, she didn't see the sugar maples or the tourists or the missing herons. She saw a memory of Mies standing before her, back when the house was still half-finished. He cocked his head and said to her, "Walk up to the terrace level so I can have a look at you." Flattered, she climbed the unfinished steps and smiled at her lover.

"Good," he said, turning away. "I just wanted to check scale."

### Figure 12: View of the Terrace

Once the house was built, it was riddled with problems. Exorbitant heating costs. The "cooker" effect of summer sun. The constant rust of the steel. Fallen leaves adhered to the terrace and stained it. Condensation. Lack of privacy. What this view does not reveal is the moths and mosquitoes that made it difficult to linger on the terrace for too long, especially at night. In response to all of Edith's complaints about the house, Mies said: "It's just an idea. You aren't supposed to live in it."

### Figure 13: View from the Living Room

What moths and mosquitoes see at night: a geometric lantern burning on the riverbed. Mies believed the house should not be burdened with screens, screens are not glass. Nor did he install ducts for air conditioning. So when the doors are left open, as they must be in summer, the moths and mosquitoes swarm toward the light. Swatting bugs away inside her living room on hot, humid nights, Edith must have regretted approving the architect's plans without clause or objection. In being drawn to the man, she was drawn to the house.

*Figure 14: The Lafayette Building*

Though he didn't excel at designing single-family homes, Mies's apartment tower in Detroit still stands resolutely just outside of the city center, a functioning residence, a success in a city where many other buildings have been deserted. With no other tall buildings on the surrounding blocks, the tower seems even taller than it is. The view of the city from an upper-story apartment is like the aerial view one sees from the window of a plane tilting into its descent. Boxy little buildings and inky black streets stretch into the distance like a plan for a city rather than the real thing. Though the view is dizzying, the room itself is cozy, filled with comfortable furniture and dozens of overgrown plants— nothing like Mies.

Scott and I both witnessed this view when we visited an older acquaintance of ours who lived alone in that building. When we arrived, it turned out her ex-husband was also visiting her—the two had stayed together for their children for years and when the children grew up, they divorced and became friends. While our friend bustled around the room, almost seeming to fly against the curtain wall of windows, her ex-husband sat on the couch talking about his new partner, a conductor. At this time Scott was still just my boyfriend, but it was his turn to be in school. We had moved to Michigan so that he could attend a graduate program, and now it was he who was too busy for me. My days in Michigan were colorless and lonely. I would later come to understand that I was suffering from intense depression, but at the time everything just seemed too stark. Our cramped apartment had few rooms and sparse furnishings, except for Scott's cluttered office. This room contained such a whirlwind of papers and books that there wasn't space for me to enter, let alone take a seat. So I tidied the rest of the house and made him dinner and hoped this might entice him to come out. It didn't.

How did I not see how doomed we were, standing in the Lafayette Tower that day with its vast perspective, visiting with a couple who had settled on friendship? A few years later Scott and I would get married, but looking back it seems like I should have known how fragile our love was, that we had partnered only to support each other, and when we no longer needed that support, our relationship would end.

### Figure 15: A Page from Edith's Memoir

Edith writes in her memoir:

> The big glossy reviews polished up their terms and phrases with such patience that the simpler minds that came to have a look expected to find the glass box light enough to stay afloat in air or water, moored to its column and enclosing its mystic space. . . . If the house had had the form of a banana rampant instead of a rectangle couchant, the proclamation would have been just as imperative. The alienation which I feel today must have had its beginnings on that shady riverbank all too soon abandoned by the herons.

### Figure 16: An Article in House Beautiful

After Edith lost her battle in court, Mary Gordon wrote a piece for *House Beautiful* that referenced the Farnsworth house. In the article Gordon attacks the International Style, calling it "cold," "barren," "sterile," "uncomfortable," "thin." She asserts that this ideal of less is more leads to "unlivibility, stripped-down emptiness, lack of storage space, and therefore lack of possessions." Gordon interviewed Edith for the piece, and she is quoted as saying, "Well, I'm six feet tall. Since my house is all 'open space,' I needed something to shield me when I had guests. I wanted to be able to change my clothes without my head looking like it was wandering over the top of the partition without a body." She goes on to say, "Mies talks about free space, but his space is very fixed." Over time, other critics stepped forward, claiming that Mies's architecture enforced a rigid idea of women as a decorative objects rather than real inhabitants. The fact that he often adorned his buildings with sculptures of women only further enforced this perception. Paula Singley, in her article, "Living in a Glass Prism," describes a few of the sculptures placed in his buildings this way: "No longer mere mantle busts or domesticated herms, his figures take on roles—as sacerdotal temple attendants or loyal servants who receive guests. In these carefully orchestrated tableaux vivants, the statues articulate a spatial tension in Mies's open yet inflexible plans."

### Figure 17: Farnsworth House with Peter Palumbo

Peter Palumbo is the man who liberated Edith of the Farnsworth House. As a van der Rohe connoisseur, he would rather own than inhabit. He adhered to all of Mies's ideals. He didn't live in the house. He didn't install air-conditioning or screens, just as Mies wanted. He hung no paintings on the primavera walls of the core and only used draperies approved by Mies. He even filled it with furniture designed by Mies. Palumbo is a wealthy London real estate developer who pays for the "infinite and eternal" upkeep necessary to prevent the house from deteriorating in his absence. Rust removal from the beams. Stain removal from the deck.

### Figure 18: 50 × 50 House

Though the Farnsworth House ended up being the only single-family house of consequence that Mies ever built in America, he did attempt to design a glass house for the whole family—the "50 × 50 house" he called it, though it was only ever realized on paper. The "50 × 50" house was designed to be scaled up: forty or fifty or sixty feet square, depending on the needs of the family. "Since there seems to be a real need for such homes," he explained to a boardroom, "we have attempted to solve the problem by developing a steel skeleton and a core that could be used for all houses." Picture a square glass model photographed and collaged into a landscape similar to Edith's. Picture the absence of family members: no children, no parents, no people.

### Figure 19: A House That Looks Like a Mies but Is Not a Mies

There is an International Style house in my neighborhood. Even before I was invited inside of it, I had always admired its boxy frame, mysterious and low-slung in comparison to the peaked rooftops of typical American A-frames. This is where I was when Scott decided to leave me. At a party. We were gathered in a living room empty aside from one red modern couch pushed up against a floor-to-ceiling window. The carpet in the room was white and vast and someone spilled wine on it. This is all I remember of that party. My husband and I lived in an apartment inside a one-hundred-year-old A-frame down the road. The house had been remodeled and divided and remodeled again so many times that the layout made no sense. All the rooms were furnished with IKEA knockoffs of mid-century classics, and we kept the rooms tidy aside from Scott's office, which was still so cluttered as to be impenetrable by all but Scott himself. When I returned home after the party that night, he told me that he wanted to leave me, that he was in love with someone else. I slapped him hard. Then I asked him to move out.

Even after he was gone, I didn't enter his office. I didn't rummage through his things to find out what he'd been hiding. By this time, I was in school again—this time for writing. I threw myself into my work, devoted all my time to poetry and graduate student readings and parties and lectures, hoping these activities would keep me afloat until my husband no longer seemed like my husband but was just some man who looked like my husband who came around from time to time to collect his many things and leave me with less.

### Figure 20: Crown Hall

Mies's less-than-successful experience in the private sector led him to immerse himself in the institutional. Crown Hall marks his highest achievement in this realm: an enormous glass-enclosed room, 120 × 220′ in area and 18′ in height. Though some critics felt Crown Hall lacked the romantic sensibilities of the Farnsworth House, Mies himself became an institution surrounded by acolytes who admired Crown Hall for its "paradox of spatial freedom and intellectual restraint."

### Figure 21: Mies and Lora at Nafplio

The two sit here on opposite sides of a table. Behind them, a Greek beach. They appear easy in their individual thoughts as they rest beneath the shade of an olive tree. Mies's checkered shirt and Lora's white sandals. His slouch and pudge. Her fit, though elderly figure. If Palumbo is the Farnsworth House's ideal occupant, Lora is Mies's ideal partner. She gained this seat by asking very little of him, her love "unqualified." Lora liked to keep a notebook of all the clever things Mies said while they were together; such was the nature of her infinite and eternal admiration of his ego. But his quips are admirable for their concision more than anything else:

On a yacht trip: "Wind caps! How sharp they go ahead!"

Lora bending over to buckle her boots: "You look nice even from the top. God must have pleasure to look at you."

After a conversation with a client: "You could hear his brain clobbering. So metallic—like a typewriter."

About a salad: "I enjoy my salad. Like a cow in the Alps."

About the weather: "It isn't raining, it's mizzling."

### Figure 22: Interior of Window with Condensation

*Mizzling* isn't a made-up word. It's Scottish English for weather that isn't drizzle or mist. This efficient use of language was likely lost on Edith, stuck as she was inside her fogged-up rooms.

### Figure 23: Boxes of Edith Farnsworth's Personal Effects at Chicago's Newberry Library

Edith currently occupies three boxes, none of them glass, each separated into fifty-nine folders, each folder more revealing than the next. I didn't know she liked poetry, but folders twenty-four to twenty-eight are marked "Memoirs, Poetry," as if the two were interchangeable. Folders thirty-four to fifty-one contain translated verses of famous Italian poets. Folders fourteen and fifteen contain "Photographs of Lumberjacks." There are two folders of family photographs, and one—folder seven—"Dog (black poodle)"—dedicated to photographs of a dog. The Farnsworth House resides in one folder of photographs and another of clippings. Though there are many folders containing photographs of Edith with various people, there are none of Mies, nor of Edith with Mies.

### Figure 24: Looking South

This is a view of the Farnsworth House today: a black leather bench (backless) placed before a window looking out over the sugar maples. The bench is an original van der Rohe piece, and the house has become a historical landmark. Even after all I've learned about the house and Mies, and even as I sympathize with Edith, I still long to live in this house and sit on this bench.

I believe that I could be lovely and pure as I stared through the glass at the copse of trees, thinking less and less, letting my identity disappear into the glass. With a loss of identity, I assume my memories would go too, and I would lose all of my regret, all of my cringing hindsight. In reality I continue to carry all of the photos and books I once shared with my husband in unsightly boxes from residence to residence, every time I move. Such excess sentiment cannot exist in a glass house. But in this view I have of myself on this bench, I believe that I could be content with nothing, no boxes, no memories. I think it wouldn't even bother me that the bench offers nothing to lean back on, and I wonder if this is what Edith thought too. I want to say I love this bench, this view, but I'm not sure love is possible here. Can we love something more because it's less? Or does love require a messy indulgence, complicated structures, more than support, more than the materials of our own making?

A few years ago after my ex-husband's attempts at new romance failed, he entered a monastery. So this view also might suggest what his life is like now: an almost impossible austerity. Any restless twitch or obsessive thought would be all too apparent here. This view demands that we strip ourselves away, that we become our most minimal selves. Does this mean our emotions will become so pure in this house that we'll lose our humanity? Sadness without a body, sadness without a mind. This house doesn't want our love as much as it wants to disappear into the landscape, to forget it was ever designed for humans at all. It doesn't understand our contradictory nature; we want so badly to love someone purely but would rather stay hidden in our comfortable rooms.

BIBLIOGRAPHY

Blake, Peter. *The Master Builders*. New York: Alfred Knopf, 1960.

Inventory of the Edith Farnsworth Papers, 1970–1977. http://www.newberry.org /collections/FindingAids/Farnsworth/Farnsworth.html.

Schultze, Franz. *Mies van der Rohe: A Critical Biography*. Chicago: University of Chicago Press, 1985.

Singley, Paula. "Living in a Glass Prism: The Female Figure in Ludwig Mies van der Rohe's Domestic Architecture." *Critical Matrix* 6, no. 2 (1992): 47.

Tegethoff, Wolf. *Mies van der Rohe: The Villas and Country Houses*. New York: MOMA, 1985.

# Son of Mr. Green Jeans

An Essay on Fatherhood, Alphabetically Arranged

DINTY W. MOORE

### Allen, Tim

Best known as the father on ABC's *Home Improvement* (1991–99), the popular comedian was born Timothy Allen Dick on June 13, 1953. When Allen was eleven years old, his father, Gerald Dick, was killed by a drunk driver while driving home from a University of Colorado football game.

### Bees

"A man, after impregnating the woman, could drop dead," critic Camille Paglia suggested to Tim Allen in a 1995 *Esquire* interview. "That is how peripheral he is to the whole thing."

"I'm a drone," Allen responded. "Like those bees?"

"You are a drone," Paglia agreed. "That's exactly right."

### Carp

After the female Japanese carp gives birth to hundreds of tiny babies, the father carp remains nearby. When he senses approaching danger, he will suck the helpless babies into his mouth and hold them safely there until the coast is clear.

### Divorce

Arizona State University psychologist Sanford Braver tells the disturbing story of a woman who felt threatened by her husband's close bond with their young son. The husband had a flexible work schedule, but the wife did not, so the boy spent the bulk of his time with the father. The mother became so jealous of the tight father-son relationship that she eventually filed for divorce and successfully fought for sole custody. The result was that instead of being in the care of his father while the mother worked, the boy was now left in daycare.

### Emperor Penguins

Once an emperor penguin male has completed the act of mating, he remains by the female's side for the next month to determine if he is indeed about to become a father. When he sees a single greenish-white egg emerge from his mate's egg pouch, he begins to sing.

Scientists have characterized his song as "ecstatic."

### Father Knows Best

In 1949 Robert Young began *Father Knows Best* as a radio show. Young played Jim Anderson, an average father in an average family. The show later moved to television, where it was a substantial hit.

Young's successful life, however, concluded in a tragedy of alcohol and depression. In January 1991, at age eighty-three, he attempted suicide by running a hose from his car's exhaust pipe to the interior of the vehicle. The attempt failed because the battery was dead and the car wouldn't start.

### Green Genes

In Dublin, Ireland, a team of geneticists has been conducting a study to determine the origins of the Irish people. By analyzing segments of DNA from residents across different parts of the Irish countryside, then comparing this DNA with corresponding DNA segments from people elsewhere in Europe, the investigators hope to determine the derivation of Ireland's true forefathers.

### Hugh Beaumont

The actor who portrayed the benevolent father on the popular TV show *Leave It to Beaver* was a Methodist minister. Tony Dow, who played older brother Wally, reports that Hugh Beaumont didn't care much for television and, contrary to his on-screen persona, he actually hated kids.

"Hugh wanted out of the show after the second season," Dow told the *Toronto Sun*. "He thought he should be doing films and things."

### Inheritance

My own Irish forefather was a newspaperman, owned a popular nightclub, ran for mayor, and smuggled rum in a speedboat during Prohibition. He smoked, drank, ate nothing but red meat, and died of a heart attack in 1938.

His one son—my father—was only a teenager when his father died. I never learned more than the barest details about my grandfather from my father, despite my persistent questions. Other relatives tell me that the relationship had been strained.

My father was a skinny, eager-to-please little boy battered by allergies, and not the tough guy his father had apparently wanted. My dad lost his mother at age three, and later developed a severe stuttering problem, perhaps as a result of his father's sharp disapproval. My father's adult vocabulary was outstanding, due to his need for alternate words when faltering over hard consonants like *b* or *d*.

The stuttering grew worse over the years, with one noteworthy exception: after downing a few shots of Canadian whiskey, my father could muster a stunning, honey-rich Irish baritone. His impromptu vocal performances became legend in local taverns, and by the time I entered the scene my father was spending every evening visiting the working-class bars. Most nights he would stumble back drunk around midnight; some nights he was so drunk he would stumble through a neighbor's back door, thinking he was home.

Our phone would ring. "You'd better come get him."

As a boy, I coped with this embarrassment by staying glued to the television—shows like *Father Knows Best* and *Leave It to Beaver* were my favorites. I desperately wanted someone like Hugh Beaumont to be my father, or maybe Robert Young.

Hugh Brannum, though, would have been my absolute first choice. Brannum played Mr. Green Jeans on *Captain Kangaroo*, and I remember him as kind, funny, and extremely reliable.

### Jaws

My other hobby, besides watching other families on television, was an aquarium. I loved watching as my tropical fish drifted aimlessly through life, and I loved watching guppy mothers give birth. Unfortunately, guppy fathers, if not moved to a separate tank, will often come along and eat their young.

### Kitten

Kitten, the youngest daughter on *Father Knows Best*, was played by Lauren Chapin.

### Lauren Chapin

Chapin's father, we later learned, molested her, and her mother was a severe alcoholic. After *Father Knows Best* ended in 1960, Chapin's life came apart. At age sixteen, she married an auto mechanic. At age eighteen, she became addicted to heroin and began working as a prostitute.

### Masculinity

Wolf fathers spend the daylight hours away from the home—hunting—but return every evening. The wolf cubs, five or six to a litter, will rush out of the den when they hear their father approaching and fling themselves at their dad, leaping up to his face. The father will back up a few feet and disgorge food for the cubs, in small, separate piles.

### Natural Selection

When my wife Renita confessed to me her desire to have children, the very first words out of my mouth were, "You must be crazy." Convinced that she had just proposed the worst idea imaginable, I stood from my chair, looked straight ahead, and marched out of the room.

This was not my best moment.

### Ozzie

Oswald Nelson, at thirteen, was the youngest person ever to become an Eagle Scout. Oswald went on to become Ozzie Nelson, the father in *Ozzie and Harriet*. Though the show aired years before the advent of reality television, Harriet was indeed Ozzie's real wife, Ricky and David were his real sons, and eventually Ricky and David's wives were played by their actual spouses. The current requirements for Eagle Scout make it impossible for anyone to ever beat Ozzie's record.

### Penguins, Again

The female emperor penguin "catches the egg with her wings before it touches the ice," Jeffrey Moussaieff Masson writes in his book *The Emperor's Embrace*. She then places the newly-laid egg on her feet to keep it from contact with the frozen ground.

At this point, both penguins will sing in unison, staring down at the egg. Eventually the male penguin will use his beak to lift the egg onto the surface of his own feet, where it will remain until hatching.

Not only does the penguin father endure the inconvenience of walking around with an egg balanced on his feet for months on end, but he also will not eat for the duration.

## Quiz

1. What is Camille Paglia's view on the need for fathers?
2. Did Hugh Beaumont hate kids, and what was it he would rather have been doing than counseling the Beav?
3. Who played Mr. Green Jeans on *Captain Kangaroo*?
4. Who would you rather have as your father: Hugh Beaumont, Hugh Brannum, a wolf, or an emperor penguin?

## Religion

In 1979 Lauren Chapin, the troubled actress who played Kitty, had a religious conversion. She credits her belief in Jesus with saving her life.

After *his* television career ended, Methodist minister Hugh Beaumont became a Christmas tree farmer.

## Sputnik

On October 4, 1957, *Leave It to Beaver* first aired. On that same day, the Soviet Union launched Sputnik 1, the world's first artificial satellite. Sputnik 1 was about the size of a basketball, took roughly ninety-eight minutes to orbit the Earth, and is often credited with escalating the Cold War and launching the U.S.-Soviet space race.

Years later, long after *Leave It to Beaver* ended its network run, a rumor persisted that Jerry Mathers, the actor who played Beaver, had died at the hands of the Soviet-backed communists in Vietnam. Actress Shelley Winters went so far as to announce it on the *Tonight Show*.

But the rumor was false.

## Toilets

*Leave It to Beaver* was the first television program to show a toilet.

## Using Drugs

The presence of a supportive father is essential to helping children avoid drug problems, according to the National Center of Addiction and Substance Abuse at Columbia University. Lauren Chapin may be a prime example here.

Tim Allen would be one, too. Fourteen years after his father died at the hands of a drunk driver, Allen was arrested for dealing drugs and spent two years in prison.

I also fit this gloomy pattern. Though I have so far managed to avoid my father's relentless problems with alcohol, I wasted about a decade of my life hiding behind marijuana, speed, and various hallucinogens.

### Vasectomies

I had a vasectomy in 1994.

### Ward's Father

In an episode titled "Beaver's Freckles," we learn that Ward Cleaver had "a hittin' father," but little else is ever revealed about Ward's fictional family. Despite Wally's constant warning—"Boy, Beav, when Dad finds out, he's gonna clobber ya!"— Ward does not follow his own father's example and never hits his sons on the show. This is an example of xenogenesis.

### Xenogenesis

(zen'u̲-jen ̮u̲-sis), n. *Biol.* 1. heterogenesis 2. the supposed generation of offspring completely and permanently different from the parent.

Believing in xenogenesis—though at the time I couldn't define it, spell it, *or* pronounce it—I changed my mind about having children roughly four years after I walked out on my wife's first suggestion of the idea.

Luckily, this was five years before my vasectomy.

### Y Chromosones

The Y chromosome of the father determines a child's gender and is unique because its genetic code remains relatively unchanged as it passes from father to son. The DNA in other chromosomes is more likely to get mixed between generations in a process called recombination. What this means, apparently, is that boys have a higher likelihood of directly inheriting their ancestral traits. Once my wife convinced me to risk being a father—this took many years and considerable prodding—my Y chromosomes chose the easy way out. Our only child is a daughter. Maria, so far, has inherited many of what people say are the Moore family's better traits—humor, a facility with words, a stubborn determination. It is yet to be seen what she will do with the negative ones.

### Zappa

Similar to the persistent "Beaver died in Vietnam" rumor of the late 1960s, during the late 1990s, Internet discussion lists were filled with assertions that the actor who played Mr. Green Jeans, Hugh "Lumpy" Brannum, was in fact the father of musician Frank Zappa.

Brannum, though, had only one son, and that son was neither Frank Zappa nor this author.

Too bad.

# Snakes & Ladders

ANUSHKA JASRAJ

⚀ ⚀

There are thirty-six possible combinations that could result from rolling a pair of six-sided dice.

⚀ ⚁

Originally known as Moksha Patam or Gyanbazi (Hindi: Game of Knowledge), Snakes & Ladders is a board game that was made popular in Victorian England by Jacques of London. It was rebranded as Chutes & Ladders before being introduced in the United States by Milton Bradley in the 1940s because a chute seemed less terrifying than a snake.

⚀ ⚂

To flirt with a man whose partner lives in another country: snake or ladder?

Later, he says: you told me you like Anaïs Nin. That's like giving someone a copy of *The Unbearable Lightness of Being* in high school. It's like saying you want to have that kind of affair.

⚀ ⚃

In his 2007 book *The Black Swan*, Nassim Nicholas Taleb defines the ludic fallacy as "the misuse of games to model real-life situations." The fallacy, Taleb explains, bases "studies of chance on the narrow world of games and dice." "Ludic," from *ludus*, meaning "play, game, sport, pastime."

In most games there are a limited number of ways to begin and infinite variations once the game has commenced. Founding cruelties: my emotional masochism, his aesthetico-evasive sadism.

⚀⚃

All moves are determined by rolling the dice. The first player to reach the final square on the board is considered the winner. Unlike chess or Parcheesi, a player's movements are not affected by those of any other players.

⚃⚀

My horoscope tells me my visions of the future are inaccurate but should always remain hopeful. An erotics of despair.

⚃⚃

In the ancient Jain version of Snakes & Ladders, the squares of vice outnumber the squares of virtue. It seems inherently flawed: a game based entirely on chance, whose goal is to deliver morality lessons.

⚃⚂

*Homo Ludens*, which translates "playing man," is a well-known treatise on games, play, and culture. It was written by cultural theorist Johan Huizinga and first published in 1938. From Huizinga I learn that dice playing was popular among the gods in Hindu mythology.

According to Susan Stewart, the difference between games and play is that the former have fixed rules and outcomes, while the latter requires remaining open to chance.

⚃⚄

We never sleep together. We write letters, we talk, we speculate. Is there such a thing as an emotional affair? Later, he says: I'm in an open relationship. Later, he says: this is against the rules of my open relationship.

"Maybe celibacy—the kind between us—is a perversion," I write in one of my letters, only half-joking. He writes back: I can't seem to remember the Lacanian definition of perversion.

He wanted to be a portrait artist, but instead he moves furniture around the room and makes paintings of a green cabinet. I agree to let him draw me but establish arbitrary rules, which are simultaneously symbolic and absurd. He is never allowed to draw my face. I never undress for him. He draws my body in fragments. He paints a portrait of my desk.

I accuse him of using me as a means to an end.

When I am angry, he outbids me with his anger. I'm sure I'll make a good anti-hero someday, he says.

Once, I met a Danish exchange student who was studying international relations. We talked about why Denmark is known as the happiest country, and he asked about my lover. I told him we broke up. He won in the end because he dumped me, I said. Oh, that's so American, the exchange student said. You both lost.

The origins of tarot can be traced to fifteenth-century Italian card games, before it came to be associated with occult practices in the eighteenth century.

I shuffle the cards while forming a question in my mind. The deck I use is nontraditional, and the cards are inscribed with fragments of text by Emily Dickinson. The Ace of Wands is a symbol of optimism.

⚀⚅

Sometimes I think of you as a man, he says, or maybe I want you to think of me as a woman.

⚀⚃

"Luck is not chance," Emily Dickinson reminds me.

⚂⚀

To have a *lusory attitude* is to accept the arbitrary rules of a game. This psychological concept was introduced by Bernard Suits in 1978. Anger is the opposite of acceptance. It is inappropriate conduct and may result in a penalty. The penalty for anger is bitterness.

⚂⚁

In game design theory the spatial boundary of the game is known as the magic circle. Meaningful play occurs within the magic circle. The chessboard, the doll's house, the playground, the stadium, the poker table, the computer screen, the page of a notebook.

⚂⚀

In theory, a cyclical game of this nature might never end. In theory, it is possible to win without ever climbing a ladder or sliding down the slippery skin of a snake. A game such as this requires no skill.

⚂⚂

There's no point in trying to avoid each other while we're both living here, he says. He paraphrases Anne Carson: You have to dance a tango to the end.

⚂⚅

The phrase "back to square one" originated with this game.

⚂⚃

"How can snakes move across very harsh and abrasive environments and still have belly skin that is shiny and smooth?" asked Stanislav Gorb, who studies biomechanics at the University of Kiel in Germany. "Is it the material the scales are made of? The tiny microstructures on them? The molecules they are coated with?"
—*Inside Science*

A group of psychologists came up with a set of thirty-six questions as part of a "practical methodology" for creating intimacy between subjects in an experimental context. The key to increased intimacy, they found, was mutual self-disclosure. To fall in love, a pair of subjects must ask each other these thirty-six questions and then stare into each other's eyes for four minutes.

We ask each other the questions, but he avoids my gaze.

He returns from a weekend trip to Canada, where his partner lives. He says: we adopted a dog named Ludo.

On my birthday he gives me a pair of blue vintage Bingo cards.

A moral dilemma is a situation where an agent must make a choice between two or more actions and is destined to fail regardless of which path she chooses.

S and I are talking about having a child, he tells me.

When the outcomes of the game are no longer uncertain, the pleasure mechanism begins to falter. Repetition compulsion, Freud tells us, can override the pleasure principle.

Richard Long is a British sculptor and land artist famous for the photographic work *A Line Made by Walking*. He paced back and forth in a field until the grass had flattened beneath his feet and created a visible line.

There are two types of cheating within games. The kind that is expected: when a player bluffs during a game of poker. The other transgresses the game: when a player overturns the board, bringing everything to a stop.

⚅⚀

Love is descensional: a falling.

⚅⚁

Games of chance can lead to psychological addiction.

⚅⚂

On our last day together, he is cleaning his studio and absentmindedly hands me a pile of papers. Lists, furniture measurements, letters I've written to him, and notes in his handwriting, addressed to no one in particular.

*There is a cruelty between couples in French films who are both having affairs— cruelty or maybe a kind of knowing. It has its own sexual quality.*

It is almost summer. We walk through Beech Forest. The trail dips halfway through, and he says something about spatially induced sadness. You weren't supposed to read that, he says, but his best friend is a Freudian psychoanalyst, and psychoanalysts don't believe in accidents.

⚅⚃

The next morning, he drives me to the airport.

⚅⚄

Only half-joking, I ask him in an email: "Do you love me yet?" You know I can't, in fairness, answer that question, he says. I send him an excerpt from Kafka's letters to Milena: about how letter writing is communication between specters.

⚅⚅

The probability of rolling doubles is 16 percent.

If a player rolls two sixes, she may repeat her turn.

# Math 1619

GWENDOLYN WALLACE

Show all of your work clearly and thoroughly. You may use an approved calculator, but the use of a tablet is not permitted. Once you have completed the problems, hand your test to the white man seated at the front of the classroom.

1. When a black girl has a question in physics class about double slits, does she not ask her question (and instead writes "HELP" on her paper next to the problem) because:

   a. everyone else seems to understand the new concept.
   b. she believes the students in her class will think that she is bad at physics *because* she is black and female.
   c. when she was ten years old, she told her parents that she was trying her best in school. They told her that her best wasn't good enough because people would always think poorly of her because she is black and female. They said that she had to do twice as well in order to get half of the credit. She isn't doing twice as well in physics, but pretending she doesn't have any questions may have the same effect.
   d. with so few black girls at her boarding school she represents her whole race and can't let the white and Asian students in her class leave Physics 230 with the idea that all black girls are inherently bad at physics.
   e. All of the above.

2. A black girl is born light-skinned, but grows 0.8 shades darker each summer when she goes to Chattanooga, Tennessee. There, she plays all day under the beating sun in the waterpark, as water squirts from the mouths of giant rock animals. If her hairdresser believes she is too dark when she is 4 shades darker than she is currently, and her aunt's standard for too dark is 1.2 times that, and her mother's standard is when her daughter is only 1 shade lighter than herself, how old will the girl be when all three people tell her to stop playing out in the sun? When will the black girl start carrying an umbrella with her when the sun is out?

3. Below is a graph of the black girl's pulse when she sees the blonde-haired woman slowly approach her from behind as she's buying a Mother's Day card. This is her first time getting followed in a store. The black girl is in a J.Crew sweater and jeans. The girl remembers to take her hands out of her pockets and slow her breathing. She softens any hardness in her eyes anyone could claim to see. The black girl smiles. The adjacent graph shows how close the saleswoman is getting to her over time. Find the speed of the girl's pulse when the saleswoman is ten feet away from her.

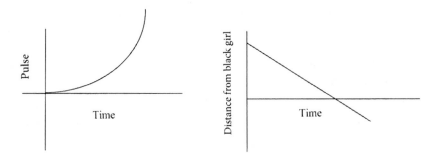

4. By the eighth grade, the black girl knows to sit at the front of the classroom once history class approaches the year 1619. That way she can't see everyone staring at her when their conversation about the start of slavery in America begins. She makes a promise to herself never to be associated with the slaves in her history textbook. Because the black girl can't subtract her skin, create a function that will let the black girl subtract everything else she thought was "too black" about herself within three years. She could start by subtracting

her black friends, subtracting rap music from her phone, or subtracting any sort of confidence she has. She could even start by adding a whole new group of white friends or perfect manners or fancy sweaters. Get creative! There are many different correct approaches and answers.

5. *Credit will be assessed on the use of a fully algebraic approach to solve this problem.* The first time the black girl tells her mother she wants to be white, it is in the car. The girl's hair is thinning from the seven years of relaxer, and she tries to push one of the limp strands behind her ear. Her mother yells at her, saying, "You can't do that, you know! You're not white!" The black girl whispers, "I wish I was," from the back seat. Her mother cries when she hears her. The second time she tells her mother she wants to be white is while attending a gymnastics camp where she becomes, for the first time, acutely aware of how black she is in the room of white faces. She calls her mother crying on the phone the very first night, says it would be easier if she looked like everyone else at camp. Her mother cries that time too. In seventh grade at summer camp, a white girl tells the black girl that she is the "whitest black girl [she has] ever met." The black girl takes it as a compliment. In eighth grade, she thinks that if she avoids all black people, she won't be associated with them. If she acts white enough, maybe she won't get followed, won't be thought of as ugly, won't be thought of as angry. In ninth grade when she comes to her fancy boarding school, she promises herself she'll have no black friends. In tenth grade, when a stranger insists the girl is in a "black prep posse," she runs sobbing to the health center to the small, cozy room of a very nice white female counselor. She tries her best to explain how she doesn't feel black enough. The counselor recommends she talk to a black teacher. She never does. In eleventh grade her friend tells her that the guy she likes "doesn't date black girls." If she is seventeen now, how long will it take her to think she is beautiful? (Hint: All of your answers must be doubled because she is black *and* female.)

How does your answer change if:

a. she is not a light-skinned black girl, but a dark-skinned black girl?

b. her parents never talked to her about how race would impact her life?

c. her hair is nappy?

Extra Credit: The black girl and her mother are traveling from their home (Point X) to a wedding (Point Y), winding down the back roads of Connecticut. The mother asks the daughter how she and her husband could do a better job of raising the girl's brother as a black boy (note that the presence of male privilege in this equation may change your problem-solving strategies. The mother apologizes for not giving her daughter any culture, any roots to hang onto, and no concept of how to embrace her blackness. She says she is scared for her children. "What can we do differently for your brother?" she asks the girl, pleading. If the car can go 55 mph on the highway but only 25 mph on the dirt roads, how long does the black girl have to explain to her mother that she doesn't think there's anything her parents can do to make growing up black less painful?

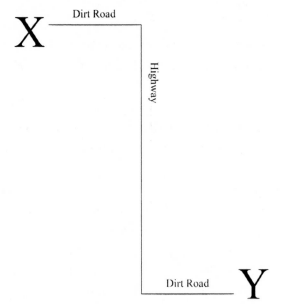

# Stagecraft

MARY PEELEN

**Dramatis Personae:** Humor the ghost that haunts you. Let's say her name is Jane. Close your eyes for a moment, entertain the idea. You can play the other character. You're a white woman, age thirty to forty-five, fatigued lately, perfect for the role.

**Stage Directions:** Wait expectantly in the dark, and when the curtain rises, permit the full contraction of your throat. Thus honed, your attention will animate the actors in the exact same way a planchette glides across the Ouija board when poised between reverent fingertips. C-A-N-C-E-R it spells out slowly, though far too early in the play.

**Synopsis:** The drama will unfold exactly as you might expect: three acts, a rise and fall in the action, heroine, villain, curtain call. Right on cue at age thirty-five, Jane is diagnosed. Your fate will remain unknown until the very last scene, but don't be afraid to go onstage. You must go on. Who else is there to speak for the dead? All they ask is that you perform your lowly pageant, drink the poison, wear all their pink crap. Don a wig.

**Set:** A lightbulb hangs from an infinitely long wire over a black stage. When you look closely, you see Jane curled up around the filament like a tiny fetus. *I have an idea,* she whispers.

**Prologue:** Platitudes delivered by the Jester, the Gravedigger, or the Voice of God, as technology allows.

**Act One:** Imagine you're a woman who always knows what to say. (Don't worry, everyone pretends. It's acting.) At the hospital follow the narrow, concrete stairway down to the place beneath logic, to the platform of your empty heart. Ignore the weepy Hallmark indignities and go ahead. Emote. On that spotlit expanse you'll become a strange kind of star, hairless and humiliated.

**Act Two:** Dialogue is careful, hushed, deadly serious. Or else it's overly cheerful. Pay attention to the subtext. With the aid of morphine, you'll hear them from the wings—voices prompting you with lines you'll need later, like *Stage 2* and *probability of metastasis*.

**Act Three:** No magic words can make the dark smudge on Jane's CT scan disappear. She's trapped in Stage 4, while you walk free, no less guilty, just luckier. Promise you'll see her again. Swear you'll bring flowers, ChapStick, magazines, Xanax, anything it takes. Then before it's too late, turn and run. *Run.* Do it now. Find a disguise, become someone else, change your wig and phone number. Do not allow yourself to be typecast.

**Epilogue:** Jane exits more suddenly than expected, drives herself to the emergency room and expires right there on the floor. Clap politely before you stand up and collect your things. Out in the lobby tighten your raincoat before you step back into the street.

# We Regret to Inform You

BRENDA MILLER

APRIL 12, 1970

*Dear Young Artist:*

Thank you for your attempt to draw a tree. We appreciate your efforts, especially the way you sat patiently on the sidewalk gazing at that tree for an hour before setting pen to paper, and the many quick strokes of charcoal you executed with enthusiasm. But your smudges look nothing like a tree. In fact they look like nothing at all, and the pleasure and pride you take in the work are not enough to redeem it. We are pleased to offer you remedial training in the arts, but we cannot accept your "drawing" for display.

With regret and best wishes,
The Art Class
Andasol Avenue Elementary School

FEBRUARY 12, 1974

*Dear Ninth-Grade Girl:*

We regret to inform you that no suitable match has been found to accompany you to the school dance. The volume of requests we receive makes individual feedback impossible, but please know that you were given careful consideration.

**79**

Do feel free to attend on your own, perhaps with another rejectee, and stand awkwardly in a corner with a glass of warm punch in your sweaty hand. Watching others have a good time is excellent preparation for the roles you will play in the future.

Best,
The Boys' Council of Patrick Henry Junior High


OCTOBER 13, 1975

*Dear Tenth-Grader:*

Thank you for your application to be the girlfriend of one of our star basketball players. As you can imagine, we have received hundreds of similar requests and so cannot possibly respond personally to every one. This letter is to inform you that you have not been chosen for one of the coveted positions, but we do invite you to continue hanging around the lockers, acting as if you belong there. This selfless act will help the team members learn the art of ignoring lovesick girls.

Sincerely,
The Granada Hills Highlanders

*P.S.: Though your brother is one of the star players, we could not take this familial relationship into account. Sorry to say no! Please do try out for one of the rebound-girlfriend positions in the future.*


NOVEMBER 15, 1975

*Dear Prospective Dancer:*

Thank you for trying out to be a Highland Dancer. Although we know you looked forward to wearing the cute kilt and argyle knee socks, the crisp white dress shirt and the tasseled shoes, we regret to inform you that you did not make the cut into the second round of auditions. Some girls simply are not coordinated enough to be a member of this elite troupe. It's not your fault; you just haven't quite "grown into" your body yet. We wish you the best of luck in finding your niche elsewhere.

The Highland Dance Team

Granada Hills High School

JANUARY 15, 1977

*Dear Future Thespian:*

Thank you for choosing drama as your major at Cal State Northridge. While we are not the most prestigious acting school in the Greater Los Angeles Area, we do take pride in having a rigorous curriculum that requires all students to be fluent in diction, singing, movement arts, and a certain indefinable "something," a *je ne sais quoi* that gives a young woman presence on the stage.

Unfortunately you do not have what it takes to be a star and will always be relegated to the "second girl" or the waitress with one or two lines that you'll belt out with imperfect timing. We understand that in high school you got to play Emily in *Our Town*, watching the townsfolk from your perch in the afterlife, and that once you had a leading role in *The Effect of Gamma Rays on Man-in-the-Moon Marigolds*, but you delivered your lines too earnestly and were too eager to please.

We appreciate that you love turning into someone else for the space of an hour or so and that you feel exhilarated once you hit your mark. But your lisping voice and rather clumsy gestures force us to look elsewhere for a leading lady.

You might have more luck in a behind-the-scenes role—perhaps writing? It's come to our attention that you once wrote a one-act play called *Backstage*, which consisted of two stagehands waiting for the stage manager to arrive; the manager never arrives, and even the play itself is an illusion! Cute.

With best wishes,

The Drama Department

Cal State Northridge

DECEMBER 10, 1978

*Dear College Dropout:*

Thank you for the short time you spent with us. We understand that you have decided to terminate your stay, a decision that seems completely reasonable, given the circumstances. After all, who knew that the semester you decided to come to UC Berkeley would be so tumultuous. That unsavory business with Jim Jones and his Bay Area followers left us all reeling. And then Harvey Milk was shot, a blast that reverberated across the Bay. It truly did feel as if the world was falling apart—we know that. We understand why you took refuge in the music of the Grateful Dead, dancing until you felt yourself leave your body, caught up in their brand of enlightenment.

And given that you were a drama major, struggling on a campus well known for histrionics and unrest—well, it's understandable that you'd need some time to "find yourself." You're really too young to be in such a big city on your own. When you had your exit interview with the Dean of Students, you were completely inarticulate about your reasons for leaving, perhaps because you still have no idea what they were. You know there is a boy you might love in Santa Cruz. You fed him peanuts at a Dead show. You imagine playing house with him, living there in the shadows of tall trees.

But of course you couldn't say that to the Dean, as he swiveled in his chair, looking so official in his gray suit. He clasped his hands on the oak desk and waited for you to explain yourself. His office looked out on the quad, where you'd heard the Talking Heads play just a week earlier, and beyond that the dorm where the gentleman you know only as "Pink Cloud" provided you with LSD, which you took in order to experience more fully the secrets the Dead whispered in your ear. You told the Dean none of this but simply shrugged your shoulders and began to cry, at which point the Dean cleared his throat and wished you luck.

We regret to inform you that it will be quite a while before you grow up, and it will take some cataclysmic events in your life before you really begin to find the role that suits you. In any case, we wish you the best in all your future educational endeavors.

Sincerely,
UC Berkeley Registrar


OCTOBER 26, 1979

*Dear Potential Mom,*

Thank you for providing a host home for each of us during the few weeks we stayed in residence. It was lovely but, in the end, didn't quite work out. Though we tried to be unobtrusive in our exit, the narrowness of your fallopian tubes made some damage unavoidable. Sorry about that. You know you were too young to have children anyway, right? And you know it wasn't your fault, not really. (Though you could have been a *tad* more careful in your carnal acts. But, no matter. Water under the bridge.)

We enjoyed our brief stay in your body and wish you the best of luck in conceiving children in the future.

With gratitude,
Ira and Isabelle


NOVEMBER 3, 1979

*Dear Patient:*

We regret to inform you that due to reproductive abnormalities, you will not be able to conceive children. *Barren* is not a word we use these days, but you may use it if you so choose. Your two miscarriages were merely symptoms of these abnormalities, which we surmise were acquired in utero. It's not your fault, but you may choose to take this misfortune as a sign of God's displeasure and torture yourself with guilt and self-loathing for many years to come.

All the best,
Student Health Center
Humboldt State University

JUNE 2, 1982

*Dear Little Raven:*

Thank you for your three-year audition to serve as the white girlfriend and savior to a Native American man twelve years your senior. Your persistence has been admirable, but we regret to inform you that we can no longer use your services.

Yes, we appreciate the fact that you smoked tobacco in a cherrywood pipe and wore a turquoise eagle around your neck. You listened to drums and chanting for hours on end and read *Black Elk Speaks* and got yourself an "Indian name." These efforts have all been noted. But the role of "pseudo-Native-American white girl" is not one we can recommend you for.

We appreciate the many times you took this man to the hospital or let him borrow your car, your money, your time. But we're sure that if you take a good hard look at your performance, you'll see that you were using this relationship as punishment for your past sins. That kind of arrangement is never good for anyone. So we bid you farewell and wish you the best of luck as you seek spiritual salvation elsewhere.

Sincerely,
Yurok Elders

MAY 23, 1986

*Dear Gatekeeper:*

Thank you for your four years of service with Orr Hot Springs Resort and in particular your role as live-in girlfriend to one of our more depressed shareholders. We also appreciate your services as a godmother to our resident toddler and confidante to his parents (a relationship that did, ahem, *transgress* some boundaries, but you shaped up when this was pointed out).

So it is with great sadness that we must inform you that your services are no longer required. This dismissal in no way reflects upon your job performance. (Well, you could have cleaned the lodge a little better and been a little more thorough when it was your turn to scrub the bathhouse.) It's simply time for you to move on.

Please pack your meager belongings into the car you bought for two hundred dollars. Please do not dramatically extend the farewells, wandering the property to "say goodbye" to inanimate objects, to the gardens, to Tub Room #2, where you spent so many mornings immersed in yourself. Please do not throw the I Ching to determine your next steps or read the tarot or take ecstasy. Simply get into your car and chug up the mountain road at first light. You will feel a sensation of tearing—like a ligament ripped from the bone—but don't worry. This is normal. You will head north. You will be fine. You will find the role that suits you.

Namasté,
Orr Hot Springs Resort
Ukiah, California


APRIL 14, 1994

*Dear Potential Wife:*

Thank you for your application to be my spouse. While I see much to admire here, I regret to inform you that you do not meet my needs at this time.

I do want to commend you for your efforts over the past five years. You did your best, but your anxiety made it difficult to proceed. Even so, we did love our coffee in the morning, our home-cooked meals in the evening, our travels through the Middle East. (Let's just forget the argument we had while walking the walls of the Old City in Jerusalem. Water under the bridge.) You laughed at my jokes; thanks for that. And of course it was fun being fledgling writers together, before reality intervened.

Try to remember that we loved the only way we could: not perfectly, nor entirely well, but genuinely. I adored your lisp and the little mole above your lip. I touched your scars, and you touched mine. We tried. But at some point in a relationship you shouldn't have to try so hard, right?

It may just be bad timing. Best wishes in your future matrimonial endeavors. I'm sure your talents will be put to good use elsewhere. I hope we can remain friends.

Your Grad School Boyfriend

JUNE 30, 1999

*Dear Applicant:*

Thank you for your query about assuming the role of stepmother to two young girls. While we found your résumé impressive, we regret to inform you that we have decided not to fill the position this year. You did ask for feedback on your application, so we have the following to suggest:

1. You do not yet understand the delicate emotional dynamic that rules a divorced father's relationship with his children. The children will always, *always*, come first, trumping any needs you may have. You will understand this in a few years, but for now you still require some training.

2. Though you have sacrificed your time and energy to support this family, it's become clear that your desire to be a stepmother stems from some deep-seated wound in yourself, a wound you are trying to heal using these children. We have enough to deal with—an absent mother, a frazzled father. We don't need your traumas in the mix.

3. Seeing the movie *Stepmom* is not an actual tutorial on stepparenting.

4. On Mother's Day you should not have expected flowers, gifts, or even a thank you. You are not our mother.

5. You are still a little delusional about the potential here for a long-term relationship. Our father is not ready to commit so soon after a messy divorce. (This should have been obvious to you when he refused to hold your hand, saying that it made him feel claustrophobic.)

We hope this feedback is helpful, and we wish you the best in your future parenting endeavors.

XXX OOO
Your Boyfriend's Daughters

JANUARY 3, 2007

*Dear New Dog Owner:*

Congratulations on adopting your first dog! She will surely provide hours of love and enjoyment and be a wonderful addition to your family.

Here are a few tips:

1. A dog is not a child, even if you do call yourself "Mom." Yes, other people will now know you as "Abbe's mom," and you'll take a great deal of foolish pride in this. But remember, a dog is not a child.

2. Though a dog is not a child, you will need to plan your life around this creature: food, water, companionship, play dates, illnesses. Yes, there will be illnesses. You will need to make crucial decisions while in tears at the vet's office. You may need to empty your savings account to insure that your dog is no longer in pain.

3. You will at some point say to yourself: *I don't need to date; I have my dog.* Be very careful about repeating this statement in public.

4. You will grow fond of this dog and overlook her shortcomings, her flaws. (Really, they are so few.) Why can't you do this with a man?

5. A pet's love, contrary to popular belief, is not unconditional. There are many conditions: expensive food, regular walks, toys, your undivided attention.

6. A dog such as Abbe makes a terrific all-natural antidepressant. At some level, of course, you already know this; otherwise you wouldn't have spent so much more time on Petfinder.com than on Match.com. When you are with her, you will feel as if something were being repaired in your body, like a ligament rejoining the bone.

7. At times you'll feel rejected by Abbe. Don't worry, this is normal. Though she is very friendly, Abbe needs her space sometimes. (As do we all!)

8. You will train to be a therapy-dog team, providing companionship and affection to people in hospitals and nursing homes. Though Abbe will be better at it than you are, you'll enjoy sitting by her side as she is petted by strangers young and old. You'll stay quiet and simply observe, playing a background role, finding satisfaction in this. You'll understand that such therapy is as much for you as it is for them.

Once again, congratulations on taking on this huge responsibility. It's an indication of maturity, of finding your niche and settling into your life as it is.

Best wishes,
Furbaby Pet Rescue of Whatcom County

# The Six Answers on the Back of a Trivia Card

CAITLIN HORROCKS

( PP ) = People and Places

( AE ) = Arts and Entertainment

( HIS ) = History

( SN ) = Science and Nature

( SL ) = Sports and Leisure

( WC ) = Wild Card

## one.

( PP ) What's considered impolite to leave stuck in your rice in Japan, except at funerals?

( AE ) This ice skater was the object of my sister's first, strange, unattainable crush on someone vaguely male but thoroughly unthreatening, much the way my first crush was on the animated fox in Disney's *Robin Hood*.

( HIS ) These are the members of what band, listed in descending order of attractiveness, by consensus of the female members of Mrs. Wilson's fourth grade class, Haisley Elementary, 1989: Donnie, Jordan, Joey, Jonathan, Danny.

(SN) As a child I studied the ways that this city siphoned off water from the Colorado River and the Sierra Nevada snowmelt, stealing it from fish like the razorback sucker and the humpback chub, from the bald eagle, and from Mexico. I wished that I could resettle this city's inhabitants in ecologically sustainable regions that grew food instead of palm trees and movie stars.

(SL) My favorite computer game in the days of floppy disks was called *Fantastic Animals*. Different slices of animals flew by as the player tried to match them. Or the player embraced the game's Frankensteinian possibilities and paired the head of an ostrich with the torso of a snake and the butt of a polar bear. This animal played a puzzlingly large role in this game. Of all the fantastic animals in the world, he appeared most frequently, heavily pixelated and tinged purple, with long horns and a shaggy coat. He looked like a dirty, wet, MS-DOS buffalo. He looked like something less than fantastic.

(WC) One Christmas my grandparents sent my family the largest single-volume dictionary I had ever seen, bigger than the dictionary in the school library that sat perpetually opened to "sex." It contained an appendix of presidential portraits and a full-color insert of world flags. The flag of this country, double pennant shaped, the only defiantly nonquadrilateral flag in the entire world, entranced me.

## two.

(PP) Who skated on CBS's *Ice Wars* to show he was "the best forty-four-year-old five-four bald skater in all the world"?

(AE) What eighties band had fans that happily called themselves "blockheads"?

(HIS) In the 1930s and '40s the government of Thailand sponsored widely mocked but ultimately successful public education campaigns persuading Thais not to eat with either their hands or these utensils but with spoon and fork, to wear Western clothing, and to kiss their wives.

The traditional Thai gesture of romantic affection was to press cheek to cheek and sniff.

(SN) My grandmother walks often to the filling station nearest her retirement complex. She goes there for company and conversation with the workers, Himalayan exiles from this country who miss their families. They fuss over my grandmother, giving her groceries and home-cooked food that they need more than she does. My grandmother lets them and then in fits of guilt tries to give them something in return. She invited them for dinner one night and served them beef. They are all Hindu.

(SL) I have personally only ever been in this city during airport layovers and a single night I spent sleeping on the floor of friends-of-friends, a couple who later left this city to live in Bratislava.

(WC) Less dashing than the rich-robbing, poor-giving fur of celebrity Disney foxes but eight times warmer than wool is the molting pelt of this animal.

## three.

(PP) What nation was required to elevate its crown prince to king shortly after he'd shot his family and mortally wounded himself in 2001?

(AE) Thai history thus explains why everyone in a Thai restaurant in Beijing mocked my group of friends when we spurned the silverware provided with our meal. We'd only been in China for a few days and didn't want to miss an opportunity to practice our newly acquired skill with these utensils. "You know," one of us said, opening the paper wrapper. "I remember reading that at least one southeastern Asian country doesn't use these. I think it might be Thailand. In which case we look pretty stupid right now."

(HIS) My single night in this city, I arrived via the Pacific Coast Highway, ate delicious sushi, and slept on the floor. That night is nondescript, anonymous, anticlimactic. It is the kind of story you tell about a night in Duluth or Albuquerque, except that the sushi wouldn't have been nearly as good. It is a night that seems somehow insufficient for the city it occurred in, a place that spawns fantastic tales.

**SN** What animal is bred for its warm, soft *qiviut* wool—the Alaskan malamute, Arctic hare, or musk ox?

**SL** This skater's height can be found variously listed as 5′4″, 5′3″, 5′3½″, 5′2½″ and 6′2″, which surely says something about the futility of knowing such trivia in the first place, carrying an ice skater's changeable height around in the brain like coins in a pocket.

**WC** To refer to this group as an eighties "band" gives me the same semantic pause as when a newscast referred to a drive-by shooting near my home as taking place "at a local restaurant." On realizing that they were referring to a Rally's fast food joint, my first thought wasn't concern for the victims or neighborhood safety but this: is a Rally's really a "restaurant"?

## four.

**PP** No one cares if you've never been to, say, Indianapolis. You are expected not to have been to Indianapolis, or to have found it boring once you got there. But this city is supposed to thrive in our imaginations, to take the shape of our longings and feed our insecurities, not be a place where millions of people suffer commutes and jobs and sushi and nights on the floor, but a city that insists on telling certain stories about itself, that quantifies its inhabitants in handprints. This city is slow to acknowledge the press of reality. Only now is it cutting down its palm trees: they take water and give nothing, no shade or oxygen, in return.

**AE** My grandmother is trying to set me up on a date with one of the filling station attendants except, she explains, he works every waking hour and sends every cent to his family abroad. Our date would have to be free and very brief, perhaps a shared Slurpee or a walk around the parking lot. He also may or may not already have a wife in this far-off country. My grandmother tells me that he is still a very admirable man, and I am sure that this is true.

(HIS) The hair of this animal is knit into clothing by the women of the Oomingmak Alaskan Producers' Co-operative. One of the knitters writes to the co-operative office: *I can still see to knit, but sometimes it is hard. When I need money the Co-Op helps me a lot, since the Governor has cut the Longevity Bonus. . . . Today we have sunshine and the Kuskokwim river ice is almost gone. . . . May God bless everyone of you.*

(SN) Unlike this man, I have limited experience with figure skating: a handful of birthday parties at rented rinks and a single disastrous winter of skating lessons. I had pneumonia and spent nearly the entire term too ill to skate. I returned for the last session less skilled than I'd been to start with. I staggered around after the other children, splaying myself frequently across the ice, humiliated at what they'd learned to do and I had not.

(SL) Lynda Highsmith owned a hot tub, a television in her bedroom, and a pink licensed watch featuring this band. This was almost too much for the girls of Mrs. Wilson's fourth grade class, until we found out that the television didn't work; its sole purpose was for Lynda to point to and say, "Look, I have a television in my room." After that, there was no hot tub in the world big enough for the derision we heaped upon Lynda.

(WC) Originally called "The Celebrated Chop Waltz," this was the sole musical composition of a sixteen-year-old British girl named Euphemia Allen. In Russia, the song was called "The Cutlet Polka."

## five.

(PP) As the girls in my fourth grade class swooned over these pop stars, discussing which they found cutest with total and fervent conviction, I memorized their choices like I was studying for a test. I thought this meant that I might grow up to be a lesbian, or that there was perhaps something truly wrong with me—that I would live a reduced life, without love or attraction, because I couldn't see their appeal. Really, I was simply nine years old, more interested in horses than in pop stars. But I couldn't escape the assumption of want, the expectation that little girls learn to be women by performing adult desires.

**AE**  My improbable familiarity with this animal is much like my relationship to the capitals of Andorra and Liechtenstein. The Christmas I asked for a Carmen Sandiego computer game, perhaps *Where in the World?* or *Where in America?*, the stores were sold out of everything except *Where in Europe?* This meant I spent two years chasing the savvy spy through small principalities and obscure republics, learning geographical facts that would prove less than useful. I didn't know the capital of California, but I knew all about Andorra la Vella and Vaduz.

**HIS**  Before Lance Armstrong, this celebrity was the ranking A-list testicular cancer survivor, with his friends Brian Boitano, Kristi Yamaguchi, Kurt Browning, and others celebrating his 1998 recovery with a televised skating special.

**SN**  It seemed like no one in my junior high school could pass a piano without sitting down to play either this, "Heart and Soul," "The Entertainer," or the first few bars of "Für Elise." These songs drove me crazy, at least partially because I was jealous I'd never learned them. A decade of piano lessons, and what I most wanted to do was impress my friends with a really smoking rendition of "Heart and Soul."

**SL**  This country's National Basketball Association was dissolved in 2006 by the National Sports Council and the Association's telephone number blocked by the national Telecom after the government was taken over by the "People's Movement," a Maoist insurgency. Some official basketball activities were allowed to resume in late 2007.

**WC**  What city is central to the books *The Black Dahlia*, *The Big Sleep*, and *Get Shorty*?

## six.

(PP)  Twelve to twenty years; four to five feet; five hundred to eight hundred pounds; eight months, two to three feet; the nineteenth century: lifespan in the wild; height at shoulder; weight; gestation period; length of hair; and period of near extinction of this animal.

(AE)  9,948,081; 29.4 minutes; 3,356,383; −1.5%; $9,433; five hundred: population; mean travel time to place of employment; number of housing units; decline in private nonfarm employment since 2000; per capita yearly retail spending; and number of movies filmed in this city yearly.

(HIS)  273 BCE; late fourteenth; 1,225 years; 1788; 1846; 2008: year Buddhism arrived in; century of rule of King Jayasthitimalla in; length of Kirat rule in; year of invasion of Tibet by; year of Kot massacre in; and year the monarchy ended and a federal republic was declared in this country.

(SN)  A solo career, a supergroup for an MTV reality show called *Totally Boyband*, *Dancing with the Stars*, acting, real estate, a comeback, a second comeback: the post breakup careers of this band's former members.

(SL)  A wig, a chicken suit, golfing tweeds, Western fringe, shining spandex: the costumes this skater has performed in.

(WC)  The ownership of worthless facts; the willful conglomeration of the unnecessary; the collecting of incoherent items: a set of statistics; a pocket of coins; an album of stamps; a jar of marbles: the thrill of possession; the sound of their jingle; the taste of the glue; the light as it falls.

# Piecing the Quilt of Valor

JUDITH SORNBERGER

*Download your free "Striped and Spangled" pattern from the Quilts of Valor Foundation, whose mission is to cover service members and veterans touched by war with comforting and healing quilts.* This pattern is a cheerful homage to our country's flag and is set vertically and sprinkled with appliquéd stars. These instructions guide you through easy piecing to make a fast and fun quilt* for your son who came back from his deployments in Iraq and Afghanistan torn and frayed, his soul ripped to tatters. Making this quilt may make you feel like you can do something to help him.

1. Assemble Fabric

*"Striped and Spangled" is made from 5.5"-wide strips. Each strip unit is made from one* WOF *(width of fabric) strip of* RED *or* WHITE *fabric and one* WOF *strip of blue background fabric (cut into two pieces). This may not make sense now. Just follow orders. The charts and illustrations will be your maps, keeping you from getting lost.* Remember the first time your son was deployed. The war hadn't yet begun, and his unit's position was top secret. Remember your panic when no map could show you where he was.

Your friend, a retired quilt shop owner and mother, will offer fabric and comforting murmurs. Let her help you select fabrics from her stash. For the strips: a

---

* Directions for the "Striped and Spangled" quilt are based on Hunter Design Studio's instructions published on the Quilt of Valor Foundation website.

rusty red with a beige pattern of hollow bullet holes; an off-white with irregular, slightly darker spots like spattered stains that wouldn't come completely out (don't think of your son's tears as he tells you of one mission, how the soldiers in his unit were "praying and spraying" as the bodies dropped); an indigo fabric sprinkled with faded blue forget-me-nots that has you humming "Where have all the flowers gone?"; and, for the stars, an old-gold fabric studded with tiny metallic-gold hearts. If you plan to make a border, use whatever fabric you want—anything but black, which would make the quilt look like the kind of bordered stationery that people once used for letter writing while in mourning.

Remember the black cotton you asked your mother to sew into a long skirt for the Moratorium demonstration you and your friends organized at your high school during the Vietnam War. You were standing on a kitchen chair while she pinned up the hem when your father arrived home from work. Seeing you, he pointed and shouted, "You're a radical!"

When you occupied the school's central staircase, singing "We Shall Overcome" and "I Ain't Gonna Study War No More" with your friends, some kids stopped to watch, some jeered as they passed, and a few joined in. Wonder what your son would have done. Try not to imagine him sneering in his Guns N' Roses T-shirt, a silver skull pulling down one earlobe, striding past you with your long, straight hair and serious bangs. Wonder if you'd have seen through his tough-guy act even back then.

## 2. Cutting Instructions

- *Blue background fabric: Cut 13 @ 5.5″ × 41″ WOF strips*
- *Red stripe fabric: Cut 7 @ 5.5″ × 40.5″ WOF strips*
- *White stripe fabric: Cut 6 @ 5.5″ × 40.5″ WOF strips*

Cut the strips as you'd cut bandages for wounds—not your son's wounds but ones that can be cleaned and wrapped by loving hands each day. Not a brain that stutters and stalls. Not a back so crushed in his fall during an explosion that he can't bend to tie his shoes. Not a liver shot beyond repair by all the drink that never kills the pain. Not a sadness no mother can comfort. These days only riding his Harley, helmetless in the mountains, can bring him to life.

Remember what a cutup he was as a kid. How he cracked you up on the way home from Thanksgiving at your parents', growling his impression of Mr. T: "I pity da foo who mess with me." Remember the time at a restaurant when his stepdad gave him and his brother quarters to play video games in the lobby while you finished your dinner. When you came out to pay the check, you found him spinning on his back, à la Michael Jackson, a small crowd of amused spectators standing in a circle around him.

### 3. Assemble Strips

*Each* STRIP *is made using one* BLUE *background strip and one* RED *or* WHITE *strip. One* BLUE *background strip is used to make both sections of one* STRIP *unit—the first* BLUE *section is cut from the* STRIP. *The remainder is used for the second section of the same* STRIP. *Cut the* BLUE *background according to the chart, and sew the* RED *or* WHITE *section between the* BLUES *accordingly.* Follow the confusing directions and hope they will all add up to something useful, if not beautiful.

Remember Matt refusing to follow rules. Remember school suspensions and his felony arrest at fourteen for having an illegal butterfly knife in his middle-school locker, his fear that a high school gang was coming after him and his buddy on the way home from school. Then his going to live with his father (who'd given him the knife) to escape the bad influence of friends.

For a while after he dropped out of high school, Matt sold household security systems. Then he thought bounty hunting was his calling till he went to apprehend the son of the Republic of Texas Militia's leader and ended up having a shotgun pulled on him. Then there was his brief but bloody career as a professional boxer. Recall how all these roles were foretold in the photo of him at six, wearing his Superman Underoos T-shirt tucked into jeans and the Superman cape his Aunt Jill had made him. How the photo shows him pushing his skinny chest out so hard it looks like his shoulders might snap off.

When he enlisted, you were actually relieved, thinking he would learn some discipline. Maybe following orders for a while was what he needed. Remember feeling elated when he tested high in linguistics and hoping they'd send him to language school. But he wanted action, not a mother's advice, and he was no sooner a member of the Air Guard Security Forces than he was deployed to the Middle East.

## 4. Assemble Stripes
*Sew the fabric* STRIPS *together in alphabetical order of the rows shown in the illustration.* As you sew the long ¼-inch-wide seams, try not to hear the sound of an M-16 firing.

Remember how you tried to keep war toys out of your young sons' hands. No guns or G.I. Joes for the sons of this daughter of the sixties. You should have known better. Broom handles became machine guns and bean bags morphed into grenades. Tell yourself it was not your fault. It was bigger than you were. Try to believe it.

Keep the rattata-rattata-rattata of your sewing machine going as you recall your son's return from his second deployment (as a volunteer that time, to look after younger soldiers in his unit, he said). You were too cowardly to ask him anything. But one day he told you anyway, his voice breaking with tears over the phone as he recalled the presumed enemy who went down in front of him, a man he killed, probably just "some poor guy like me who only wanted to get home to his family." At some point, they found a "foreign body" in Matt's shoulder. He still can't remember being hit.

*Note: Don't press the seams open. Press them away from* WHITE *toward* RED *so that the* RED *will not bleed through.*

## 5. Appliqué Stars
*Using the star template on the last page, cut thirteen* STARS *from the* GOLD *fabric to add to your quilt. Sprinkle the* STARS *randomly across the quilt top.* As you zig-zag stitch around them, try not to think of fire that isn't fireworks, tearing open the sky, thundering through stars. Wonder how he bore it as you recall his terror of loud noises ever since being startled by a gun going off the first and last time he went to the circus—a play shootout between the clowns. He was so shaken, you had to leave immediately. After that he even dreaded the Fourth of July.

Tell yourself you're giving him stars for doing what he believed was right, even when you were standing on a downtown corner of your small town, holding a sign that read: "Iraq is Arabic for Vietnam." Tell yourself the stars aren't like the medals he earned for bravery or the Purple Heart bestowed on him for being injured. You're giving him stars for *valor*, a word from the Latin *valere*, meaning "to be of worth." Once, years after the last deployment, he called you, slurring his words so badly you had to listen hard to understand: when he'd gone to live with his dad after his arrest as a teenager, his dad had gotten "so pissed off once he punched [him] over and over with a closed fist." Remember feeling you might vomit, like you'd been punched in the gut. "All I ever wanted," he said, "was for him to be proud of me." Know damn well that the stars you'll send him can't come close to granting that wish.

*YOUR QUILT TOP IS COMPLETE! NOW ONTO CONSTRUCTION!*

### 6. Creating a Quilt Sandwich

*Backing: Choose a quilt backing fabric of the same weight as your quilt top. A printed backing will disguise imperfect stitching.* By now you know how fallible you are. For God's sake, choose the printed backing.

*Batting: Cotton and wool are natural choices, but pay heed to any washing instructions.* If the quilt shrinks and bunches, after all your blood, sweat, and tears, you'll be devastated.

### 7. Assembling the Layers

*Place the backing down on a flat surface. Smooth it out* as you once soothed your babies into sleep. Remember the night Matt and his twin were born six weeks early, how each one was swooped away to an Isolette before you could touch him, how no one expected them to live. When you asked the doctor the next morning how they were doing, he shook his head and spoke the first words of hope: "Well, they're fighters!" Back then those words pointed to their strength and their heart. Back then they meant survival.

*Cut the batting slightly smaller than the backing and place it centrally on top of the back. Center the quilt top on the batting. Use quilter's safety pins to hold the layers together while you baste them.* Remember struggling to hold things together during your years as a single mother. You thought you were protecting your sons when you divorced their father—a man who'd once threatened you with a loaded gun and was later arrested for selling drugs. But after an exhausting day at the clerical job you despised, picking up your sons from after-school care, stopping at the grocery store to find something nourishing and quick to make for supper with the few bucks left in your purse, you felt your soul unraveling. Remember the night, as you tucked Matt's red, white, and blue superhero comforter around him, when he said, "Dad said we could all be together again, if only you'd agree." All you could say was, "I'm sorry, sweetie, that's just not possible." Then you retreated to your bedroom where you fell apart, pouring tears into the puff quilt your grandmother made you.

## 8. Birthing the Quilt

*If you choose not to bind your quilt, trim all edges and stitch around it, leaving an open space of 8″ on one side. Tightly roll the quilt toward the opening, tucking in the sides as you roll. Slowly and carefully ease the quilt through the small opening to turn it right side out.* Remember the epidural the doctor insisted on giving you before you delivered your sons—not for pain, but because he didn't want you pushing on their still-soft heads. As if his forceps would be gentler than your body's wisdom. Up until this point, you'd followed all your Lamaze teacher's instructions, and you'd really wanted to give birth drug free. But you were willing to disobey your body's directives to protect them. Remember doubting your ability to mend the rips in your family's fabric in later years—the times you followed advice from teachers, principals, doctors, and therapists instead of listening to your heart.

*Fold in and pin the edges of the quilt's opening and slipstitch it closed.* Tuck in a prayer with each blind stitch.

## 9. Quilting

*Quilting protects the seams and holds the filling in place. The easiest method—recommended for the novice quilter—is to "stitch in the ditch," which involves stitching along seam lines. If your stitches swerve off track, get back on as soon as possible.* Don't picture your son lying in a ditch beside his Harley. *Most mistakes can be easily remedied by using your seam ripper and restitching.* Remember that this is why you love quilting.

### AND YOUR QUILT IS FINISHED!

Know the flag this quilt is based on got him where he is. Try to believe it stands for more than all these wars—all these deaths, all these wounds. Now bundle the quilt into white tissue paper and send it to your son. Imagine yourself tucking it around him. Hope the quilt reaches him safely, though you no longer believe in the idea of safety. Know it will not heal him. Or you. Hope it gives him some measure of comfort.

# Self-Portrait as a 1970s Cineplex Movie Theatre (an Abecedarian)

STEVE FELLNER

*Agatha* (1979)

It all starts with a single mystery.

And then another. And another. And then another.

I can still remember seeing my mother cry as *Agatha*'s ending credits rolled. My mother said, "My tragic flaw: I hold no mystery."

*Agatha* is a biopic that offers a theory as to what happened to the mystery writer Agatha Christie during her eleven-day disappearance in 1926. Some said it was a kidnapping. Others a mere publicity stunt. Most recently, it's been said it was a result of amnesia, a psychogenic trance. *Agatha* claims that she left to plot the murder of her philanderer husband. "Not everything revolves around a man," my mother said.

*Ben* (1972)

I was obsessed with the title song to *Ben*. It has a young Michael Jackson crooning lyrics like "We both found what we were looking for. With a friend to call my own, I'll never be alone . . ." And, "I used to say I and me, now it's us, now it's we." I knew the lyrics by heart.

There was a man I loved. I didn't know how to tell him I loved him. His name was Ben, too. It was the 90s. *Ben* was released in the 70s. There was no way he would link the two.

I wrote out all the lyrics and told him that I had written a poem for him. As I read it, he gave me a funny look. "Are you sure you wrote that song?" he said.

"Of course. It took me weeks."

There was a long pause. "That's the song from that movie about killer rats. It's about some loser who has nothing. So he befriends a rat. A rat. Is his only friend." He enunciated that last part very, very slowly.

"Really?" I said.

"Really," he said. "You know what? I don't get on with liars." He walked out of my apartment.

The next day, there was a cage covered with a sheet on my front porch. I could hear some frantic scraping. It was a rat. And not the pet store, domesticated kind; it was a back alley rat, black-furred and crazy with fear. There was a note that said: "LOVE THIS, YOU ASSHOLE!"

### Coma (1978)

When I had my first manic episode, I couldn't sleep. I tried and tried. I took sleeping pills, listened to music, exercised for hours, drank warm milk, devoured melatonin. I stayed up all night long for three days, watching TV. Once *Coma* was on. It's a mystery/thriller revolving around a series of healthy people who mysteriously go brain-dead after minor surgeries.

This was all I could think: *They are so lucky. They are so lucky.*

### Deliverance (1972)

In *Deliverance* Burt Reynolds plays a beefy alpha male who is obsessed with seeing the Cahulawassee River before it's turned into one huge lake. He takes his posse river rafting; they meet various and dangerous people along their way. My favorite: a deformed, mute banjo kid. Everybody remembers the "squeal like a pig" guy in *Deliverance,* but the banjo kid doesn't need a catchphrase. He never speaks. He just strums. One of the guys in Reynolds's crew has his own banjo. They go back and forth and back again, calling and responding to each other for a scene that lasts for over five minutes. You would never expect music to be in a place so remote, so distant.

Once I had a dream and all I could hear were those banjos being strummed, the strain of the strings, and then the death of silence. It's the one time in my life I wondered if God had spoken to me.

*Every Which Way but Loose* (1978)

I always wanted to own a pet. The closest thing I've ever gotten was a goldfish. My brother named it Doorbell. Every morning he would get up and feed it. He'd say, "Hi, Doorbell. How are you doing today?" The fish never answered, but that never stopped him from asking the question.

One day we went and saw *Every Which Way but Loose*, a star vehicle for Clint Eastwood, who plays a tough guy roaming around the American West looking for a lost lover. Of course the real star of the movie is his best friend, an orangutan named Clyde. Clyde and Eastwood have a perfect comic rapport.

When we got home from the movie, my brother changed the name of his goldfish from Doorbell to Clyde. A few weeks later the fish died. I told my brother it was from natural causes. I lied. I still think the cause of death was identity confusion.

*Fiddler on the Roof* (1971)

When I saw the movie in high school, I convinced my drama director to do the play. I wanted to be the lead. I wanted to play the role that Zero Mostel made famous. Operatic in nature, always larger than life, I wanted to be Tevye. I wanted to be the ultimate Jewish patriarchal figure who ruled over his family with an ironclad fist, refusing to assimilate.

I didn't let the fact that I was supposed to be Catholic stop me. If I had to convert to Judaism to get the lead role in the school play, so be it.

The first day of the production I lost my voice. "God isn't on your side," my director said. I prayed to God to help me. There was no answer. No voice, no fiddle-playing coming from the roof or anywhere else. Not even a banjo.

*The Godfather* (1975)

This is a fact: the horse's head was real. The horse had died, and they cut it off and froze it and then brought it to the set. Jesus Christ.

The things people will do for art.

I can never remember anything in the scene other than the horse's head. Not even the basics, really: I know an Italian Mafioso wakes up to find blood in the sheets and then the wrapped towels at the end of the bed. And then something else happens, and so on and so forth. There are a lot of famous scenes in *The Godfather*. But all I remember is that head of the horse.

Am I allowed to say it? Once I dreamt that I was the head of the horse. My eyes did not blink. My mouth did not move. All I could feel was the angry freezer burn of the ice.

## H.O.T.S. (1979)

I remember asking my father to tell me about the birds and the bees. I don't think I really even cared to hear about sex. I was just curious about the metaphors. Who were the bees and who were the birds?

My father looked a little puzzled when I asked the question. He grabbed a newspaper, scanned the movie listings and said, "This one looks good. It'll tell you more about the birds and the bees than I can."

*H.O.T.S.* is a stupid soft-core sex comedy that features Danny Bonaduce from *The Partridge Family*. It also stars three Playboy Playmates. My father told me their names. I couldn't remember them. In the movie they were in some kind of sorority, and they wore tight shirts and red shorts. (My father later told me about a theory he'd developed regarding these uniforms: "I think the owners of Hooters must have ripped them off. They're practically identical.")

I kept on almost falling asleep during the movie. My father was spellbound. He nudged me a few times because I was snoring.

It was the first time I told my father I was gay, only not in so many words.

## I Spit on Your Grave (1978)

When I was an undergraduate, I rented a videotape of *I Spit on Your Grave*. The film focuses on a young woman who is raped and beaten by a group of men whom she later runs down and kills one by one. I'm not sure why I thought it would make a good date movie.

My boyfriend fell asleep during the film. I had to nudge him every so often to keep him from snoring. I was pissed.

"How could you nod off during that film?" I asked.

"I'd rather not see this kind of shit," he said. "Something happened to me a long time ago. I never fought back."

Once he said that, I knew we would never go on another date again. I needed to believe I was the only one who suffered in certain ways. I needed to have a secret. And I didn't want to share mine. We broke up after that night. I never saw him again.

### The Jerk (1979)

My husband's father died weeks before we started dating. His father's favorite movie was *The Jerk*. I had never seen it.

The movie stars Steve Martin as a white idiot who is an adopted son of a black family of Mississippian sharecroppers. When he comes to the realization that he is tone-deaf, he is forced to face the fact that he doesn't belong and sets out on his own adventures to find love and success.

I watch Phil watch the movie. He tells me what his father's favorite jokes were. I don't know if he realizes that a lot of these are what he would have found funny anyway, without his father's cues. So I watch my husband watching this movie through his father's eyes. Does he experience this silly slapstick comedy as a profane, necessary elegy? I do.

### Kramer vs. Kramer (1979)

"They make the movie so dramatic. Like divorce is a big tragedy. Like it warrants a two-hour-plus running time," my mother said. "You can boil it down to two scenes: when he stops saying 'I love you' and when she says 'Leave.' No one deserves an Academy Award for that script. I could have written it. After all, I lived it."

### Love Story (1970)

Even I cry during this dishonorable tearjerker. But the one thing that really bothers me is that after Ali MacGraw's character dies, and Ryan O'Neal leaves the hospital, the drama turns into a resolution of a father-son conflict. Instead, I want the movie to focus on the period of time it takes O'Neal to walk from the hospital bed to his car. I want them to film it in real-time, so we see O'Neal walking and walking and walking, for maybe twenty minutes. No dialogue. When I imagine grieving over my husband Phil's death, that's what I see as the most difficult distance: the bed he dies in and the exit to the hospital. I imagine, even now, that as long as I don't leave the building, he won't be dead.

I imagine hiding in nurses' stations, bathrooms, storage rooms for days on end, because if I'm not found, how can he be lost?

### Magic (1978)

Who wouldn't be excited by Anthony Hopkins playing a ventriloquist tortured by a murderous dummy? Me more than most, I guess.

I've always wanted to be someone else's puppet. All jerks and strings. The pleasure of being moved by the hands of a familiar stranger. The pleasure of not having to think of words. The pleasure of making noise for someone else's satisfaction. And yet it goes both ways. I don't know how many I've longed for over the years: dummies with sculpted bodies.

### Norma Rae (1979)

Once I went to human resources to complain about the way I was being treated. I was told to talk to someone named Lisa. I wanted to be able to have a genuinely fair shot at overtime work just like everybody else. Lisa asked me to tell her my story. "Every single detail," she said. I told her every single detail.

"You feel better?" she asked.

"Why would I feel better?" I said. "I still don't have what I deserve."

"Sometimes it feels good just to tell your side of the story," she said.

I walked out of the office and decided that I needed to contact a union rep. I imagined myself as a contemporary Norma Rae. I imagined myself standing on a large conference table with a huge, unwieldy sign that said, "Union." I imagined being so proud about the way the magic marker made the most beautiful lines.

The union rep listened to my side of the story. "Tell me every single detail," he said.

I told him every single detail.

"You have a case," he said.

I was happy. He said that we'd meet with Lisa and find out how I could be given an equal opportunity. "I'll be there for you, for support," he said.

Before the meeting, I decided I wanted to look like Norma Rae. I put gel in my hair and pulled it back. I practiced angry and determined looks in the mirror.

When the three of us met to talk, the union rep completely changed his tune from what he'd told me only a day earlier on the phone. He now said I didn't have a case. He said he'd chatted with Lisa. They reviewed every single detail and realized everything was completely fine, nothing to worry about. He smiled. "Sorry," said the union rep and Lisa in near unison. "But if you want to tell us your story again, please do. It's always good to have an emotional release."

### One Flew over the Cuckoo's Nest (1975)

I wanted to be Nurse Ratched. I was obsessed with her uniform: the aggressive whiteness, the tough material, the stubborn zipper, the perfect creases. Everything was surface and hidden threat. I could never imagine her taking off her cap. She rolled out of bed with it on. Her skin was dull sheen. Like the floors she walked on. Like the windows the patients stared out of.

She was a woman who always had a destination. She never looked around. She always looked forward. She was a woman who had mastered the art of locking a door: she knew never to look back.

I admired the way she watched the patients take their pills. Follow the rules. Under her watch, no one would choke. You could hear the silence broken by swallowing.

She was all about time, the clicking of a clock.

She was the measurement, the fit, the pattern. Numbers came as easily to her as madness did for her patients. She was as large as God. The sound of her shoes on the bare floor: the echo of wounded angels landing.

### The Paper Chase (1973)

I worshipped John Houseman's performance as the brilliant, didactic, intimidating law professor Dr. Charles W. Kingsfield Jr. in *The Paper Chase*. I've always wanted to scare my own students into intellectual submission. When at the start of the film Dr. Kingsfield puts one of his students on the spot using the Socratic method we know we're on a wild ride.

I try to think of things Dr. Kingsfield would say. This is one of my best lines. When I compliment students on their writing, they'll often say thank you. My response: "That was not a compliment. It was a fact. Never thank me again."

If a student misses class and asks me if they missed anything important, I say, "Every single thing I say is important. Class is sixty minutes long. You missed at least sixty things crucial to your development as a writer and by extension a human being."

There's a part of them that believes me. So: I believe them. And that's why I choose to be a teacher.

### Quadrophenia (1979)

I was never the rebel. I was scared of people who could change their lives on a dime, like Jimmy Cooper in *Quadrophenia*. He jettisons his "respectable" career as a post room boy in a firm to be a London Mod, a gang leader.

I do, however, like the idea of having definite rivals. Mod or Rocker? Rocker or Mod? Make your decision, boy. Which are you? It's harder to make mistakes in life when your enemies are clearly marked.

Of course, it never turns out the way you want it. In *Quadrophrenia*, during a violent fight, a member in one of the rival gangs dies, and it turns out that it's Jimmy's best friend. He doesn't stick around. He takes off.

Just as Jimmy thinks he's escaped from his former disrupted and disappointing life, he ends up being catapulted over a ditch on his motorbike. The ending is a little ambiguous. While some say the beginning of the film hints that Jimmy survives, others have argued that Jimmy kills himself in that final scene.

### Rollerball (1975)

Once I asked a colleague: "Do you think I'd be a good dad?," to which he replied: "A perfect pushy stage mom. A dad, no. But Phil could be."

I fantasize about Phil, myself, and a child—our child—holding hands, an invincible trio, roller-skating with sheer bravado past the skyscrapers full of evil Republicans.

That's the movies for you: giving you defenses you'll never have.

People always ask us if we're going to have a child. They always tell Phil he'd be such a good dad. And he would. If some malicious goon came darting toward our kid on a roller rink, Phil would swoop the child away with perfect timing. Also, he has patience.

Sometimes I think to myself: *I am so sorry, Phil.* And then: *I wish I wasn't gay. I could be so much more.* And then: *Shut the hell up, you idiot!*

We have stuffed animals that we put to bed at night. One by one. We have a teddy bear that we call Mr. Pokey. We give him little adventures.

### Smokey and the Bandit (1977)

When I think of the movie *Smokey and the Bandit*, I think of wind. I do not think about the silly plot involving a massive car race over a tractor trailer of beer. I do not think of Sally Field and Burt Reynolds and the lack of spark in their romance. I do not think of the brilliant editing, showing us the hot pursuits with precise crosscutting.

There is nothing more beautiful than wind. Perhaps this is why I am afraid to drive. In *Smokey and the Bandit*, I like watching the wind tousling the hair of the actors, sending the vehicles into a tailspin, or disappearing feet before the flag falls at the end of the race. I imagine the wind as God's breath overtaking my car, blowing me to the heavens above. The wind reaches everything. No movie, even *Smokey and the Bandit*, can quite capture the wind's stillness or its aggression, its fierce determination to do what no human can: move beyond itself.

### The Texas Chain Saw Massacre (1974)

Everyone thinks there's so much blood in this movie. But whenever I see the film, I'm always in awe how little blood there actually is. In fact, there is none. For me, the scariest moment has nothing to do with any sort of gore. This is the setup: we see one of the women who escaped from Leatherface in the forest. She runs into a gas station/convenience store. She's scared to death. She has forgotten to close and lock the door. She hides behind the counter. She gets up and tries to see if he's coming. It's dead silent. She waits. And waits. As we do. And we already know she will soon be dead, and she pretty likely knows it, too.

Death is not a cheap scare. Death is not a lot of dumb shocks. Death is the moment between waiting for something to happen and what happens when it does.

### Up in Smoke (1978)

Cheech and Chong were my heroes. I remember catching their debut *Up in Smoke* on late-night cable. The Latino comedians inspired me to try to light my first bong. My hands were awkward and the fire singed my best friend Sean's hair and burned her ear.

I worried our friendship was over after I'd almost killed her for a dumb puff. The comedy duo possessed a certain grace when they handed the bong back and forth, inhaling and exhaling with a perfect rhythmic intensity. It wasn't something you could learn. It was a God-given gift. They had the perfect rapport. No woman got in their way.

Years ago I found out they had broken up. It ended in a truly nasty, irreconcilable way. How could my friendship remain if theirs didn't?

Sean and I never looked at each other blurry eyed and hungry, laughing over nothing, wrapped in a cloud of sweet air. We were sober and desperate, marching through smokeless gay bars, inhaling the fumes of bad cologne and stale poppers.

### Viva Knievel! (1977)

Imagine being the most talented motorcycle stuntman in the history of the world and finding out that villainous people are luring you to Mexico, where they want to kill you and then pack cocaine in your corpse for easy traveling over county borders. You know, that old story.

How good it would feel to do jumps and flips and wheelies like Evel Knievel, all in the name of escape and transcendence.

Sometimes Mr. Knievel doesn't even hold on to the handlebars. I guess that's my tragic flaw: I always do. And my grasp is always so tight.

### A Woman under the Influence (1974)

Gena Rowlands as Mabel in *A Woman under the Influence* suffers from severe mental illness. The first half of the movie focuses on her preparing dinner for a dozen men in her husband's construction crew. You can see how untethered she is. Everything sends her reeling. We don't know if she's going to make it past serving them an initial drink.

The next time we see her, she has just been discharged from a psychiatric hospital. Her family has thrown her a welcome home party. It's a nice idea. But the sheer pressure of having to show gratitude and joy overwhelms her.

She's probably been pushed over the edge again. We don't know for sure. The movie ends before we are certain.

Like most of Cassavetes's films, the scenes go on and on. There are only two set pieces in the entire movie: the kitchen table and the living room where the party takes place. Once I got a stopwatch and timed how many seconds it took before Mabel started to go truly mad.

I recorded it in my journal. I liked to keep track of madness. I wanted to see when it was, exactly, that she broke. I was looking for the demarcation between sanity and doom. I didn't know it then, but I was preparing to cross that line myself.

If you think about the movies that mean the most to you, every single scene of your favorite becomes meaningful foreshadowing, and equally, every moment becomes a useless epilogue, not enough to hold onto when the film suddenly ends.


### X, Y, and Zee (1972)

The setup: a rich man (Michael Caine) who is married to a rich woman (Elizabeth Taylor) falls in love with a young rich woman (Susannah York).

What the directors failed to realize: you can't create a measured, precise three-way love triangle if one of the lovers is Elizabeth Taylor. No offense to Susannah York, but more than one point of the triangle has to matter. Elizabeth Taylor is the point. The single point. She's always the point of any movie she is in. Nothing else counts, no matter how exquisite the shape, no matter how ruined the lines of the triangle may be.

On the day of my high school prom, my father moved out of our house. My mother was taking pictures of me and the three other couples as my father threw his clothes into the back of his Volvo. At one point we were all on the driveway. You could say there was a triangulation: it was uncanny. Our collective grief somehow made my father, mother, and me an equal distance apart. And even though we could count the steps that could bring us back together again, we were all frozen in a simple shape none of us could make sense of.


### You'll Like My Mother (1972)

"My mother isn't going to like you," Phil said to me.

Phil's from Knoxville, Tennessee. I figured she'd have something against me. The South = homophobia.

"She's not *that* weird about gay people," he said. "I meant your personality. You're not quite right."

"Is that a good thing or a bad thing?"

We had been going out for a year.

"I'm not sure," he said.

So: we went to see his mother.

I was like Patty Duke in the horror movie *You'll Like My Mother*. I was travelling across the nation to meet a possibly nasty, oppressive force. The first thing she said: "You're not black."

"No," I said.

"Good," she said. "You're a grad student?"

"Yes."

"What subject?"

"English."

"That's one strike against you."

During my entire stay it went like that. She even started saying, "That's one in the plus column. That's one in the negative column."

Once I asked, "What happens if it turns out there's more negatives than pluses?"

"You'll disappear," she said and then snapped her fingers: "Just like that."

## *Zardoz* (1974)

I've never liked collecting movie stills. But I do own one. It's from *Zardoz*, a sci-fi movie that takes place in 2035. Sean Connery plays the hero. I've watched the film three times and still cannot explain the plot in any concise way. There are so many characters that if you asked even the best Mormon genealogist, he'd quit his job and laugh bitterly to himself every time Pioneer Day rolled around. Let's just say this: *Zardoz* involves well-intentioned assassins, phony gods, magic stones, badly staged fight scenes, and a secret society of immortals.

But I don't really care what happens in the movie. That's not what's important.

What matters is Sean Connery's costume.

He is scantily clad in a flaming red bandolier and matching jock strap, knee-high black boots. His hair is in a ponytail. It is, perhaps, the single strang-est costume ever worn by a major male Hollywood star in an action movie.

Some might say this was a bungled attempt by Connery to draw attention to himself as a groovy seventies sci-fi hero. Others might say it was a way for him (or the director) to publicly work out private sexual kinks.

But a rare few might simply call it stripping down and getting ridiculous for no other reason than a profoundly mad love for the movies.

I keep the picture on my writing desk. For inspiration.

# The Forgetting Test

LEE UPTON

Are you the sort of person who forgets things easily? Does your capacity to forget burn through each day like acid? Do you mindlessly fill out multiple memory tests online? Try our forgetting test instead. Answer the following questions truthfully then score your responses!

*When you're introduced to someone, does the person's name:*
1) Disappear from your memory like a snowflake in a hot frying pan,
2) Become conflated with other names so that for years you'll call Kirstin "Kristen" and Harrison "Thompson" and Ahmad "Amir" and Eddie "Dwayne,"
3) Grip your memory with the force of a too-tiny sports bra on a giant,
4) Or maybe you agree with Michel de Montaigne that "Nothing fixes a thing so intensely in the memory as the wish to forget it" and as a result try to make meeting new people an especially unpleasant experience? That is, when you meet someone do you tend to turn hostile? Perhaps this is the attitude that prompted the novelist Dawn Powell to write in her journal: "I'd love to meet him personally and shake him by the neck."

*How sharp are your memories of your first camping trip?*
1) Crystalline. I even remember the bear attack.
2) I've never camped. Oh, sorry, I did. Once. No, twice.
3) We spent the night in a hotel after we saw the facilities.

4) We forget more than we remember. I started forgetting as an infant, maybe even earlier than that. Forgetting came naturally to me. Thus I am proud to report that I don't remember my first camping trip.

5) I would rather be hogtied to a trailer truck than camp—or is that the same thing?

*What form does the act of forgetting most often take for you?*

1) A solid.

2) A liquid.

3) A semi-solid. Once, years ago, at dawn, I opened my car, and on the door handle I touched a perfect ledge of sludgy water, not quite fluid, not quite solid, and I felt like the physical world could be poked through and that I could touch another world on the other side of this world, I think.

*What best describes your response to the moment you remember you forgot something crucial?*

1) Calculation: If I drive slowly I won't get pulled over, and no one will know I forgot my wallet with my driver's license in it.

2) Panic: I just remembered I'm not supposed to be asleep while driving this bus to Atlantic City!

3) Curiosity: Why is it so important to remember that:
   a) I'm driving
   b) I'm uninsured
   c) I'm using a sleep medication that has convinced me I'm playing pinochle in Osaka, Japan?

4) In the movie *Eraserhead* erasers are made from the main character's brain.

*Proust's famously detailed recollection of his childhood—its every particular—was spurred by the taste and scent of a madeleine dipped in tea. Is your capacity to remember heightened by:*

1) Feeling the texture of your old grade school uniform against your skin?

2) Opening your first diary with a tiny key?

3) Your high school yearbook?

4) An ability to lie?

5) The sight of a snow cone in the hand of a grinning clown?

*Forgetting, like memory, is made partly of the imagination; forgetting prunes memory to create another, sturdier, more well-defined, more muscular narrative.*

1) I agree.
2) I agree somewhat.
3) I don't think so.
4) If Oliver Sacks says so ("It is startling to realize that some of our most cherished memories may never have happened—or have happened to someone else").
5) You lost me at the word *prunes*.

*If memory is mother of the muses, then:*

1) Forgetting is the daughter/son/grandchild/grandmother/ornery uncle of the muses.
2) Forgetting is the forgotten muse.
3) Forgetting is a god, a cousin to Bacchus, and the cast-off inventor of stupefying after-dinner drinks.
4) Forgetting is the power of an untold story, an alternative version, a secret account. For example, what if there was a forgotten story about the Judgment of Paris? What if instead of choosing from among three goddesses, Paris chose from among three gods: Mars, the god of war; Vulcan, the god of craftsmanship; or Mercury, the god of commerce? Paris would have chosen war—which requires repression and denial and subsumes craftsmanship and commerce for its own purposes. And depends on the power of our forgetting the nature of war. Our powerful forgetting.
4) Forgetting is a river in hell.

*If forgetting is a terrain, it is:*

1) A desert.
2) Swampland.
3) Mountainous.
4) Farmland. When something comes into memory where has it been? Forgetting is like the soil from which memories spring . . . seeds planted in the loam of forgetfulness.
5) A verdant forest that you can't see because of the trees.

6) Forgetting may more profitably be considered an aquatic phenomenon. We forget so that memory can do its work, arising from the ocean of the forgotten like a new island. The joy of re-remembering requires forgetting.

*Hyperthymesia—the rare ability to remember one's own personal life in incredible detail over many years—would:*

1) Be wonderful!
2) Frighten me halfway to death.
3) Make it possible at last to win an argument.
4) I remember the first time I heard the word *hyperthymesia.* It was August 2, a Tuesday, and I was wearing my gym uniform, and my lunch consisted of an olive loaf sandwich, an overripe banana, and one of those hostess snowball desserts with the marshmallow lid that you peel off like it's your own little pink igloo, which reminds me of August 25, 1996, which was a Sunday, and I was listening to "Macarena" by Los del Río when . . .
5) It's simple. Some things are worth forgetting. Even so, that may mean you remember them and record them in your journal. I can't remember if I mentioned the novelist Dawn Powell earlier. Did I? At any rate Dawn Powell knew this well. She hated a date on the calendar. Referring to January 26, 1938, she wrote: "For no reason at all I hated this day as if it was a person— its wind, its insecurity, its flabbiness, its hints of an insane universe."

*What militates against forgetting?*

1) Grief: during the eulogy the priest said of the deeply loved woman we were mourning, "She's on her way to heaven." The widower interrupted and said, "She's already there."
2) Censorship: I won't forget what you're trying to deny me.
3) Imagination: revenge on memory's clinging dependency to the illusions of actuality.
4) Telling yourself again and again: Don't forget! Recording a reminder. Stating your intention to a personal enemy who will mock you in front of your friends if you forget. Hiring a personal memory trainer.
5) Acceptance.
6) Gratitude.

Your Score:

Forget about scoring yourself. I have. Are you being competitive about forgetting? Forget about it. Forgetting always wins. Anyway, who would be so arrogant as to score forgetting for you? Not me!

Forgetting: a mystery of our lives associated with sadness and affliction and aligned with disease and decay, with fears of no longer being able to bring to mind what we treasure about the ones we've loved, their faces and habits and words. And yet forgetting is memory's accomplice, and out of forgetting's depths memory rises. Forgive and forget? So unlikely. More likely: forget and forget. How to conceptualize this absence that may in some instances be painful and may in other instances make our minds bearable?

The forgetting and the forgotten. The untold stories of those excluded. The lost languages. The lost rituals. The extinct animals. The dusky sea sparrow in a bottle in a natural history museum. The extinct song of the dusky sea sparrow.

I once met a woman who told me she was married to a minister and that her husband preferred funerals to weddings. I was surprised and asked why. She said, "Because at funerals people listen to him."

Her words made me remember that I'd forgotten how much I like weddings; how weddings enshrine a pledge against loss and small-mindedness in favor of loyalty and our sympathetic angels, the ones most likely to raise the sword of forgetfulness against our more cynical natures, against our remembering too vividly the flaws of others.

How to make peace with the sort of forgetting that is itself a form of peace? How to admit the other wages of forgetting? Attention to our lives includes attention to the act of forgetting. The lingering mystery of forgetting and of the ever-increasing forgotten.

The last dusky seaside sparrow, weighing one ounce, blind in one eye, in captivity, possibly as old as thirteen—which is very old for a sparrow, as if he intended to live as long as he could for his forgotten kind—died on June 17, 1987.

# #miscarriage.exe

INGRID JENDRZEJEWSKI

```
import from library daily_routine: wake, wash, dry, move, flush
import from library motherhood: hug, kiss, read

#Define subroutines

define subroutine: cry()
   if sad:
      if alone:
         sob
      else:
         use(tissues)
         stifle(sobs)

define subroutine: pain_management(time_since_last_painkiller)
   if cramping:
      if (time_since_last_painkiller_in_hours>=4):
         take(codeine)
         take(water)
      else:
         subroutine cry()

define subroutine: toilet()
   use(toilet)
   subroutine cry()
```

```
      search(toilet for remains of baby)
      subroutine cry()
      if baby:
         pause()
      flush(toilet)
      subroutine cry()
      change(sanitary pad)
      wash(hands)
      if tears:
         dry(face)

  #Define modified daily subroutines

  define subroutine: dress(person)
     if time in range(6am,5pm):
        open(wardrobe)
        outfit=choose random(clothes)
        combine(person,outfit)
     else:
        open(dresser)
        outfit=choose random(pajamas)
        combine(person,outfit)

  define subroutine: feed(person)
     open(refrigerator)
     list(options)
     query(person)
     give(person, whatever_they_want)
     fuck(balanced_diet)

  #Begin Program

  #6:30 am

  wake(self)
  subroutine cry()
```

```
subroutine toilet()
subroutine pain_management(time)
subroutine dress(self)
if daughter asleep:
   wake(daughter)
hug(daughter)
kiss(daughter)
try(not_to_cry)
subroutine feed(daughter)
subroutine dress(daughter)
subroutine toilet()
if hungry:
   subroutine feed(self)

#8:00 am

drive(daughter,preschool)
hug(daughter)
kiss(daughter)
return(home)
subroutine toilet()
subroutine cry()
subroutine pain_management(time)

try(sleep)
if sleep==possible:
   while(time<11:50am):
      sleep
   wake(self)
else:
   while(time<11:50am):
      subroutine toilet()
      subroutine cry()
      subroutine pain_management(time)
      pause()
```

```
subroutine toilet()
subroutine cry()
subroutine pain_management()

#12:00 pm

try(not_to_cry)
drive(self,preschool)
hug(daughter)
return(daughter,home)
subroutine feed(daughter)
move(daughter,television)
if hungry:
    subroutine feed(self)
subroutine toilet()
subroutine cry()
subroutine pain_management(time)
while daughter==watching_television
    pause()

#5:00 pm

subroutine feed(daughter)
subroutine feed(husband)
if hungry:
    subroutine feed(self)
stack(dishes)
hug(daughter)
move(daughter,husband)
subroutine toilet()
subroutine cry()
subroutine pain_management(time)
move(self,television)
watch(television)
    if baby_on_television==true:
        subroutine cry()
```

```
#6:30 pm

run(bath)
wash(daughter)
dry(daughter)
subroutine dress(daughter)
move(daughter,bed)
hug(daughter)
kiss(daughter)
while daughter==awake:
   current_book=choose random(book)
   read(current_book)
kiss(daughter)
subroutine toilet()
subroutine cry()
subroutine pain_management()

#9:00 pm

subroutine toilet()
subroutine cry()
subroutine pain_management()
subroutine dress(self)
move(self,bed)
if husband==present:
   if bleeding:
      print("I'm still bleeding.")
   if cramping:
      print("I'm still cramping.")
   if crying:
      print("I can't stop crying.")
   open library(affection)
   from library(affection) import hold(person)
   hug(husband)
   hold(husband)
```

```
try(not_to_cry)
try(sleep)
try(sleep)
try(sleep)
try(sleep)
try(sleep)
try(sleep)
try(sleep)
try(sleep)
try(sleep)
try(sleep)

#End program
```

# SECTION 404

CHEYENNE NIMES

1  *Section 404 of the Clean Water Act and the Santa Cruz River Sand Shark*
2  ***"This troublesome regulatory constraint"***
3  SENATE JOINT MEMORIAL 01–666
4  *"The home builders have a long history of trying to avoid any Clean Water Act regulation,*
5  *so it's not surprising that they would do this. As evidenced by the condition of our rivers*
6  *in Arizona, it's never been easy to protect them. And a big reason for that is the efforts*
7  *of the home builders to avoid regulation."*—Sandy Bahr of the Sierra Club's Grand
8  Canyon Chapter
9
10  WHEREAS, Dear Santa Cruz River, test case for national policy on river
11  protection:
12      A. because *navigable rivers are covered under section 404 of the Clean*
13          *Water Act* but you're an "ephemeral" river—& streams flow only during
14          intense rainfall, into deep ravines and arroyos—& you spend part of
15          your time underground north of Tubac as you proceed toward Tucson,
16      B. so you've been tricked, you've been a token in this scheme because
17          they want you to be someone you're not, &
18      C. it's a different river, the wrong river, a river far from this one, &
19      D. on & on *that* river flowed, now golden like the aisle to someone's
20          God's distant altar; and

21    WHEREAS, *The* EPA *declared two portions of the Santa Cruz River—one stretching*
22    *from Tubac to Continental Road and the other from the Roger Road sewage*
23    *treatment plant to the county line—navigable in December, after taking on the*
24    *river as a "special case"*; and

25

26    WHEREAS, Henceforth, agency officials removed the designations without
27    explanation: "This document has been temporality [*sic*] removed pending
28    further policy review"; and

29

30    WHEREAS, That constitutes crime scene evidence like lying in wait, &

31

32        A. you need to research the story you are being told, &
33        B. see who benefits from your deception; and

34

35    WHEREAS, Only humans & seals have salty tears; and

36

37    WHEREAS, The National Mining Association, the American Farm Bureau
38    Federation, the National Cattlemen's Beef Association, the Public Lands
39    Council, the American Forest and Paper Association, the American Public
40    Power Association, the Edison Electric Institute, the National Association
41    of Home Builders, the National Association of Realtors, and the National
42    Association of Counties are now—in a kind of back-up vocabulary—termed
43    "grass roots" and turning the waters to blood, and the river, & they prefer a
44    river to nowhere; and

45

46    WHEREAS, The aforementioned big businesses are no match for Ducks
47    Unlimited, the Tucson Audubon Society, the Tohono O'odham Nation, the
48    National Wildlife Federation, Pronatura Noroeste, the Friends of the Santa Cruz
49    River, the Akimel O'odham, the Ak-Chin O'odham, the Environmental Defense
50    Fund, the Coalition for Sonoran Desert Protection, the Theodore Roosevelt
51    Conservation Partnership, Los Falcones, the LightHawk Organization, the
52    Arizona-Sonora Workgroup, the Nogales International Wastewater Treatment
53    Plant, the Kino Heritage Fruit Trees Project, the U.S. National Parks Service-
54    Tumacacori, the Sobaipuri, the Arizona Department of Environmental Quality,
55    the Arizona Department of Water Resources, Trout Unlimited, the Sonoran

Institute's Sonoran Desert Ecoregion Program, Arizona State Park, the Nature
Conservancy, the Sky Island Institute, El Colegio de la Frontera Norte, the Hia
C-ed O'odham, Henry Waxman of California, Raúl Grijalva of Arizona, James
Oberstar of Minnesota, and the Clean Water Network—a coalition of more
than one thousand and two hundred public interest organizations across the
country representing more than five million people; and

WHEREAS, It would be remiss to disinclude the migratory yellow-breasted chat,
Lucy's warbler, Bell's vireo, or Abert's towhee in the flyway sky North–South
every Fall–Spring, as the river indeed orients North–South, nor shall it slip
our mind about a rare woodland raptor—the northern goshawk—& other
living beings like the lesser long-nosed bat & aquatic creatures such as the
endangered Gila topminnow, Gila chub, the Sonoran salamander, &

    A. lest we forget the white-tailed deer, the mule deer, the pronghorn, the
        javelina, the Mexican gray wolf, the black bear, the bobcat, the coyote,
        the ocelots & jaguars & mountain lions,
    B. & the fifteen now-endangered species, the Pima pineapple cactus, the
        rare Wilcox's fishhook cactus, the endangered Huachuca water umbel,
        & the Madrean ladies' tresses, &
    C. can we get back to the birds, the yellow-billed cuckoo & vermilion
        flycatcher, the insects, oh, the bugs & bees, the trees, the catclaw
        acacia, willow, mesquite shrubs & bosques, the hackberry, amaranth,
        & native grasses along the
    D. three, count them, *three* distinct biomes the Santa Cruz river crosses
        through, under, over, & above, & at an altitude low of 3,000 feet, yet at
        times 9,453 feet; and

WHEREAS, More than *80%* of species in Arizona depend on riparian habitat
at some point in their life cycle, &

    A. the American Bird Conservatory lists Southwestern riparian habitat
        as the fifth-most threatened habitat in the U.S., &
    B. freshwater animals are disappearing five times faster—*on the double,*
        *now*—than land animals, &

91   C. that means *this* one river & all dark-shadowed rivers, ones that *was,*
92      *then wasn't, then was*; &
93   D. so we will not forget that when the Santa Cruz does run, it will arrive at
94      the sea eventually, & in that sea appear 90 percent of *all* living things, &
95   E. of those life forms, 85 percent of *all* life on Earth is, in fact, *plankton*; and
96

97   WHEREAS, What happens to the microcosm happens to the macrocosm, &

98

99   A. this fact has never changed; &

100

101  WHEREAS, Will never change; and

102

103  WHEREAS, The Rapanos disaster tried to change surface water quality protec-
104  tions implemented in Arizona & on every American river since 1972,

105

106  A. as if a wetland were isolated from surrounding ecosystems—not a
107     galaxy striking the edge of another galaxy; and

108

109  WHEREAS, Most rivers begin accidentally &

110

111  A. they all glow a certain way &
112  B. there are colors to each of them, their watersheds &
113  C. a drainage basin is in its own longitudinal zone,
114  D. a water of the United States; which includes, but is not limited to:
115  E. a sandy bottom wash, a small wash, a lake, a tributary, a two-foot-wide
116     wash, a storm water retention basin, bays, beaches, runoffs, kills, runs,
117     reaches, brooks, riffles, natural pools, storm water retention ponds,
118     natural ponds, farm ponds, standing waters, backwaters, anabranches,
119     channels, wastewater treatment systems, streams, headwater streams,
120     intermittent streams, peripheral streams, streambeds, stream terraces,
121     streets and gutters, gulches, gullies, irrigation canals, endorheic
122     basins, swamps, inland swamps, back swamps, backwaters, bayous,
123     cypress swamps, cypress domes, springs, flooded grasslands, glades,
124     wet meadows, adjacent wetlands, small wetlands intermixed with
125     uplands, remote wetlands, small, discontinuous wetlands, "isolated"

wetlands, "isolated" intrastate pools, puddles of rainwater, marshes,
coastal marshes, fringing marshes, estuaries, tidal bores, northern
bogs, southern riverine bottomlands, yazoos, oases, floods, flooded
river valleys, meanders, *rincones*, lagoons, sand flats, swales,
watersheds, creeks, cricks, small rivers, rills, mudflats, fjords, *rias*,
terraces, river bifurcations, street washes, cutoffs, eddies, floodplains,
rivulets, prairie potholes, playa lakes, wet meadows, sloughs, oxbows,
drainage basins, irrigation ditches, desert washes, damp places, deltas,
discharges, draws, depressions filled with water on an intermittent
basis, distributaries, & thousands of fluvial landform water bodies
which flow into other streams, which in turn

F. combine to form larger streams then

G. these larger streams unite to form rivers &

H. a stream is smaller than a river,

I. a creek is smaller than a stream,

J. but larger than a brook;

K. *stream*, *brook*, *creek*, and *rivulet* are applied interchangeably to any
small river &

L. a truly comprehensive list of water collections—or the point between
two rivers—could not be contained on this page alone &

M. in fact, I don't believe that it could be contained at all; and


WHEREAS, About 60% of the nation's streams are nonpermanent according
to the National Hydrology Dataset, &


A. between 80 and 95 percent of streams in arid western states like
Arizona, Utah, and New Mexico do not flow year-round,

B. repeat, do not flow year-round; &

C. again, seasonal streams are common in the western United States; and


WHEREAS, The 1972 Clean Water Act was intended to "restore and maintain
the chemical, physical, and biological integrity of the nation's waters," & were
it violated, it would result in the removal of 95 percent of the state of Arizona's
surface waters from Clean Water Act protections which means they *couldn't
prohibit wastewater discharges* into the cleanest rivers like Sabino Creek and

161 the Little Colorado River & all aforementioned ninety-eight names in Section
162 Thirteen; and
163
164 WHEREAS, To the Kogi Indians of Columbia the three entities at the beginning
165 of life are
166
167     A. mother,
168     B. night, &
169     C. water; and
170
171 WHEREAS, Where a season crosses over, lines in the river crack like a weed
172 in the ground—you can't even recognize her face anymore—& they may even
173 say it is worthless & therefore doesn't exist—try & pretend that something is
174 not when it is—but you cannot replace something that "is" with something
175 that "is not" because
176
177     A. "what is" & "what is not" are two completely different configurations &
178     B. you do not change one into the other &
179     C. it doesn't have to have a name because
180     D. it is "water" & that is enough &
181     E. it goes into the underworld &
182     F. returning, brought & brings & will bring life, &
183     G. 96 percent of the streams in Arizona *are* non-perennial & subterranean
184         water—1,680,000 cubic miles of it—*is* groundwater; and
185
186 WHEREAS, The hardest situation for the human to understand is the human
187 cannot understand it all but that
188
189     A. where there is no water, there is no life; and
190
191 WHEREAS, That is the one situation that is true & in all instances & is therefore
192
193     A. the one sole phenomenon the human should, in theory, grasp; and

WHEREAS, 10–16 percent of the earth is true desert & evaporation of the seas goes on all the time,

A. enough to drain all oceans completely every three thousand years; and

WHEREAS, Evaporation is a distinct, regular, normal part of the hydrologic cycle; and

WHEREAS, *"In Arizona alone, according to the experts at the EPA, we stand to lose protection of approximately 95% of our streams and rivers under current federal agency interpretations, which would allow pollution to greatly increase"(Raúl Grijalva, chair of the House National Parks, Forests, and Public Lands Subcommittee)*; and

WHEREAS, That would be absurd; and

WHEREAS, Water created *three billion years ago* (where or how no one knows) is still in existence & large rivers flow faster than small ones—that's clear—& as water moves, it slows down or speeds up, becomes shallower or deeper, & deep water is dark, &

A. human babies learn to swim before they can walk or sit upright, &
B. know not to try to breathe underwater, know how to come to the surface on instinct, &
C. we kept the hair on our heads to give babies something to cling to as we swim, &
D. adults are 65–70 percent $H_2O$, same as elephants, &
E. all parties in Section Six say with a straight face they "haven't seen any elephants"; and

WHEREAS, The Pima County Waste Water Department already quotes themselves: "The water in the Santa Cruz river is clean, but we advise against drinking, or playing in it"; and

227   WHEREAS, The Santa Cruz River decision will set a precedent for how all
228   other rivers, streams, and wetlands will be evaluated in the United States &
229

230        A. if the Santa Cruz is a navigable river,
231        B. it gains Traditional Navigable Waters (TNW) status,
232        C. the most restrictive designation in the Clean Water Act; and
233

234   WHEREAS, Precedents have a way of setting precedents ad infinitum; and
235

236   WHEREAS, *"A controversial 2006 Supreme Court decision in the Rapanos case*
237   *reinterpreted the 1972 Clean Water Act,"* & *"The Rapanos decision potentially*
238   *excluded from the Clean Water Act waterways that are either non-navigable or*
239   *don't have a 'significant nexus' between a streambed and a 'navigable water of*
240   *the United States,'"* & *"Suddenly, Justice Anthony Kennedy caused every potential*
241   *streambed in the country to be analyzed to see if it was connected to another that*
242   *could have or has had watercraft on it before it could be protected from pollution*
243   *or disruption, creating legal chaos for arid Western states, including Arizona,"* &
244   *"From 1975 until this decision, such a connection was not needed in streambeds*
245   *that were ephemeral or often dry,"* & apparently the Supremes
246

247        A. expected God to be a creature, have a face, & be singular in 3D,
248        B. just like themselves, &
249        C. God must be under the water they said, &
250        D. you can't count God glancing up at skeeters gliding across as
251            *watercraft*; and
252

253   WHEREAS, If God is underwater or there is no water whatsoever it is because
254   she is drowning in elusive legal standards, jurisdictional uncertainty, & the
255   lowering of priority of enforcement action due to stone ignorance whether
256   the waters remain within the scope of the Clean Water Act, therefore allowing
257

258        A. violators of enforceable actions to use the lack of Clean Water Act
259            jurisdiction as their defense, &

260  B. because the Clean Water Act enforcement docket has been backed
261     up with over four hundred cases in the Los Angeles area alone, she
262     cannot lift herself up out of the sewage &
263  C. subsequently is a violation if
264  D. God invented the human so the water could walk place to place; and
265

266  WHEREAS, It is water, is it not, thus must be clean to continue to keep all of
267  us alive; and
268

269  WHEREAS, Water molecules cling tightly to one another & to hydrogen atoms
270  and their bonds, & two hydrogen atoms are angled 104.5 degrees from each
271  other at all times with billions of tiny bonds between, &
272

273  A. no one has ever seen a water molecule, &
274  B. all we know is that atoms are laced together &
275  C. they look like rivers under a microscope or on an X-ray & thus are
276  D. comparable to branching patterns of trees or blood vessels in animal
277     tissue & other natural networks, &
278  E. two hydrogen atoms & one oxygen atom cling to one another & need
279     to get heated up to 2,900 degrees Fahrenheit to be pulled apart; and
280

281  WHEREAS, Water molecules cling tightly to one another; and
282

283  WHEREAS, As many as fifty thousand midge larvae can congregate on one
284  single square yard of a river's bottom &
285

286  A. we started out as blue-green algae, the slimy coating on rocks &
287  B. 7 percent of all humans are born with webbed feet & have rudimentary
288     webs between fingers & thumbs, & parties to Section Six also forgot
289     about the tail, didn't they &
290  C. when we're eight months old, we're still 81 percent water &
291  D. every cell has a fluid interior with hydrogen, oxygen, nitrogen, carbon,
292     magnesium, iron, phosphorous, sulphur, silica, calcium iodine,

293     fluorine, chlorine, bromine, silver, cobalt, vanadium, & gold, & sixty
294     thousand miles of arteries & veins wind through in each of us; and
295
296 WHEREAS, They cling tightly; and
297
298 WHEREAS, Over 85 percent of the fish fauna in Arizona are threatened & all
299 three ecoregions have a conservation status of either *critical* or *endangered*
300 with a high likelihood of future threats; and
301
302 WHEREAS, They cling; and
303
304 WHEREAS, Not long ago philosophers thought water came directly from the
305 center of the earth: in 1580, Bernard Palissy said water in rivers & springs came
306 from rainfall, while Edmond Halley later figured out that the amount falling
307 equaled the amount in the rivers, & that water traveled through the atmosphere;
308 water, then, arrives not from Earth's center but from clouds—storm clouds that
309 hold water vapor that returns water to land, & to sea as rain, to the oceans, to
310 the land, to the air, & this cycle makes perennial streams flow year-round &
311 intermittent streams flow only during the wet season, or after heavy rain, or
312 leave behind dry riverbed ghosts, &
313
314     A. a skeeter touching down, & innumerable others of known Kingdoms
315        and Phylums cannot possibly be expected to side-trip it to Walmart
316        Super Center for Hazmat suits in their size, &
317     B. talking to *you*, EPA; and
318
319 WHEREAS, The ongoing human depletion of the aquifer is the reason the Santa
320 Cruz dried out *except* after storms, &
321     A. common sense like this, for some reason, needs to be stated in this
322        SENATE JOINT MEMORIAL; and
323
324 WHEREAS, Water is not uniformly available in all areas of the United States; and
325
326 WHEREAS, They cling tightly for dear life; and

327    WHEREAS, Water molecules cling tightly to one another because they know
328    degradation & protection of any potential watershed always begins at its
329    ninth-order tributaries; and

330

331    WHEREAS, It bears repeating that degradation & protection of any potential
332    watershed always begins at its ninth-order tributaries; and

333

334    WHEREAS, They cling for safety because

335

336        A. there is safety in numbers &
337        B. moving targets remain whole; and

338

339    WHEREAS, Just because the Southwest has ninth-order ephemeral streams
340    with no monstrous berths the RMS *Queen Elizabeth 2* can cruise down does
341    not call for their degradation & destruction, causing local residents to ingest
342    toxins *like there's nothing wrong with this at all,* as if

343

344        A. the National Mining Association, American Farm Bureau Federation,
345           National Cattlemen's Beef Association, Public Lands Council, American
346           Forest and Paper Association, American Public Power Association,
347           Edison Electric Institute, National Association of Home Builders,
348           National Association of Realtors, the National Association of Counties,
349           the Environmental Protection Agency, & Justice Anthony Kennedy
350        B. understand better than we do, all of it, better than
351        C. Ducks, Unlimited,
352        D. the Kogi Indians of Columbia, &
353        E. you, again, with your tailbone; and

354

355    WHEREAS, Riparian areas—that's riverbeds & streambeds—restore the aquifer
356    arena *everywhere,* as do the riparian zones that are land-adjacent to streams—
357    which contain wildlife & wildlands, which contain finned critters, furred friends,
358    & winged things, who

359

360        A. if polluted & destroyed, so too shall ground water aquifers be polluted
361           & destroyed,

362   B. & flora & fauna & anamalia & fishalia & all such living in & around it,
363     as well as
364   C. nutrients dissolving in said $H_2O$, &
365   D. the rock & soil carried by riparian area flow, including, but not limited to,
366   E. the entire ecosystem; and
367
368 WHEREAS, They continue to cling tightly to one another; and
369
370 WHEREAS, Seventy inches of rain in one day fell on the island of Reunion in
371 the Indian Ocean, which set a record, but
372
373   A. this is not Reunion Island in the Indian Ocean; and
374
375 WHEREAS, The larger the body count, the worse for the state,
376
377   A. the country,
378   B. this world, &
379   C. all other dimensional worlds, &
380   D. do they really need a dimension anyway, as the ideology "if you can't
381     measure it, it can't
382   E. *exist*" is the province of deep, deep, traditionally
383   F. Caucasian male ignorance &
384   G. their priceless advice; and
385
386 WHEREAS, Water molecules don't let go no matter *who* comes for them; and
387
388 WHEREAS, Homebuilder organizations declared war against treating streams
389 with intermittent flows—like the Santa Cruz—as *navigable* waters & the
390 Southern Arizona Home Builders Association, the Home Builders Association
391 of Central Arizona & the National Association of Home Builders filed a lawsuit
392 in DC for an injunction against the Environmental Protection Agency & the
393 U.S. Army Corps of Engineers; and
394
395 WHEREAS, These molecule bonds are stronger than parties to Section Six—
396 whom shall henceforth be called *Section Eight*—humans, &

A. various other parts standing for the whole such as the IRS, the B of A,
     AIG, & corporations referred to as personages, & here, somehow, the
     powers that be suddenly have no issue *whatsoever*

B. seeing the trees for the forest; and

WHEREAS, "... *Memos came to light that some Pima County officials had urged the Corps and the Environmental Protection Agency to favor policies that would, in effect, eliminate CWA enforcement on Tucson waterways,*" & "*Some viewed the memos as another example of the public works and transportation departments working at cross-purposes with county planners over conservation issues*"; & these same officials referred to the Clean Water Act as "this troublesome regulatory constraint"; and

WHEREAS, We may say that *some Pima County officials* suffer from a profound thought disorder &

A. remain dumb as a load of gravel &
B. prefer toxic chemicals,
C. raw sewage,
D. oil, & Stage IV vestigial tail cancer over
E. *water*; and

WHEREAS, Someone was going to get caught, &

A. they did, &
B. were called to the carpet; and

WHEREAS, Someone smart said, "*This was really good news to have back the protections that we lost when the Corps rescinded the designation. I see this as an important interim step while they study whether the rest of the river should have this protection. I'm very hopeful for the whole river to get the traditional navigable waterway [designation], but with this, all the tributaries should be protected because they all eventually touch these two portions*"; and

WHEREAS, Decades ago quantum physicists decided everything touches everything *anyway*, no matter what the Corps puts in their studies, so I don't care *who* this report is brought to you by, &

    A. it's just *sentido común*, or in Utahan, *horse sense*,

    B. eerily absent in Orrin Hatch (R-Utah), who was "disappointed" at the Obama Administration's gall in *actually enforcing* the Clean Water Act, protecting those eight thousand square miles currently impaired with

    C. ammonia, chlorine, chlorophyll, copper, dissolved oxygen, *Escherichia coli* bacteria, mercury, nitrogen, low pH, phosphorus, zinc, &

    D. Mister Hatch, selling wolf tickets, said, "I will continue to fight this egregious abuse," so in June, 2015, Utah became ninth-state-plaintiff to block the newest Act incarnation, &

    E. into the watershed thirty-five thousand users discharged raw sewage like bombing by daylight, and there sat Senator Hatch in the limo tint, &

    F. it's unbelievable, how it gets sometimes,

    G. *what kind of a person comes up with a plan like this and carries it out?*

    H. after over *thirteen thousand years hunter-gatherers* traversed to and fro on this river, &

    I. what *created* this river was ebb and flow waters, millions of years ago, moving bits of mountain into basins along with the gargantuan inland seas, &

    J. the proof is in boulders there, where people scratched in human figures by gripping small, triangular projectile points, the obsidian, the rocks at the fire circle pits, at night,

    K. sounds nearby—mammoths & camels, lions & bison, the long-fanged dire wolves circling, tracing the scent, always the ceaseless circle (can you hear them?); and

WHEREAS, No, really, WHEREAS, Every normal man must be tempted at times to spit on his hands, hoist the black flag, and begin slitting throats,

    A. as Mencken said, tooled up for a final blood prize, but

    B. *if they kill you, you just might come back*, others have said in the meantime; and

465  WHEREAS, The average stay of a water molecule in the air is ten days; and

466

467  WHEREAS, It will eventually come down again, we swear, before the court, to

468  tell the whole truth & nothing but the truth, so help us God; and

469

470  WHEREAS, *"The Environmental Protection Agency has deemed two portions of*

471  *the Santa Cruz River navigable, which means the usually dry 'waterway' deserves*

472  *full protection under the federal Clean Water Act,"* & *"The designation—based on*

473  *flows created by sewage treatment plants in Tucson and Nogales and the historic*

474  *use of the river for recreation—means stepped up restrictions on building along the*

475  *river and its tributaries, and more required permits for private and government*

476  *construction"*; and

477

478  WHEREAS, "Stepped up restrictions" shall make water pleased to let go & fall

479  upon our 'lil heads; and

480

481  WHEREAS, The amended Clean Water Restoration Act replaces the term "navi-

482  gable waters" with "waters of the United States," & the Obama Administration's

483  Clean Water Rule—legislation passed clean through—defines "navigable waters"

484

485  A. as navigable waters & their tributaries,

486  B. *duh,*

487  C. because someone caught on that federal protections apply to all

488  waters (& that someone was not the Section Eight party), as Congress

489  intended in 1972 to protect *all* of America's waters from pollution, not

490  solely those "navigable" to corporate interest, so:

491  D. Dear Utah, Georgia, Alabama, South Carolina, Wisconsin, Kentucky,

492  Kansas, & Florida: the Tenth Amendment shall not be overridden

493  or reinterpreted by greed no matter how many decades you try to

494  addendum-twist the system, &

495  E. you might want to remember that those etched human figures in those

496  boulders will be here long after you're gone, &

497  F. it's so way past time to restore this act's original intention in this world

498  and in other dimensional worlds; and

WHEREAS, The twelve- to fifteen-foot-wide rivulets & the life that is exceedingly
obvious in said rivulets *on Mars*—no matter whether life shows up on their
"gold standard tests"—cannot be included in this SENATE JOINT MEMORIAL
as such except to note that while Ducks, Unlimited and other parties to Section
Seven have not the funds now, nor will Ducks, Unlimited, et al., secure such
funds in the 2030s to join NASA up, up, and away, the Hatches of this world
do because there ain't no rest for the wicked, &

    A. duck duck duck duck
    B. GOOSE; and

NOW, THEREFORE, BE IT RESOLVED BY THE LEGISLATURE OF THE STATE
OF ARIZONA that those days draw near when the waters will rise & break
through, & that

    A. water molecules cling tightly to one another &
    B. this is how life moves, this is the law &
    C. these are the bonds, bonds,
    D. bodies, bodies, bodies, bodies, &
    E. dear god, the bonds, and

BE IT FURTHER RESOLVED that:

    A. the river's beginning, it's not far now

# The Body (an Excerpt)

JENNY BOULLY

1   It was the particular feel of him that made me want to go back: everything that is said is said underneath, where, if it does matter, to acknowledge it is to let on to your embarrassment. That I love you makes me want to run and hide.

2   It is not the story I know or the story you tell me that matters; it is what I already know, what I don't want to hear you say. Let it exist this way, concealed; let me always be embarrassed, knowing that you know that I know but pretend not to know.

3   One thing the great poet confessed before biting into her doughnut: a good poem writes itself as if it doesn't care—never let on that within this finite space, your whole being is heavy with a need to emote infinitely.

4   I never uttered that loose word; I only said, "I opened my legs and let him."

5   One thing the great poet would never confess was that afterwards, she took me into the back room and slapped me for loving her.

6   The illustration also represents various states of being. The student of art should be
    particularly cautious of interpreting such depictions without proper background
    training, as it is often easy to confuse source light with light from another world, as
    in movies when it is easy to confuse internal sound with external sound.[a] Sometimes
    the artist, as does the director, plays tricks for symbolic purposes.[b]

    a In cinematic terms, "actual sound" refers to sound which comes from a visible or
    identifiable source˙ within the film. "Commentative sound" is sound which does
    not come from an identifiable source within the film but is added for dramatic
    effect.˙˙

    b See footnote 1.

       * By "identifiable source" it is meant that there exists a presupposition, an under-
       standing that an opposing "unidentifiable source" exists.

       ** By "commentative sound" it is meant that there exists a presupposition, an
       understanding of a "commentator" who is thereby executing the "commentary."

7   The visit to the circus is of particular import if one considers this passage from a letter written to the man whom she regarded as her guardian angel (to whom she also
dedicated a great number of poems). Dated in her 23rd year, the letter states:

> . . . I told Lousine that I was terrified of clowns; no, not just childishly afraid like
> being afraid of the dark, but really, really fearful, like starting-your-period-for-the-
> first-time scared. Anyhow, she looked at me serious-like and made me promise in
> that strong Armenian-Brooklyn way of hers that I would never reveal this to any-
> one because anyone could be an enemy. She made me swear up and down and on
> graves and holy books and the needle in the eye and all sorts of crazy shit that drove
> me insane. I can't help but think now that something bad is waiting to happen and
> that there's this little man staring at me from between the fence slats. I can see his
> little eyeball sometimes, showing up in the various holes in my apartment. But you
> know what scares me the most? It's that clown in *Antony and Cleopatra* who says
> to Cleopatra, "You must not think I am so simple but I know the devil himself will
> not eat a woman. I know that a woman is a dish for the gods, if the devil dress her
> not. But truly, these same whoreson devils do the gods great harm in their women;
> for in every ten that they make, the devils mar five." So you see, Andy, I have been
> seriously stressed. Am I marred? E. says he cannot love me now and that I have a
> dark side he is afraid of . . .

8   It wasn't that the ice-cream man came every day; he came whenever the child heard his music.

9   The confessions denoted here are lies, as it would be senseless to list my true regrets. The true regrets are indexed under the subject heading "BUT EVERYONE DIES LIKE THIS," found at the end of the text.

10  Given this information, the definition of "footnote" is of particular interest to the overall understanding of "bedlam." Consider, for instance, this denotation: *n. 2. Something related to but of lesser importance than a larger work or occurrence.*

11  See also De Sica's *Bicycle Thieves*; thus the leitmotif of this body: *What will I have found in the end if I am seeking as if I am seeking one thing in particular?*

12  The great pre-Socratic philosopher Empedocles did not keep the commentative sound of his life a secret. He says of the source of mortal things, one should "know these things distinctly, having heard the story from a god" (as told by Simplicius, *Commentary on Aristotle's Physics* 160.1-1 = 31B23).

13  It should be understood that Heraclitus also lost a bicycle. In *Miscellanies* (2.17.4 = 22B18), Clement of Alexandria quotes Heraclitus as saying, "Unless he hopes for the unhoped for, he will not find it, since it is not to be hunted out and is impassable."

14    *I Corinthians 13:5* "Doth not behave itself unseemly, seeketh not her own, is not
easily provoked, thinketh no evil"; *13:7* "Beareth all things, believeth all things,
hopeth all things, endureth all things"; *13:11* "When I was a child, I spake as a child, I
understood as a child, I thought as a child: but when I became a woman, I put away
childish things"; *13:12* "For now we see through a glass, darkly; but then face to face:
now I know in part; but then shall I know even as also I am known." Given these passages, it is easy for the reader to infer that the protagonist, aside from despising her
pubic hair, also believed that she was being watched and thus began her odd behavior
of hiding and casting her voice into a void.

15    Ms. Boully must have been confused, as it was actually _____, not _____,
who uttered "_____" and thus became
such a symbolic figure in her youth; however, critic and playwright Lucia Del Vecchio
(who is known to transcribe some of her dialogue directly from audiocassettes she
and Boully recorded during their undergraduate years), argues that Boully was well
acquainted in _____. As this is a suspicious oversight, Del Vecchio cites
evidence from a recorded conversation where Boully argues _____
_____.

16   Although the text implies a great flood here, know this is seen through a child's eyes, and here she actually played in sprinklers while loving Heraclitus: "A lifetime [or eternity] is a child playing, playing checkers; the kingdom belongs to a child" (Hippolytus, *Refutation* 9.9.4 = 22B52).

17   The circus net, under the trapeze artists and tightrope walkers, is to be interpreted as "a safe way to know falling."

18   Although the narrative is rich with detail and historical accounts, the author is blatantly supplying false information. For example, the peaches were not rotten and there were no flies or rain for that matter. The man she claims to have kissed never existed, or rather, the man existed; however, she never kissed him, and because she never kissed him, she could only go on living by deluding herself into believing that he never existed.

19   The last time I saw the great poet I brought her strawberries, hoping she would ask me to bed. Instead, she only suggested that I touch how soft her fuzzy pink sweater was. I broke down crying as soon as I made my confession. I told her that I had written a bad poem, that in the space between me and him, I emoted too much through speech and touch, and I made it known that I was willing to emote infinitely; the poem was so bad, he left. I was hoping that the great poet would kiss me then, but instead, she slapped me and forbade me from telling anyone that I was her student. I left her, and I never told her that I was on my hands and knees, picking those berries for her.

20  After the author's death, it was Tristram who went through her various papers and
    came across the many folders labeled "footnotes." It wasn't until years later, when he
    was curious as to which papers the footnotes corresponded, that Tristram discovered
    that the "footnotes" were actually daily journals of the author's dreams. Del Vecchio
    recalls a later audiocassette recording with the author saying, "I have it all worked
    out. I write down my dreams because I understand them once symbols become
    written. They're all so sexually charged and I almost always feel ugly in them; they're
    embarrassing and filthy. But I have it all worked out. No one will know. I've relabeled
    everything in my study, including my books—you think you're getting Shakespeare,
    but really, it's astrophysics and cosmology, or you open Hesse and you actually get
    Kierkegaard. I'm not so off am I? But really, I must confess . . ." Del Vecchio, in her
    words, says, "And then she started going on and on about this Robert Kelly[c] guy."

  c The following excerpt from Robert Kelly's "Edmund Wilson on Alfred de Mus-
    set: The Dream" was pasted above the author's various beds in the various places
    she lived: "Dreams themselves are footnotes. But not footnotes to life. Some other
    transactions they are so busy annotating all night long."

21  Besides the obvious lost marbles or stolen purse or misplaced lottery ticket, the
theme of loss preoccupied her even in sleep. The following is from a dream dated in
the author's 33rd year:

> (But then, I remembered in my dream that this was only a dream and that when
> you lose something in a dream, when you wake up, you realize it's still there. Of
> course, the reverse is true as well, as when I dreamt I had silver eyes and wings, but
> upon waking up, upon looking into the mirror, I discovered brown eyes, no wings.
> So, in my dream, I woke up from my dream in my dream, thereby correcting the
> situation on my own.
>
> This reminds me of Kafka's *Trial*, in a passage deleted by the author: ". . . it is
> really remarkable that when you wake up in the morning you nearly always find
> everything in exactly the same place as the evening before.")

22  Ezra Pound: Questing and passive. . . . / "Ah, poor Jenny's case" . . .

# Questionnaire for My Grandfather

KIM ADRIAN

Please answer all questions as simply as possible; do not use digression as a means of evasion. Feel free, however, to elaborate on the point at hand to a reasonable degree so as to provide the clearest and most informative answer you can. Do not lie. Any lies will render this questionnaire null and void and require that you submit to its inquiries again. (I am a patient person; I have asked these questions all my life. I can keep asking them.)

Is it true that you were born and raised in the port city of Göteborg, Sweden, toward the southwestern tip of that country at some point during the second or third decade of the last century?

Is it true, as family legend states, that you ran away from home at the age of thirteen?

Why did you run away?

Is it true that the means of your escape was provided by the Portuguese merchant marines? Did you (as for some reason I always imagine) climb on board that first ship in the Göteborg harbor shoeless and wearing woolen britches rather too short for you, carrying nothing but a small parcel of personal belongings wrapped in flannel cloth? Did this parcel contain the thick, lightly gilded, leather-bound Bible, a Swedish translation that my mother still has (protected by triplicate layers of plastic wrap) in her possession?

Is it also true that the broad Göteborg harbor was (as for some reason I am imagining right now) shining a deep sort of teal gray blue and that sunlight was scattershot across it like so many silver coins the day you left it behind?

Is it a fact that while working for the Portuguese merchant marines, you learned the craft of metallurgy?

What is metallurgy?

Can you now or could you ever speak Portuguese?

Are you really, as my mother once told me, what is known as a "Black Swede," meaning small, wiry, and dark? Is the term "Black Swede" a pejorative one?

How tall are you?

Your hair, I know from the one photograph I have of you, is dark and slightly waved. Your eyes are light. But are they blue or green?

Whether blue or green, do you sometimes suspect that your otherwise attractive face may be marred, as are the otherwise attractive faces of six of your seven children (including my mother), by those eyes? Are they, perhaps, a little too large, too light in color, too vigilant in expression? Have you ever noticed that your eyes, in other words, make other people uneasy?

Is it a fact that your father was a minister? Was he a good one? Did he rouse the crowds? Or rather, the humble congregation? (I picture a small church: whitewashed walls, wooden pews. Dark inside. Not many windows. Just a few, and filled with plain, not stained, glass. If there is a crucifix, it is small and simple, probably wooden or silver plate.)

Is it true, as family legend states, that your father regularly beat you and your brothers twice a day as a matter of basic discipline?

Is it true, as family legend also states, that you were required to say your morning prayers at 4:30 a.m. and that if you happened to fall asleep during those prayers, you were sure to receive a third beating that day?

Is it true (as you must have told your children since they told me, or at least talked about it amongst themselves some long-ago Christmas Eve or Thanksgiving, and I overheard it) that your father used flexible twigs, stripped-down saplings, or something like reeds to beat you?

Is it true—or at least possible—that your mother sometimes wore a very long brown dress, quite plain, with a simple ruffle at the hem? Is it true that on top of this dress she would often wear a gingham apron? Did she occasionally wear an old-fashioned white cap on her head, and was her hair a soft mass of mousy brown usually tied in a bun at the nape of her neck? (I ask because when I concentrate on the phantom of your mother that I carry in my own head, this is invariably how she appears.)

Did your mother knit? (I knit.)

If so, did she do so by the fire? Was that fire an open hearth? Or was it one of those old-fashioned Swedish stoves made as much for sitting as for heating and cooking—the kind covered with large, brightly glazed ceramic tiles and surrounded by benches?

Was your mother, as my mother once told me you told her, kind and loving but meek to a fault?

What exactly did you mean by "meek"?

Was she a good cook?

What were some of your favorite childhood dishes?

Did you eat rabbit? (I have a Swedish cookbook that—though very poorly translated—has some excellent recipes, including a cream-based rabbit stew flavored with juniper berries. Whenever I make this dish, which might be once every other year, I think of you and wonder whether you may have eaten something like it when you were a child.)

Did your father, as I have always assumed, beat your mother in your presence? If so, can you say with any certainty whether or not he was drunk when he did so?

In your opinion, was your father an alcoholic?

In your opinion, was your mother an alcoholic?

Is it true, as family legend has it, that you drank nearly a bottle of vodka a day?

It must have been very cheap vodka, no?

Did you ever have any drinking buddies or were you, as my mother has described you, too deeply misanthropic for that?

Did you really, as my mother once told me, enjoy "playing" with people "as a cat plays with mice"? Were you, as she also claims, weirdly driven in these kinds of games, while at the same time seemingly devoid of all emotion? Almost robotic in your manipulations? Keyed up, yet totally calm, detached, but then nearly gleeful (I almost said orgasmic) whenever you went in for the kill, which is to say, when you found some way of humiliating the person you had targeted?

Would you agree, as is generally thought to be the case, that vodka has no taste and that it leaves no hint of itself on a person's breath? Were these qualities ever of any advantage to you?

Were you, as I believe I've heard it said, one of four sons? Was it difficult having so many brothers? Did you sometimes feel you couldn't live up to your brothers? Were they bigger than you? Smarter? Kinder or crueler or simply better liked?

Were you the oldest, the youngest, or one of the middle brothers?

Are you aware of the fact that one of your brothers—I think his name is Thor—became a well-known Evangelical singer in your native country?

Did you ever have a sense, as a child, that something might be wrong with you? Did you ever feel that your thoughts didn't obey you or that you weren't entirely in control of your own actions? Did you ever have the sense that something was not right in your head?

As a child, did you have many friends? Do you remember any of these friends in particular? What sorts of games did you play with them?

Did you do well in school?

Did you have a favorite teacher? What was his or her name? Why did you like this teacher so much? Did he or she see something in you that nobody else saw? What was that thing—that quality or condition or personal quirk? Was it something your father did not see? Did your mother see it?

Did you (as I do, despite never having met him) hate your father? Was your father (as I feel convinced he must have been, albeit on very scant evidence) a religious fanatic? A pious madman? Would you have liked to kill him? Did murderous thoughts ever occur to you in moments of great duress—for instance, while he was beating you?

Did you ever dream, as a child, of someday becoming, like your father, the minister of a small church? Or did you perhaps dream of being a doctor? Or an artist of some kind? Or maybe an astronaut? Did children even think about astronauts back then? Or were sailors the astronauts of your day?

Although your formal education obviously stopped when you ran away from home, were you ever tempted, as some men are in similar situations (I am thinking of other sailors, like yourself, or prisoners), to read the Bible as one would read a great novel? Or to read the dictionary word by word? Or to contemplate Zen koans for hours, even days on end? What I mean is: Did you ever make any attempt to raise yourself intellectually or spiritually? Did you ever conduct personal philosophical investigations of any kind? Or did you enjoy, as your future wife would, degrading your own mind to the greatest extent possible?

What most attracted you to my grandmother?

Is it true that you met her on shore leave in New Orleans? This would have been in the early 1940s, correct?

Is it true that she was at that time working in that city as a prostitute?

Is it true that your first encounter with my grandmother was as a customer? Didn't you find her ugly—with her long, thin face and dramatic underbite?

Or did you like her legs, which were superb? Did the graceful lines of her body help you to overlook the homeliness of her face?

Did you sense—perhaps because of her long face and remarkable underbite— that in my grandmother you had finally found somebody who needed you in a way nobody else had ever needed you? Somebody who would be as loyal to you as a dog and, like a dog, absorb your abuse without ever misplacing her loyalty?

Did you make my grandmother laugh? Did you court her? Did you ever shower her with presents, compliments, or caresses?

Did she make you laugh? Did she beg you to love her, to stay with her, marry her?

Are the very, very tiny golden earrings shaped like daises, the centers of which are little green emeralds not much bigger than a grain of coarse salt—earrings that are swimming around somewhere in the blue-and-white Chinese porcelain bowl on the shelf above the sink in my bathroom (the bowl in which I keep jewelry I never wear), earrings that are tarnished and misshapen (the wire is very thin), and one of which is broken—were these earrings really what you gave my grandmother in lieu of a wedding ring?

Why earrings?

Why emeralds?

How soon after meeting her did you first realize that my grandmother was an unusually intelligent woman? How soon after that did you understand that she was the kind of person who enjoyed destroying her own best qualities, including her intelligence?

Would you say that your wife's masochism was in some ways the linchpin of your marriage?

Did you ever feel hopeful with my grandmother? Was hope or happiness at any point central—or even tangential—to your relationship with her?

When you first met her, was my grandmother already a bitter woman? Could you taste the bitterness in her mouth? Could you smell it on her skin and clothing, the way I could when I was a child? Could you see it growing in the dark shadows under her eyes?

Did she, even then, enjoy telling tall tales, often of a gruesome or morbid nature? Did she, even then, speak obsessively about the sadness of her own childhood? Did she, even then, speak with great hatred of her aunts, who had raised her?

Was this something the two of you shared? An inconsolable sadness regarding your respective childhoods and what was stolen from you during that time?

True or False?
You sexually molested all four of your daughters.

True or False?
You often beat your wife when you were drunk.

True or False?
You were drunk most days.

True or False?
You raped your youngest daughter, Elsa, before you ran away. (You ran away shortly after I was born; your youngest daughter was eleven when I was born.)

Are you aware that your youngest daughter, my strangest and funniest and, by my childhood standards, coolest aunt, died nearly ten years ago of a heroin overdose at the age of forty-three? Are you aware that she died curled up in a dry bathtub, naked, and covered with bruises? Did you know that the heroin she used was of an almost unheard-of purity? Are you aware that she herself was acutely aware of this extreme purity because one of her best friends had died of an overdose on this same batch of heroin only two weeks earlier?

Do you consider your youngest daughter's death a suicide?

Do you consider yourself in any way responsible for that death?

How did you die?

Were you lonely?

Were you sad?

As you were dying, did you think of your meek mother and your own long-lost childhood? On your deathbed, did you yearn for some of the ancient comforts you had known then?

Or, alternately, were you filled with remorse and paralyzing regret in regards to the whole of your adult life?

Are you aware that my mother is mentally ill and has been for a long time, perhaps even since childhood?

Are you aware that she has been hospitalized—rough count—eight times? Are you aware that she has tried to kill herself at least three times? Are you aware that she inherited many of your worst traits, including addiction (to prescription drugs, not alcohol), a gift for verbal abuse, a perverse and insatiable need to manipulate the people around her if for no other reason than her own amusement, a compulsion to lie nearly every time she opens her mouth, and a voracious narcissism?

Would you agree with the following assertions?
1. Despite your death and preceding decades-long absence, you have acted as a kind of puppet master, using my mother as a kind of puppet, for her entire life.
2. I was raised by a broken puppet of a woman.
3. I was raised (it logically follows) by you.

I always say I never met you, but in fact, I did meet you once, when I was a newborn. You held me briefly—just until my mother (then eighteen years old) noticed what you were doing and "tore" me out of your arms. Do you remember that encounter?

Do you remember me?

Do you think it's possible for huge but unmappable portions of a person's life to be shaped by a grandfather she never knew?

Do you think it's possible that you don't actually—never actually—existed but are merely a kind of mythical bogeyman? An extended nightmare? A lesson in evil that I have never managed to get through? Or one in forgiveness?

If you are a lesson (of one kind or another), why is it that I can never get the pages of this lesson straight? That the order of these pages is always changing and rearranging? That these pages are constantly falling out of my hands and scattering at my feet, and when I bend to pick them up, it's a given that the wind will sweep them away before I reach them. My hair is always in my eyes when I try to understand you; I can't see a thing.

Did you know that I dream of you, on average, about once a year, and that in these dreams you are always a small, strangely insistent little man? Sometimes you are bald and almost golden in color. Sometimes your skin is stretched very tightly over your bones, as skin stretches over the bones of a corpse. Other times you are dark and faceless. I frequently find you loitering in filthy public toilets. You do things like steal tangerines and evade questions, disappear, and make my mother weep. Once, in one of these dreams, I cracked all the bones in your body. I broke them like charred chicken bones; they crumbled in my fingers. You didn't even notice. My mother kept crying.

Would you like to hear something about me, my life?

Would you like to hear about my kids? I won't tell you about them. Pick something else.

How about knitting?

Are you familiar with two-end knitting? It's an old Swedish technique. You knit with two ends of a single ball of yarn, twisting the stitches around each other and in this way creating a flexible, double-thick fabric. With a little extra effort, a line of purled stitches can be made to look like a delicate chain, and isolated purl stitches against a stockinette fabric look like tiny, playful o's. These can be arranged to create elegant patterns of almost infinite variety. Indeed, some of the simplest but most subtly beautiful effects in all of knitting can be achieved with this old-fashioned method, although hardly anybody knows how to do it anymore. I myself have never knitted in this way, but I cherish a fantasy of someday traveling to Sweden in order to learn how to do it.

True or False?
You had your own shelf in the family's often otherwise empty refrigerator, and on this shelf you kept specialty items, delicacies imported from your homeland, such as Getost cheese, anise-flavored limpa bread, lingonberries, pickled herring, blood sausage, and raw sirloin, which you chopped very fine and ate with onions, capers, and raw eggs.

True or False?
Although as a metallurgist (what *is* a metallurgist?) you made a decent salary, most of your money went to liquor, so that at times there was nothing much for your wife and seven children to eat. Sometimes all there was to eat were potatoes. Sometimes your wife didn't bother to cook these, and the children ate them raw, like apples.

True or False?
You also had your own spot in the living room (which doubled as your bedroom and which was paneled, when I knew it, with cheap, white, wood-grain-patterned paneling on which was duct taped a poster of running horses in a Wild West landscape saturated with the golden pink light of a setting sun) . . . anyway . . . in this room, in the top drawer of a dresser, you kept your bottles of vodka, cartons of cigarettes, and boxes of thin mints, all of which were forbidden to your children and all of which were carefully pilfered by them anyway.

Are you actually human, or was your humanity at some point (perhaps very early in your life) destroyed?

Did your father ever molest you?

If you are no longer human, do you have any advice for those of us who are? For instance, how can we best keep ourselves human?

Does evil actually exist, or just bad and worse luck? Put another way, do you consider yourself evil? Do you think of yourself as being a bad person? (Wait. I know. That is not a fair question; bad and evil are not the same thing. Evil, like goodness or love, is an abstract concept—more of a noun than an adjective; there is an inhuman purity about it. Bad, on the other hand, is very human. It is optional; it is sometimes. Bad is poor decision making, poor judgment. Bad is lazy, somewhat random, and most of all selfish.) In any case, I am wondering about the other possibility: that you are neither bad nor evil, but very weak and very unlucky. Your thoughts?

Do you think that a certain ugliness can be said to characterize our family? And that this ugliness—be it sexual or physical abuse, mental illness, addiction, apathy, cruelty, or what have you—is a kind of inheritance, a gigantic and terrible medicine ball that has been passed down, generation to generation, for as far back as anyone can imagine?

In your opinion, do crooked genes play any part in the sad story of our family's history, in its medicine-ball legacy, or has it mostly been a matter of crappy socioeconomic conditions—of poverty, lack of opportunity, and so on?

Do you think Hitler's family had a similar medicine ball? Stalin's? Attila the Hun's?

How do you think such a medicine ball comes into being in the first place? In your opinion, what is the best way to destroy this kind of medicine ball?

You met my paternal grandparents briefly, I believe, at my parents' rushed and somewhat embarrassed wedding (my mother was already four months pregnant with me) and again at a dinner party at their house either shortly before or shortly after that event. It is my belief that when my sister and I lived with my paternal grandparents for the first several years of our lives, our family's medicine ball (which both Tracy and I were born carrying) actually shrank to a nearly manageable size because of our grandparents' patience and ability to love—to give, that is to say, without taking. Do you feel any gratitude at all that these people (who were kind and simple and more or less happy) managed this magic trick with our family's bad, bad medicine ball? Or, as I rather suspect, do you not really give a fuck?

Do you consider it likely that my mother tried to marry you when she married my father? (My father had his problems, sure, but he was better than you. For instance, he never touched Tracy or me, not the way you touched your girls.)

Speaking of which, what, exactly, were you after when you molested your daughters? A physical rush? A sense of omnipotence? An infantile form (clearly misguided) of revenge? Whenever I see or hear or eat or touch something very tender (I am thinking, here, of how it was to nurse my children, of how I felt when their little bird mouths groped for my breast and they were frantic, nearly desperate to feed), what I usually feel is a softening, a widening or opening somewhere in the vicinity of my heart, at the back of my throat, around my jaw, and behind my eyes. It is a feeling I might describe, roughly, as a state of delicate awe, and whenever I experience it (which happens more often than not at odd moments in the face of odd things, things of a not-easily-discussed nature, such as an infant finding my nipple with his mouth), I sense everything go nearly still, both inside me and outside, all around me. I am, in other words, transported, however briefly, directly into the present, where I recognize something that may or may not be called my soul, something that seems, in any case, to be a large and gentle, unknown yet utterly familiar spiritual environment. It has occurred to me (though I suspect I give you far too much credit) that in an absurdly twisted way, when you pulled your daughters onto your lap and tugged down their panties, you were reaching for moments like this. Well, were you?

What do you think your father used to think about when he hit you with that willow switch or whatever it was?

What did you think about when he hit you with it?

What do you think your sons, the two oldest ones anyway (because according to the youngest, you spared him everything you visited so recklessly on the others; why?), might have thought about when you hit them?

What do you suppose your daughters thought about when you did the things you did to them?

What did you do to them, exactly? My mother's obsessive belief that her teeth are rotting, her disturbingly successful attempts to destroy those teeth, her conviction that the germs in her mouth are killing her—all these coupled with a recurring dream she once told me about (one she described this way: she is young again, a girl again, at a beach; a boy holds her down and pours sand into her throat; she can't breathe and believes she is dying; she wakes suicidal)—these things clearly suggest certain acts. But this is just guesswork. Freudian assumptions. Are they correct?

Can you imagine your father as a little boy? What about your father's father?

What questions would you have liked to ask your grandfather on a questionnaire of your own making? (Please be specific.)

In asking these questions, would you be attempting, do you think, to give shape to a void? To define that void by describing the negative space around its negative space?

My mother as a little girl—please tell me some nice stories about her. Was there ever a time when she wasn't completely focused on herself, when she wasn't the self-hating narcissist (I'm sure you know just what I mean) I have always known, when she was somebody—a person with a self—not just the emptiness I have always known, when she was still curious, when she gave (nothing too big—a joke, a smile, a thoughtful response) without taking? What was she like then? When she was happy, when she was whole, what were her eyes like?

Did you ever sing to her?

You were fragile, weren't you? Like her, you were born weaker than some.

Still, I would like to make you pay for what you did, even though, of course, it's much too late for that. I would like, at least, to make you cry—and I would like your tears to be the bitterest kind and endless. Let's say, hypothetically, that I could hurt you in some way—what would be the most effective way to do that? Or does someone like you live in a self-made purgatory where things can't possibly get any worse, no matter how inventive I got?

Do you ever find yourself curious about other people? Someone on a bus, maybe, or the person in front of you in line at the grocery store? Do you ever wonder about anybody beside yourself—what his or her life might be like, his or her struggles? Do you ever feel a secret tenderness for a perfect stranger, for some tiny part of a perfect stranger? A tuft of hair? A limp? A downy cheek? Do old people ever remind you of old dogs, and in this way inspire a quiet affection in you? When you were an old man, were you old like that? Did you shuffle in a charming way? Did your singsong accent trip over your shriveled tongue and wrinkled lips and endear you to strangers? Did you have a faint twinkle in your clouded eye? Did young women find you cute? Had you, by that point, forgiven yourself for all you had done? Had you, by then, forgotten?

# The Petoskey Catechism, 1958

ELIZABETH KERLIKOWSKE

*Does God exist?*

Of course. How else could a woman in high heels walk across the lawn?

He's tucked into the little girls' hat bands and it is He who will watch them
walk toward the lake while their mother makes eye contact with an old
flame. God waits on the far shore, and He does not judge. He is also
the old flame.

*How is He manifest?*

A fisherman trolling. A family picnic. His eyes are everywhere so when
the girls disappear below the bluff, they're actually safer. God is in the clover
crushed in one girl's hand. In the stains on their lips from blackberries, in
the drama.

*And where shall we worship?*

Under the blue trees at twilight just as the storm rolls in. In the ripples a rock
makes talking to the lake. In the presence of rough angels below the bluff.
Beside still waters. Together.

# What Signifies (Three Parables)

DAVID SHIELDS

1.

One summer, a friend of Laurie's worked as a graphic artist in a T-shirt shop in Juneau, Alaska. Cruise ships would dock, unloading old passengers, who would take taxis or buses a dozen or so miles to Mendenhall Glacier, which is a hundred square kilometers—twenty-five thousand acres—and whose highest point rises a hundred feet above Mendenhall Lake. Once, a tourist said about the glacier, "It looks so dirty. Don't they ever wash it?" On their way back to the boat, one or two ancient mariners would invariably come into the shop and ask Laurie's friend if he would mail their postcards for them. Able to replicate people's handwriting exactly, he would add postscripts to the postcards: "Got laid in Ketchikan," "Gave head in Sitka," etc.

What do I love so much about this story? I could say, as I'm supposed to say, "I don't know—it just makes me laugh," but really I do know. It's an ode on my favorite idea: language is all we have to connect us, and it doesn't, not quite.

2.

The kicker made the field goal, and as the game went to commercial, the kick was shown again in slow motion. The camera was positioned in such a way that the ball kept spinning higher into the upper right-hand corner of the screen. At the end of the replay the ball was out of view, and for a held moment the screen showed only black on a Monday night, November 6, 1989, in San Francisco, three weeks after the earthquake. For a second, there was just the night in all its elegiac beauty. The shot conveyed terror but only for a moment. Then graphics came up.

3.

When I lived for a few years in New York, I'd go out every night at eleven and come back with the next day's *Times* and a pint of ice cream, then eat the whole carton while reading the paper, which had the odd but, I suppose, desired effect of blotting out tomorrow before it had even happened. All my nightmares—an endless network of honeycombs, a thousand cracks in a desiccated lake, a set of rotten teeth—are specifically about uncontrolled proliferation. Two questions constantly occur to me: What would this look like filmed? What would the soundtrack be? I grew up at a very busy intersection, and to me aesthetic bliss was hearing the sound of brakes screeching, then waiting for the sound of the crash.

I've read every bumper sticker I've ever seen.

# The Marriage License

JUDY BOLTON-FASMAN

Connecticut State Department of Health
Bureau of Vital Statistics—Hartford, Connecticut, U.S.A.

This flimsy piece of paper is the only documentation that my parents were married: smudged black-and-white proof that once there was love and then it was lost—a tremendous amount of it hemorrhaging like blood after an accident or a miscarriage.

When my father as groom witnessed Hamden Town judge John H. Peck sign this marriage license, did he know his wife would turn out to be unstable? Did he know during this civil ceremony (a mere formality as his bride refused to consummate the marriage until she stood under a marriage canopy in a synagogue) he would abandon her at the altar in Havana the following month because it would be easier to get an annulment without the second ceremony? Did he know he would go on to marry her in a synagogue anyway three months later? Could he possibly have guessed the next year he would become a father and then go on to have two more children with this woman?

GROOM'S NAME: Kenneth Harold Bolton
My father rarely used his first name. His signature read K. Harold Bolton. The initial *K*, ramrod straight, stood for the disciplined navy man he was during the Second World War. The meticulous accountant he would later become to support a family.

(A) DATE OF BIRTH: 1/19/19        (B) AGE: 40

My mother may have been flattered that my father had been shaving five years off his age, telling her that he was thirty-five so as not to scare his young bride. But this bride was looking for a father figure—her own father blurred the line between parent and spouse. In the early years of their marriage my father had a tight rein on my mother until she broke away in full bipolar fury.

RACE: White

Race was a construct for my father. At Yale he tried to fit in as a WASP. Two decades later in the 1950s, he traveled extensively in Guatemala. These were his *soltero* or bachelor days. Days that were bleached with sun and cloaked by the mystery of what he was actually doing there. As a spy my father tried to fit in as a self-styled *mestizo* in Central America. (My mother says when they were first married he had a tanning lamp). When he came home to New Haven for good he waved away his parents' objections to him marrying an immigrant girl from Cuba. "She's a peasant," declared my grandmother when she met my mother.

OCCUPATION: Accountant

After the Havana fiasco, there was a brief marriage ceremony in New York City's Spanish Portuguese Synagogue, followed by a Catskills honeymoon where the bride passed her days playing Simon Says in the hotel lobby with the other guests and planning the days with her new husband around the resort's gut-busting meals served family style. By the end of the week my parents had conceived me. If he had any thoughts of escaping the marriage, my father quickly dismissed them and found sustained employment. It turns out my dad was superb at organizing other people's finances yet had trouble making his own money. Bill collectors called incessantly, sending my mother into spasms of hysteria. She raged, "Cubans just off the plane are more successful than you are." His own father tried to help by sending examples of household budgets for his forty-something son to follow. A check was frequently enclosed.

BIRTHPLACE: New Haven, Connecticut

My father was born and raised in New Haven. But as newlyweds, my parents were unwelcomed in New Haven by Dad's family, and so they moved to Hartford. My mother—the Cubana with her wild moods—was, in every sense of the word, alien. Nevertheless, my father insisted that his three children be born in in New Haven. In labor my mother made the forty-mile trek three times to give birth in Dad's ancestral home.

Years later when my parents seemed settled and the notion of home was all consuming for my father, he left the marriage in spirit. Every day after work he called me over while he was still on the porch and asked, "What kind of mood is your mother in?" I was afraid to tell him that she was still in her housecoat, exhausted from crying and frantically cleaning. The summer I was nine, she took the three of us down to her relatives in Miami, and we stayed there for six weeks. When my father finally came down to reclaim us and bring us back to Connecticut, she hung on his neck whispering, "*No te vayas*—Don't leave."

RESIDENCE: 35 Stimson Road, New Haven, Connecticut

My childhood refuge from 1735 Asylum Avenue was 35 Stimson Road. Our home on Asylum Avenue was cluttered with my parents' arguments and my anxiety, but Grandpa and Grandma Bolton's sweet, pristine house smelled like lemon Pledge and chicken soup. Nothing out of order in that fairytale-like cottage where Grandma allowed me to read forbidden books like *Love Story* and *Marjorie Morningstar*: alternative glimpses into the intricacies of love and romance.

PREVIOUS MARITAL STATUS: Never Married

That was technically true, but there was a lot of energy and drama around the appearance one summer of a teenage girl from Guatemala named Ana, who showed up at our doorstep and to whom my usually taciturn father was very kind and protective. No one said outright that Ana was my father's daughter. I was ten and I adored everything about Ana from her colorful skirts to her eyes as black as the dark olives my sister and I loved to eat out of the can. But Ana's arrival was not unexpected. My mother ranted for years that a half-sibling would show up at the door and steal a place among us. That summer—the summer of Ana—my parents' fights were vigorous as ever. Yet as I lay in bed, uncharacteristic whispers also spilled out under the door like light.

FATHER'S NAME: William M. Bolton

My grandfather. The engineer, the poet, the musician. The perfect husband who forgave my grandmother the fact that she moved out of their bedroom when she was only thirty-eight years old. "Menopause drove your grandmother out of her mind," my mother once told me gleefully. My grandfather donned a clear plastic apron and did the dishes every night. My father tried so hard to emulate grandpa, but he never had a chance with my mother, who threw plates at him.

MOTHER'S MAIDEN NAME: Anna Rosen

When I named my daughter after my grandmother, my mother said I had betrayed her. "How could you name my granddaughter after a woman who tried to break up my marriage and treated me like *basura*?" I knew the name thrilled my father even though by then his mind had deteriorated along with his Parkinson's-addled body. He thought his mother was still alive when he heard me call my daughter Anna. This set off my mother whose tantrums by now were atomic. "You crazy old man," she screamed as my shaky father held the new baby with my help, "your mother is dead. This is Judy's baby, your granddaughter." My father's voice, soft and hoarse from disease, said, "Anna is a beautiful name for a beautiful girl."

BRIDE'S NAME: Matilde Alboukrek

Matilde claimed that her original family name was Albuquerque—not for the New Mexican city but the Spanish Duke. It was just one of the stories she spun to herself of ghosts and drunks and more, to help herself survive a mother who she always told me was in and out of hospitals and a father who never failed to come into her room and stumble into her bed, passing out there after a night of drinking.

Matilde always said her mother was "a sick woman." Sick with what, I wonder. I still picture her sitting in a chair with its stuffing spilling out, draped in a bedspread she'd made of green satin. She was terrified of *microbios* and did not bathe for days during the winter. Cold weather germs, she believed, seeped through the skin to sap her very breath.

My grandmother named her baby Matilde to honor the ghost of her dead sister, a sister who died of the dreaded *microbios* in the prime of her life when she was seven months pregnant. My grandmother even claimed that her sister haunted her throughout seven days and seven nights of her own labor—a biblical, holy amount of time.

It's no surprise that my mother was willing to shed her rich and historic name to become Mrs. K. Harold Bolton. With that Anglicized last name everyone back in Havana would know that she had snagged an *Americano*.

### (A) DATE OF BIRTH: 8/19/35     (B) AGE: 24

My mother always swore that she was born in 1936. Her father mixed up the year of her birth when he finally registered her at age twelve into Cuba's version of the Bureau of Vital Statistics. She claimed such things happened in a Havana where the setting sun brought neon and chaos and lawlessness. Perhaps that's why she never followed rules or abided by official records. But as I keep going through the license, I can't help thinking that my mother was covering up something. Was my grandmother pregnant with her oldest child when she married my grandfather? Did my grandmother get pregnant against her will? Each time I try to ask my mother, she calls me a *mentirosa*, a liar.

### RACE: White

Correction: My mother always claimed she was royalty.

### OCCUPATION: Office Secretary

My mother told me that when she came from Cuba in 1958, she was supposed to be a translator at the United Nations, but someone lost her paperwork. (Who is the *mentirosa* now?)

### BIRTHPLACE: Havana, Cuba

My mother's was the first and last generation of Alboukreks to be born in Havana. In mom's stories Havana was a fairytale kingdom and her small second-floor apartment a towering castle with marble stairs polished to a high sheen. Reality came crashing down when my grandparents left Old Havana by shutting the door on thirty years of life. They, the perennial refugees, were forced to leave yet another home intact. When they landed in Miami in 1962 *mis abuelos* had one small suitcase between them.

RESIDENCE: 585 Snediker Avenue, Brooklyn 7, New York

My aunt Reina, Matilde's younger sister, once told me that the oldest daughter in Sephardic families is always in charge. My mother mercilessly bullied her sister, who, unlike her, had a fiancé. She taunted Reina that she had been improper with Miguel and wore revealing bathing suits in front of him. It was a false accusation that upended the entrenched double standards of their tradition-bound world. In that world Reina could not marry before her older sister. What shame that would bring on Matilde and on her old-world parents, who placed so much importance on birth order. When Matilde immigrated to the United States, Reina said she sat on the beach for hours, savoring her new-found freedom from her sister.

PREVIOUS MARITAL STATUS: Never Married

When the family had had enough of her antics, my mother was sent away to America like an unwieldy package to live with cousins in Brooklyn. When she finally married (in the nick of time—four months before her sister), she was thrilled to say goodbye to the cold-water flats and acrid subway stations of Brooklyn. Her fantasies of a star-spangled, Doris Day life included the two-story colonial in suburban Connecticut in which she eventually lived, complete with gleaming kitchen appliances and a damp but finished basement.

FATHER'S NAME: Jacobo Alboukrek

Born in Ankara, Turkey. Illiterate. He was the grandfather who attempted to give me toothless saliva-drenched kisses smack-dab on the mouth. "*Tu eres la grande. El numero uno*," he always told me, his first grandchild. He tried to curry further favor by dispensing M&M's and encouraging me to puff on his Marlboros. When Jacobo came to our house, my father hid the liquor.

**MOTHER'S MAIDEN NAME: Corina Behar**

Born in Greece. My grandmother first came to Sagua La Grande, north of Havana, when she was twelve years old. A decade later her family moved to Havana, where she took care of infirm parents and supported herself as a seamstress. When she was finally free to marry, only Jacobo was left. My grandmother told me that the first time she met him he tried to force a kiss on her in an elevator. She was twenty-eight. Corina was not an affectionate woman. She may well have been content never to marry, never to become a mother. She liked that Harold was strict with her daughter. He was just the kind of man her willful daughter needed. When my father left my mother at the altar in Havana, my grandmother understood: he could not spend the rest of his life with a loose cannon of a woman.

**SUPERVISION OR CONTROL OF GUARDIAN OR CONSERVATOR: No**

My wedding was on an Indian summer day—my parents' scruffy backyard was lightly carpeted with leaves that had once been bursting with New England colors of gold and orange and red. My mother installed herself in a white plastic chair on the porch and paged through circulars from discount stores. She hunted down bargains as if it were the only thing she had to do that Saturday. My wedding gown hung from the lintel, suspended between the living room and the hallway, where my father lurked. With cufflinks gripped in one hand for his tuxedo shirt, he shuffled by the gown every few minutes to finger the silk as if he could hardly believe that my nuptials were real. But I knew by the way he hovered he also expected my mother to explode. She was keen to remember his abandonment of her at the altar.

"Who knows if he'll show up," my mother said about my groom.

Suddenly a funereal murmuring buzzed in my head. "Ken's not here. Ken's not here."

"I hope," said my mother, bringing me back to my wedding day, "that you will not have my *mazal*."

Later that afternoon a dozen roses from my groom arrived with a note that said he could not wait to marry me.

My hair was done, my veil pinned into place. I gave my mother one of the roses. "Be careful," I told her. "There are always thorns."

\* \*

I HEREBY CERTIFY THAT MR. KENNETH HAROLD BOLTON AND MISS MATILDE ALBOUKREK, THE ABOVE NAMED PARTIES, WERE LEGALLY JOINED IN MARRIAGE BY ME AT *New Haven* THIS 19th DAY OF NOVEMBER 1959.

JOHN H. PECK
Judge, Town Court of Hamden, Connecticut

There are so few official papers documenting the life events in my family. Bound up in this marriage certificate is the lost *ketubah*, the official Jewish wedding contract my father must have signed in front of two male witnesses just before he stood waiting for his bride under the marriage canopy. Bound up in this marriage certificate is also love—a love about which my father muttered just loud enough at the end of his life to assure me it once existed.

# The Heart as a Torn Muscle

RANDON BILLINGS NOBLE

Overview

Your heart was already full, but then you saw him and your heart beat code, not Morse but a more insistent pulse: Oh yes. That's him. That one.

Not The One (The One you already have—and love), but of all the people in that large room far from home, he was the one for you. And your heart stretched more than it should have, tore a little, and let him in.

Symptoms
- Swelling, bruising, or redness. The feeling that your lungs contain a higher percentage of oxygen and have somehow grown in their capacity to respire. A heightened sensitivity to glances, postures, gestures, attitudes, and casual remarks from observers. A propensity to blush.
- Pain at rest. General restlessness. An inability to sleep. Fever dreams. Sleep-walking. Conscious walking: out of your bedroom, out of doors, into the moonlight or an unmown field shrouded in mist and ache (or fantasies of same).
- Pain when the specific muscle is used. When your heart beats to force blood through your femoral arteries, to your iliopsoas muscles, your sartorius muscles, your peroneus muscles, each expanding and contracting to force your legs to walk away, from him, from thrill, from all the promise and potential of an alternate future.

- Inability to use the muscle at all. Lethargy. Apathy. Malaise. Especially after having walked away from the one in question.

Self-Care

- Apply ice: cool it. The early application of heat can increase swelling and pain. [Note: ice or heat should not be applied to bare skin. Always use a protective layer—latex only as a very last resort. Clothing is better, or, better still, several feet, a piece of furniture, a wall, or a building. Ideally: a state line, a continent.]
- Try an anti-inflammatory such as herbal tea or a pro/con list. Cool showers and brisk walks in bracing air may help. Do not take depressants in the form of alcohol or otherwise. Avoid stimulants: caffeine, chocolate, Cheetos.
- Protect the strained muscle from further injury by refusing to jump into anything. Avoid the activities that caused the strain and other activities that are painful.
- Hold yourself together.
- Rise above.

When to Seek Care

If home remedies bring no relief in twenty-four hours, call your youngest and most bohemian friend.

If you hear a "popping" sound, signifying a break from your primary relationship, the one (The One) you truly know and truly love, call your closest and most trusted friend.

Exams and Tests

Your youngest and most bohemian friend asks,

Are you going to run away together, tryst in motels, meet up in Paris, open a PO box, wear trench coats, give each other code names, assume different identities?

Would he be up for a threesome?

Want to use my place?

Says, It's so romantic.

Says, Tell me everything!

Your closest and most trusted friend asks,

What do you mean, "met someone"?

Have you thought this through?

Is this choice supporting, adding to, enriching, complicating, marring, degrading, or not even leaving a blip on the screen in the way you will see your life in the years to come?

What will you be left with? Regret? Memory? Or absolutely nothing?

Says, Time wounds all heels.

Says, Don't fuck up.

## Recommended Reading
- *Anna Karenina* by Leo Tolstoy
- *The Bridges of Madison County* by Robert James Waller
- *Time Will Darken It* by William Maxwell
- *The Lone Pilgrim* by Laurie Colwin
- *Mrs. Dalloway* by Virginia Woolf
- "The Littoral Zone" by Andrea Barrett
- *The End of the Affair* by Graham Greene

No horoscopes. No tarot cards or tea leaves. If you must, you may steep yourself in stories of passion and price. Years from now you can indulge in what-ifs. But for now, right now, put your hand to your chest and feel what beats. The only muscle you can't live without needs to stay whole.

# The Spectrum
# (of Miracles and Mysteries)

STEVE EDWARDS

Psych Central—Short Autism Screening Test
1. It is difficult for me to understand how other
people are feeling when we are talking.

The sunlight edged my father's skin in gold as he stood hunched over the telephone in the kitchen, receiving the news. I'd climbed out of bed and slipped down the hall at the sound of his voice. I was ten. An early riser. He glanced at me a second when I appeared, and in his face was something—a confusion and brokenness—I'd never seen before. He shook his head slightly, said, "It's your grandma." I thought she was on the phone, even though I knew she was in the hospital, and that she had lung cancer, and that she didn't want us, her grandkids, to see her in such shape, and that a few weeks before my mother and aunts had tried to lift her spirits by dyeing her gray hair black so she might feel young again. And since I'd only recently gotten over a cold, I said to my father in the kitchen, "Did she catch my cold?" He turned away as my mother swept in from the other room to tell me, "No, no, honey. Grandma died—early this morning."

2. Some ordinary textures that do not bother others
feel very offensive when they touch my skin.

Growing up, we had a chamois I never liked to touch. It was yellow and stiff, scratchy-feeling. I don't know if it felt *offensive* to me. Maybe. Its home was a shelf in the garage alongside buckets of tulip bulbs dug up from my mother's flower garden, and seed packets that rattled, and rusty pruning shears, trowels, and work gloves the years had worn smooth. In the rafters, desiccated spiders hung crumpled in smoke-like webs. Brown wasps tapped at exposed studs. I remember one fall with my father. It was cool out, coming on evening, the light from the garage's bare bulb leaching out into the driveway and up the deep-grooved trunk of a locust tree. Below the spiders and the chamois and the twisted, alien shapes of my mother's tulip bulbs were cases of empty pop bottles that every few weeks we took to the grocery store to redeem for five cents apiece. And I remember the dusk of that one fall evening, coming back from working in the yard—having built up a sweat in our flannel shirts—we found a bottle of Sprite, unopened, in among the empties. My father popped the cap and took a slug and passed it to me. The glass was green and dusty and dimpled—and cold to the touch. The light of that bare bulb. The Sprite slick and cold on my tongue. Coolness blossoming in the depths of me.

3. It is very difficult for me to work and function in groups.

Once my brother said to me, "You can't play football with us. You have glasses!" Once I broke his finger by dropping a rock on it. Once, out in the woods with some friends, we found the camp of these runaway girls from Florida and dug through their pile of clothes and pulled out black see-through bras, and I found a box of maxi-pads and stuck them to tree trunks and smashed red berries against them. Once we stuck an M-80 down the throat of a gasping bluegill and exploded it on a picnic table. Once we soaped pentagrams on an elderly neighbor's car. Left a hotdog in a jockstrap on a porch. Burned books in a fire pit. Shot mourning doves with a BB gun. Robins. Blackbirds, too. Watched encrypted satellite porn after my parents had gone to sleep. Gave each other wet willies and purple nurples. Smashed bottles against railroad cars stopped along the tracks back behind the church. None of it was difficult in the sense that I didn't know what to do or how to join in the fun. What was difficult was how easy it was.

4. It is difficult to figure out what other people expect of me.

My mother was determined to be a good mother, to protect me and tame me and keep me from being an embarrassment to myself and the family. The fall

I was nine or ten, she was out raking leaves while my brother and I were next door playing football. Then came one of the Schwartz brothers—Doug or Jeff, I can't remember which. Doug probably. Their father owned the Wendy's in town and they were older, in high school, and had dirt bikes and snowmobiles they were always buzzing around on. One of them, who knows why, picked me up by my ankles and started swinging me around and around and around. I was screaming, terrified. I don't know. Finally he tossed me in the grass, and I popped up in a huff and said, "You goddamn fucking son of a bitch!" And my mother, who had been blissfully oblivious to me getting manhandled, somehow heard this statement and called my name and said, "Get over here. Now." And the Schwartzes and the boys I was playing football with all laughed as I marched home, head slung low, to meet my fate. When I got to my mother, she reached into a tree and snapped off a switch. I started running, and she said, "You want me to do this in front of your friends?" I wanted to tell her if she thought those were my friends, she was crazy. I didn't have friends, just planets I orbited, gravities that pulled me along. All the same, no, I did not want her to beat me in front of them, so I stood there and took it.

5. I often don't know how to act in social situations.

One spring break in college I went with my girlfriend to Iowa to meet her extended family, who were all dairy farmers. On Sunday morning after church we drove out to this truck-stop fried chicken joint. The men sat at one table. The women sat at another. I didn't know any of the men, and it wasn't like they were a gregarious bunch. They were old farmers in coveralls and seed company ball caps. They communicated in a series of one-note hems and haws while glancing at me sideways through the steam rising off their Styrofoam cups of coffee. So I sat with the women. As a burgeoning feminist I sat with my girlfriend and the women—these respectable, older, floral-printed and heavily perfumed country ladies who gossiped and tittered over their plates of chicken and runny slaw. I sat there and said nothing, and nothing was said to me. The unspoken sentiment around both tables was that we would pretend that I did not exist and had not, by existing and choosing to sit with the women, opened a rift in the space-time continuum that is early March in central Iowa. Early March: the furrows in empty black fields, stretching to the horizon; windblown weeds gyrating in an irrigation ditch. And so the talk went on as though I weren't there. Stories about the undocumented Mexican field hands—the "illegals"—my girlfriend's family employed, and how eight or ten or twelve of them all crammed themselves into a ramshackle trailer out on some corner of the back forty, the kids always hollering and needing a doctor, their mothers always looking for someone to sponsor them for a green card or a driver's license, and their fathers always getting drunk and crashing the tractor. I listened and stared at the fried blood in the joints of my chicken bones—the stories all a kind of lark, humorous, as though to these perfumed ladies the lives of the Mexican field workers who made their lives possible somehow weren't real. Their pain and struggle, their meager dreams of a better life. "You probably should've sat with the men," my girlfriend said on the long drive home to Indiana. And it's a much longer story, but to this day—even though I've got a wife and a son, and a thousand years have passed since that trip to Iowa—her mother still swears I'm gay.

6. I can chat and make small talk with people.

In my twenties, I had a part-time job at the YWCA selling candy to parents and kids for a youth basketball league. One Saturday a woman came in late and everyone else was in the gym. She strolled up to my table, leaned in conspiratorially and sadly and said, "Did you hear? The Columbia space shuttle exploded and all the astronauts aboard were killed." I said that was terrible, and she agreed. "It really is terrible," she said. Then she asked how much the Snickers cost and fished a dollar from her purse and went into the gym to cheer her daughter's team.

7. When I feel overwhelmed by my senses, I have
to isolate myself to shut them down.

Last night my wife went out to dinner with some friends, and by our son's bedtime she wasn't home. The boy is six and still blossoming into an awareness of himself. While we were at the sink getting ready to brush his teeth, he started bawling: "I miss Mommy!" Down came the tears, the snot, the choked sobs. I tried to comfort him. We tried to call my wife so he could leave her a message. Finally he tore away from me and ran to his room and slammed the door. I gave him a minute to catch his breath, and when I peeked in he was under the blankets with a paperweight music box his great-grandmother had given him. Inside the snow globe stood a pair of wolves with their backs arched, howling. And the music it played—the tinkling little song—my god, it was the saddest melody I'd ever heard. "What are you doing, Bud?" I said. And he said, "I'm just listening to this and trying to calm down my brain." And it was as though I was standing outside of myself, seeing in my son every time I'd done something similar. Like when my grandmother died when I was ten and I ran down the hall to my bedroom and covered myself in blankets and tried to somehow swim to her through the blackness of my closed eyes.

8. How to make friends and socialize is a mystery to me.

In middle school this kid started saying—semi-ironically—"I'm superior." And it became a thing. Everybody said "I'm superior," and we said it in the halls and at lunch and after school at football practice. Then we started doing the Panama pass out. You bend over and take ten deep breaths, then you cross your arms over your chest and someone behind you squeezes you until you lose consciousness. And somehow that makes you friends. I don't know. There was this other kid in my class, Jamie Davis, who always sat near me because our last names edged up to each other alphabetically. He was thirteen but already over six feet tall. His clothes smelled and were old, as though maybe they'd been his father's back in the 70s. These wrinkled white button-up shirts and shitbrown pants. It hurt just to look at him. Glasses. Acne. Wash your goddamn hair, Jamie. And please god no, no, don't put a Band-Aid across your forehead because a zit you popped started bleeding and wouldn't stop. We were in health class one year. He was always trying to talk to me—because he was always talking, and because I was nicer than a lot of the other kids at my school who would've just ignored him or scowled at him or told him to fuck off. But I sat there and listened. I was polite. One day he said his leg hurt and asked me to take his quiz up front and put it on the teacher's desk. Misty Flack, one of the cheerleaders, one of the hot girls, looked at me when Jamie asked me to take his paper up, and because she looked at me—because it made me feel uncool to be talking to Jamie, to acknowledge his existence—I said, "Take your own quiz up front. I'm not your slave." And he shrugged and limped up front and

handed in his paper. Then I don't know. He was absent the next day. A week
went by, and we didn't see him. Or maybe it was longer before we noticed his
absence because ignoring him was something we'd been doing all year. But
finally word got out: Jamie had some kind of bone cancer. It was in one of his
long, impossibly lanky legs. The next time we saw him was in the gym toward
the end of the year. He was in a wheelchair and chemo had balded him, and
where his leg had once been now only a stump remained. I remember everyone
crowding around him, saying hi, asking him how he was doing. The kid who
said "I'm superior" was there. Misty Flack was there. People were so happy to
see him, and so messed up by his illness that they were laughing and crying
at the same time. I remember Jamie stood up on his one good leg and said,
"Watch this!" and wildly swung the stump back and forth. The miracle of that
moment. In two months, he'd be dead.

9. When talking to someone, I have a hard time
telling when it is my turn to talk or to listen.

One summer in grad school I volunteered at the Indiana Veterans' Home and
worked with a disabled World War II vet named Rocky who had a notebook of
poems he wanted Willie Nelson to turn into songs. A former bantam weight
boxer in the navy, he now spent his days in a wheelchair watching *The Price
Is Right* in the common room and flirting with his nurse's aides. A stroke had
paralyzed the left side of his body. Emphysema scorched his lungs. His poems
were about love and gratitude. Once he told me his ship had been hit by a
Japanese kamikaze but the closest he ever came to dying in the war was the
night he spent with a prostitute in Spain. I would come in on Wednesdays
and chat with him for an hour or two, then take him down the hall for a Coke
from the machine. He would introduce me to his fellow vets by saying, "This
here's the *arthur* who's going to make me famous." And once they heard I
liked stories they all had stories to tell, and their stories had no beginnings or
middles or endings, just strings of details by turns horrifying and sublime and
banal. Gene, the Korean War vet, had seen his captain using pliers to peel off
the black, frostbitten skin of a boy's trigger finger. Then he'd come home from
the war and taken a job at Frisch's Big Boy—and he walked us through his days
of getting up in the morning, eating breakfast, hitching to work, working all

day with a mop. And on it went like that, unrelenting, as though these men could reconstitute their former lives if only someone would listen. And I tried to, every Wednesday, for as long as I could stand it. I listened and tried not to judge them or ask questions that might break their heart to answer. Then one day before we went down the hall for a Coke—because the world is impossibly small—Rocky's nurse's aide walked in. And it was Misty Flack. I almost didn't recognize her. At the end of high school she'd been in a bad car accident, and it damaged her severely, and anyway it had been years since we'd seen each other. But she recognized me and came right over and gave me a hug. We stood grinning at each other stupidly enough that Rocky—dirty old man that he was—said, "You want me to get out of here, Steve, and give you two some time alone? I can pull the curtain, you know." And I remember blushing like I hadn't since middle school.

10. Sometimes I have to cover my ears to block out painful noises
(like vacuum cleaners or people talking too much or too loudly).

For the first three years of his life, my son had an undiagnosed gastrointestinal problem and screamed—in agony—day and night. I couldn't cover my ears because I was holding him, feeding him a bottle, burping him, singing to him in the night, gently bouncing him in my arms, changing his diaper, putting on his tiny socks. "It's like his voice is choking me," I'd tell my wife. "Suffocating me. I can't breathe." Instead of covering my ears, I sometimes screamed back at him.

11. It can be very hard to read someone's face, hand,
and body movements when we are talking.

Last December I stood at an intersection and looked across the street at a middle-aged woman who'd caught my eye and smiled at me. She wore a long white winter coat, and under the coat flashed the ruffled hem of a blue dress. Straight dark hair hung to her jaw. When she smiled at me, I looked down. When I looked up, she smiled again. And pointed at me. And nodded. With her finger she made a cross in the air. One vertical line straight down, one horizontal line straight across. Then she pointed at me again and nodded as though to say, "Yes, you." And as we waited for the light to change, she kept smiling and making crosses and pointing at me. When the light finally turned, we walked toward one another, and I thought maybe she was going to pull a knife. I didn't know. I tried to keep to the edge of the crosswalk, but she dipped into my line of sight and whispered: "You're going to burn in fire." I said, "Pardon?" She said, "Just wait: you're going to burn in fire." And then she kept walking, off toward the rest of her afternoon. I stopped in the intersection and called after her: "I'm ready! *I'm ready!*"

12. I focus on details rather than the overall idea.

When I was ten and my grandmother died, the overall idea was that I'd never see her again, never see her in the kitchen of her little white house on that cobbled brick street near the railroad tracks in Effingham, Illinois; in that kitchen, smoking, steel-gray hair in a loose bun, hunched over a cast iron skillet frying squirrel legs, the squirrels from a gunny sack my dad had brought back from a hunting trip, shotgun shot lodged in their skulls; never again in that little kitchen, smoking, frying squirrels, and talking to my dad and me while we cradled bottles of Pepsi and enjoyed a late-afternoon breeze through the curtains, and the way the breeze twisted the smoke from her cigarettes into coils and ropes and question marks; never again in that little kitchen smelling of cigarettes and grease, the skillet popping, sizzling; the skillet, in its blackness, a universe; never again the thin, waxy translucence of her skin and the webbing of veins in her arms; never again the arms that wrapped themselves around me and pulled me tight . . .

13. I take things too literally, so I often miss what people are trying to say.

Several years ago I went to see a psychologist—Dr. Wilson—to talk about Asperger syndrome and the possibility that I might have it. She said, "Do you suspect any of your family members have Asperger's?" This was before the DSM eliminated Asperger's from its official language and talk turned to being "on the spectrum." I said I suspected my dad had Asperger's. "And what does he do?" Dr. Wilson asked. I said that he sniffed his fingers and rubbed his belly, and she smiled knowingly, reassuringly, and said, "For a living. What does your father do—*for a living?*"

14. I get extremely upset when the way I like
to do things is suddenly changed.

The other morning our coffeemaker stopped working. It hissed and gurgled and made all the right sounds, but nothing came out. I fiddled with it. Nothing. On a typical morning I have plenty to do: I make my son breakfast, get him dressed, pack him lunch for the day; make my wife breakfast (including coffee) and pack her a lunch; and make my own breakfast and lunch, and iron my clothes for work; and by the time I've dropped our son at school and gotten to my office, I'm tired. There's no place in my schedule for a coffeemaker break down. And it was all my fault because the day before I'd let my son help me make the coffee, and he'd touched things, and that was probably why something wasn't right. Usually he doesn't show half an interest in what I'm doing. Yesterday he wanted to help with the coffee. So I let him. On some primordial level, all I want is for him to know me. All I want from anyone is to be known, acknowledged. Loved. But the other morning, the coffeemaker stopped working, and I couldn't fix it, and because my son had messed it up—because (the self-incriminating story ran) in my impossible hunger for love I had let him mess it up—everything suddenly felt wrong. I fiddled with the machine, got angry. My son wanted to see if he could fix it, and I snapped at him. My wife came into the kitchen to help, and I snapped at her. Meanwhile the radio brought a story of the Syrian refugee crisis, which doubled my shame because a broken coffeemaker isn't anything to get mad about, and I knew that, and yet I was still so mad I was shaking. Then I don't know. My wife suggested we boil some water and pour it through the grinds, and we did it, and it worked, and there was coffee. It was just another morning. I kissed her on the cheek, and I apologized to my son for snapping at him. And the breakfasts and lunches got made. The clothes got ironed. Inscrutable as ever, the day began.

# "Easy as Pie," That's a Lie

AMY WALLEN

Darth Vader to Obi-Wan Kenobi: "If you're not with me, then you're my enemy."

Obi-Wan: "Only a Sith deals in absolutes."

—*Star Wars: Episode III—Revenge of the Sith*

Directions:

*1. In a large bowl sift 2 c. flour and ¼ t. salt together.*

Americana Chicken Pot Pie—in the aftermath of the 9/11 terrorist attacks what better dish to serve your Republican in-laws? I don't mean voted-for-Bush-both-terms Republican in-laws, I mean wrote-Newt-Gingrich's-Contract-with-America-at-the-Heritage-Foundation-religious-right in-laws. My husband, on the other hand, saved whales alongside Al Gore and Bobby Kennedy Jr.

I'm a Rodney King devotee. I believe we should all get along. No matter how diverse or strong our passions and ideals, our opinions shouldn't make us enemies. My politics are left, and I'm a card-carrying ACLU member who, at the time, worked in international development creating water supplies and gardens in Latin American villages. In the daily news I don't dwell on the politics and debates; I roll my eyes at the buffoonery of Gingriches and Clintons alike; I skip celebrity drama; but I'm faithful to certain comic strips, often searching the obits for character artifacts; and I religiously read the food section on Thursdays.

Savory pies are my specialty. Chicken and thyme, salmon and portobello,

Persian lamb and eggplant—the combinations are as endless as flavors. Something about the mixture of all the ingredients inside the warm crust brings folks at the table together, sharing through that most vulnerable organ—our stomachs. I told myself and my husband that it would show bipartisanship to dine together, to welcome our in-laws into our home—to serve them pie.

These brothers rarely visited one another—one on the East Coast, the other on the West. Their rivalry could make Cain and Abel resemble foxhole comrades. One brother even bore the scar from a pair of round-tipped grade-school scissors stabbed into his back. But: who the sinner and who the martyr?

After 9/11, people did strange things under the guise of solidarity.

Either you are
with us, or you are with
the terrorists.

George W. Bush, September 20, 2001

*2. Cut in ¾ c. chilled fat until the mixture resembles coarse crumbs.*

In the summer of 2002 "WMD" was not yet part of our nation's vocabulary, but "preemptive strikes" as a topic of discussion had begun. A heated discussion. The color wheel of national security alerts remained stuck on red and orange. The Patriot Act had been signed into law, making it easier for the federal government to spy on ordinary citizens. Anthrax made special appearances in personal mail. The shoe bomber had struck, giving all air travelers good reason to wear Odor-Eaters. And the axis of evil, as a label, was created.

He that is not with me
is against me; and he that
gathereth not with me
scattereth abroad.

Jesus Christ, Matthew 12:30

*3. Sprinkle ½ c. ice water over the flour mixture just until the pastry holds together.*

I grew up on frozen potpies, Swanson to be exact. An obsession, really. As I got older, my tastes became more sophisticated, and I turned to making my own pies. But my piecrusts looked like Frankenstein's face—crosshatched and glued together. My brother, who had been a dessert chef in his younger life, told me, "It takes practice to make a piecrust." He knew pastry. "Start with a Cuisinart," he said, "a food processor. It'll make the job much easier."

I refused to get a machine for a task that grandmothers for centuries had been achieving with vein-riddled hands and a pastry cutter.

Still, no matter what I did, the dough always stuck to the rolling pin and wouldn't flatten out into anything resembling a circle. The more flour I added, the more the crust broke apart.

"Add more water," my brother advised on the phone, calling from the Midwest. "You live in a dry climate." I added the maximum amount of ice water the recipe called for and then some. "Use shortening; it's easier than butter," he suggested. But still my pie dough wouldn't cooperate. It crumbled in my hands, and when I tried stitching it back together with wet fingertips, I only made a bigger mess of gloppy sections versus dry sections. When I'd finally get the whole thing stuck together and then lift the circle of dough to lay it in the pie pan, it would break in a new place.

"The harder it is to handle, the better the crust will be," my brother said on a closing note. As much as I tried, nothing worked. First I cried "uncle." Then I recited the platitude: it's what's inside that matters.

I found a substitute—Pillsbury refrigerated piecrust. In its red box the Pillsbury crust is rolled-up rounds of dough ready to be laid out in the pie pan, filled, and pinched around the edges. I had perfected the filling: aromatic garlic cream sauce with a hint of thyme; chicken breast marinated in white wine; cauliflower, carrots, parsnips, peas, and, of course, lima beans, all steamed to a fresh crunch. I laid a handful of shredded Irish cheddar cheese on the bottom crust before layering in the ingredients and dousing it all with cream sauce. Then I placed the perfectly round Pillsbury top crust and sealed it with fluted edges.

Who needed a homemade crust? I still made a good pie. It always got compliments. When friends asked if I had made the crust from scratch, I'd laugh and say, "No, no. 'Easy as pie'—that's a lie. It's a store-bought crust." Inevitably they would say, "You wouldn't know; it tasted great." I had nothing to hide.

*4. Mix with your hands, a pastry cutter, or a food processor, adding more water if needed.*

My brother-in-law is a constitutional scholar. He's written a best-selling book on how to interpret the U.S. Constitution literally line-by-line, much like fundamentalists do with the Bible. He also wrote a tome on George Washington's Farewell Address, within it warning that we should not get involved in foreign affairs, lest we suffer the likes of 9/11. My husband, an international law expert, brokered a deal with the Mexican government to maintain a UNESCO whale sanctuary. And here we all were in the same house, our house, doing our best to pretend we had the same interests at heart: chopped-down cherry trees and *Moby-Dick*.

Seated in our living room, we chatted over cocktails, the usual banter about the flight from DC, which then veered into a discussion about delays caused by increased airport security. My husband was the first to cross the divide, stating his opinion on the ridiculousness of having to remove his shoes in line. My sister-in-law chimed in, "I'd gladly relinquish all my rights," showing off her stripes as a scholar of Christian conservative politics, "if it means safe air travel and protection of my country." She saw herself as an arbiter of wisdom and reason. I saw her as someone who disapproved of anyone who thought differently—always ready to expose any flaw, dedicated to the righteousness of her point of view.

Blunt-tipped scissors had been drawn from their scabbards!

I shrugged and smiled—after all it was only for one evening, then they'd be on their way to lecture on public policy at their alma mater, the conservative Claremont McKenna College.

But my husband continued the bifurcation of the room by opining on the fear created by the administration in establishing their power. My sister-in-law, with textbook clarity, diagrammed for him proof of real fear factors. When she added the anthrax scare to the mix, my experience growing up blue-collar with hunters and ranchers in Texas prompted me to consider mentioning that anthrax was a common bacteria found in all mammals, not some new biological weapon—but I thought it would sound proletarian. My brother-in-law asked my husband, "Are we not supposed to be afraid when we live one mile from the Pentagon that was just rammed by a 757 jet?" I watched the meticulousness, the even keel of the conversation, the throwing of stones without anyone ever lifting a fist. I clam up in such situations, so I remained an observer. A peacekeeper, I told myself at the time.

No matter what I said—"I hope there's not a bra bomber!"—or wanted to say—"Bombed skyscrapers are the norm in Latin America"—bad attempts at humor to keep the mood light or a relaying of personal experience from my work in El Salvador, I received cool glances, eyes refraining from a good roll. Intellects pulsed, and not a single voice rose. The scholars, my husband included, fought a battle of the minds. This low simmer of insults was not what I had in mind when I pictured us gathered together.

On first appearance my brother-in-law would have been considered the most civil among us. With calm and pedantry he offered his explanation for the necessity of the Patriot Act: *we must protect our country against those who are jealous of our freedom.* I hated this statement, this propaganda that was the administration's line. But the pause, the look, the demeanor after the words—all communicated that his was not an opinion, but fact. He had probably even written the line for the Republicans.

"Let's eat!" I said.

Dinner conversation followed the same grand strategy. Besides pie the menu consisted of civil rights appetizers stabbed with toothpicks, a wilted salad of national security risks, and for dessert, pokeweed berries piled over constitutional amendments. I would be scraping founding fathers off the walls for weeks.

After dinner my sister-in-law helped me clear the table, taking the empty plates to the kitchen. I tried to tell her no, but she insisted. In the other room she didn't speak about politics. She implied that women didn't talk politics. Now it was just us chickens in the kitchen, and she babbled about curtains, paint colors, and homeschooling her future kids—like we had removed our armor and donned aprons in a 1950s kitchen. She and my brother-in-law had many plans for their home remodel—all bigger and of better quality than any my husband and I had for ours. Her foil still thrust. I pictured my kitchen scissors in the closed drawer.

The usual compliment came. "Delicious pie," she said. "Did you make the crust from scratch?"

The words came out of my mouth before I could stop them. "Yes," I said, my back to her, "yes, I did."

Liar! Just like that I became a liar.

You may think a simple white lie like this was no big deal, but lying is not my modus operandi. I can be honest to a fault. I can swear as well as any of my redneck cousins. I can blurt out embarrassing remarks at the most inopportune times. But I have trouble with lying.

"I'm impressed," she said. "I can never get a piecrust to come out right."

"It just takes practice," I said, Miss Know-It-All.

Their visit had no potential for future solidarity. Not when their team sat in the Oval Office making laws meant to absolve their actions with single-sided moral justification. I was done.

She asked if she should scrape the plates before putting them in the dishwasher. Our old house didn't have a garbage disposal, so I pointed to the trash can. As I faced the sink, I heard her step on the pedal that opened the lid to the stainless steel can, and with a sickening feeling I pictured the red Pillsbury box, sitting atop the trash where I had placed it.

My sister-in-law did not say a word. She could have called me on my lie. Or perhaps she didn't see the box, or recognize it for what it was, but I doubt it. I didn't admit anything. I could have easily made a joke. But I didn't.

The next morning I dropped the in-laws at the airport, and then before going home, I stopped at the mall and bought a Cuisinart.

> If you hamper the
> war effort of one side
> you automatically help that
> of the other . . . . In practice,
> 'he that is not with me
> is against me.'

George Orwell, *Pacifism and the War*, 1942

*5. Knead just until a dough forms. Be careful not to overhandle.*

I've never purchased another crust. I make everything from scratch now. In fact, with plenty of practice under my elastic waistband I can tell by the weather and the consistency of the dough and the type of ingredients I'm using—whole wheat, sour cream, cornmeal, or maybe a butter crust—how much liquid I need. No more Frankenstein crusts. Instead I fashion glossy, lattice-striped or intricate cut-out top crusts with fluted edges.

But the conditions have to be just right to create a perfect version of the classic flaky butter crust. The climate dictates the moisture level, and the fat must be kept chilled throughout the process. It's the hard flecks of butter, which burst when baking, that create the flakiness. Too soft and the ingredients will not form a dough that can be rolled out into a pastry. The work bowl should also be kept as cold as possible to maintain the ingredients at their stiffest for blending. And the dough, as soon as it's the right consistency—not too wet, but forming into a ball—must rest, or it will become tough when baked. On occasion those four simple ingredients—flour, salt, fat, and water—do not come together. With practice you begin to know at what point it's time to abort the attempt.

*6. Cover and chill for an hour or overnight.*

It's not just the filling—beef curry, cheddar and roasted vegetables, carne asada, caramelized leeks with roasted potatoes, whatever. It's not just the pinch of thyme or garlic roux. What's outside should complement what's inside.

Now when someone says, "My crusts never turn out like this—what's your secret?" I say, quite honestly, "It takes practice to recognize when it will work and when it won't."

# Outline toward a Theory of the Mine versus the Mind and the Harvard Outline

ANDER MONSON

I. Start with the Roman numeral I with an authoritative period trailing just after it. This is the Harvard Outline, which comes in Caps and is a method of organizing information
   a. remembered from high school as a major step toward creating an essay
      i. though there was a decimal method, too
   b. but I've never been comfortable with the thing—its seeming rigor, its scaffolding so white against the language
      i. never felt the top-down structuralist method of constructing writing to be useful or effective; the mind, so idiosyncratic, unusual
         1. its strangeness and its often-incoherence
            a. the lovely anomaly
   c. and the Harvard Outline is the reason that I get fifty-five five-paragraph essays every month
   d. it is, I think, suspect, (its
   e. headings
      i. subheadings
         1. sub-subheadings
            a. etc.
            b. though there is a pleasure to this iteration, this recursion— like mathematics and the algorithms I played with and

admired in computer science classes, writing functions that called themselves

   i. which called themselves

      1. which called themselves

         a. until they were satisfied

      2. and exited

   ii. right back

  c. out

    i. like those Russian nesting (matryoshka) dolls; a lovely symmetry; such satisfaction comes in nesting

    ii. such starkness

       1. elegance)

f. all those steps out and down across the page—like the writing task is that of going downhill, like a waterfall in its rush

   i. or the incremental, slow plod down the slope, skis buried behind in some drift

g. While technically called "the Harvard Outline"

   i. it has nothing to do with Harvard

      1. according to their archivists, "it appears to be a generic term"

   ii. so it's difficult to track it down in the history of organizing information

      1. which is what this culture spends increasing time (and money!) doing

         a. witness the amazing success of the search engine Google

            i. as created by Larry Page and Sergey Brin

            ii. with its elegant mechanism of concordance

               1. of ranking searches by the number of pages that link to each individual page or site in order to establish the relative importance of that initial page or site

                  a. and look—there's no need for parentheses in 1. above thanks to the Harvard Outline

                  b. again that attraction to self-examination

                  c. again that attraction to what elegance there is to find

II. My family has a background in the Michigan mining industry
   a. a history in copper, iron, the cast-off leftover materials necessary to process ore from rock
   b. though less my recent family
      i. not my father who is a professor—whose job, like mine, is the mining and refining, then the distribution of information for (small sums of) money
         1. though perhaps this is a cynical view of the profession
            a. and the light-as-knowledge metaphor is hardly breaking new ground
               i. nor does "breaking new ground" break new ground
         2. still I like the image of the light-helmeted professor plowing through the darkness
            a. though it is romantic to say the least
         3. "like mine" (from above)—mining is a story of possession
            a. of legal ownership of land and rights, the permission to go below the crust
         4. "breaking new ground" (from above)—again the construction terminology
            a. the invocation of the building, of the engineering
         5. my father teaches at Michigan Technological University, formerly the Michigan College of Mines, a school that is just about to lose its Mining Engineering program
            a. which is older than the oldest living humans
            b. which is "one of only 15 mining engineering programs in the U.S. that has been uninterrupted since the beginning of the century and has also held accreditation with the Accreditation Board for Engineering and Technology (ABET) since 1936" according to the MTU Mining Engineering website
               i. this tidbit brought to you through Google
               ii. this tidbit being no longer accurate (now we should use past tense, as the program has now been retired, killed, phased out): this is an information shift between the writing of this essay and its publication

   c. but further back

      i. since nearly everyone who emigrated to Upper Michigan from (mostly) Scandinavia worked in the mines or worked in industries that supported mining

         1. the mining boom in the nineteenth century was so big that Calumet, Michigan, population of 879 as of the 2000 census, was nearly named the capital of Michigan

            a. as the story goes (turns out on drilling deeper that it is not true)

         2. and there are stories of exploitation and immense hardship

            a. as there always are

         3. though just after World War II, the price of copper declined, and so—though there's still plenty underneath the northern earth—the mines slowly shut their doors

            a. now there are no active producing mines left in the Keweenaw

               i. the railroads no longer run

               ii. even the Greyhound bus service has stopped

               iii. it felt at times while growing up like living in a dead letter office

                  1. another information shift: evidently there are still two mines that remain in operation, one of which my high school friend Jeremy, his father a metallurgist, is working for

            b. though the shells they left behind—the fine network of tunnels that still riddle the earth—are havens for millions of bats

               i. who come out at night through the chicken wire that often covers up the mines' mouths

               ii. and were—until recently, when the method of closing off the mines was changed to be a bit more bat-friendly—picked off by hundreds of raccoons that would sit at the chicken wire, waiting for the daily exodus and feast

            c. and now Upper Michigan is a destination for bat-watching tourists

d. and anyone growing up in the Keweenaw has had ready access to mines

  i. either through the tours of the few remaining open (now purely tourist) mines

    1. which are absolutely worth doing, though expensive (to the tune of twenty-five dollars), because to be submerged a mile underneath the earth is a necessary experience

      a. to get that absolute darkness

        i. even if you think you know what it's like

      b. and to get that absolute *chill*

      c. to know what your ancestors went through

        i. or at least to have an idea—isn't this an honor or an obligation?

  ii. or more likely illegally

    1. breaking the locks off the doors

      a. because there are dozens of old shafts sunk in the land that haven't been filled

    2. drinking inside (also arguably a family obligation), or exploring with rope, flashlights, and a constant sense of possibility

      a. for there is something beautiful, nearly unbearable, about a hole in the earth

        i. about darkness

          1. that unknown

            a. black box

            b. big X

        ii. maybe it's a male fixation

      b. that it must bear exploration, no matter how far down it goes

        i. maybe it's too many Hardy Boys books, or Jules Verne

      c. and also there's the danger

        i. a definite attraction

          1. one cure for boredom

          2. a cheapie and dangerous carnival ride

      iii. or possibly through the few research mines maintained by the University

         1. one of which I discovered while hiking in Hancock, Michigan

           a. while it's not a public mine, it is not gated or barred off

           b. walk within a quarter of a mile and you'll feel the drop in temperature caused by the cool air streaming out

              i. a counterintuitive finding—remember high school geology, the earth's crust, mantle, core, etc., and lava bursting out through craters

              ii. or Jules Verne again

                 1. while less than absolutely reliable

              iii. and how it gets hotter now

                 1. the farther

                    a. in

                       i. you go

              iv. how there's a pressure from the outside structure

                 1. how the structure

                    a. either binds you in or wants to expel you like a sickness

                    b. think the mine, the outline, as a body

                    c. an ecosystem

                    d. or a mechanical spring

                       i. compress

                       ii. release

                       iii. repeat

              v. and that structure creates pressure; how architecture is the elegant distribution of stress

III. The outline, so like a mine

    a. defined by penetration

      i. deeper in

      ii. both laterally and vertically

         1. for harder information

      iii. yes, how male, again, you dirty bird

b. and mining is interested mostly in the horizontal.

    i. Mineral deposits—in the absence of fault or other geologic strangeness—lay naturally in planes

    ii. and since similar materials respond similarly to pressure, they settle horizontally

    iii. and the goal of the miner is to identify the deposit

        1. in terms of *dip* and *strike*

           a. the straight line of maximum inclination (*dip*)

           b. the horizontal line, the contour line (*strike*)

c. and the vertical when necessary, to either follow the vein

    i. or to proceed deeper into the earth once the vein has been exhausted

        1. and repeat, recursively

d. though the terminology of the mine is far more lovely than that of the outline

    i. *level, incline, drif, shaft, crosscut, winze, raise* and *mouth* and *face, gossan, apex, adit, gangue, stope*

    ii. "Shallow Boring in Soft Rocks: Boring by Hand Auger"

        1. a chapter subheading from the "Boring" chapter of *Introduction to Mining* by Bohuslav Stočes

    iii. having an essential mystery

        1. due to their earthy inaccessibility

           a. compare to that of the Harvard Outline, designed particularly (one imagines—though it's not clear who designed it) to be easily negotiable

        2. and the aura of danger, of esoteric, academic, secret knowledge about it

           a. these terms literally describe loci of danger, pits and sinkholes; they offer both treasure and death

               i. both of which have a lure

    iv. and I was obsessed with mining for the first ten years of my life

        1. visiting the A. E. Seaman Mineralogical Museum at Michigan Technological University

          a.  which has a seventeen-ton copper boulder, the largest mineral specimen ever taken from Lake Superior

          b.  an emblem of the Keweenaw, one of the world's richest copper deposits

      2.  trying to convince my dad to buy me various geological supplies

          a.  such as the rock tumbler I never really used—a sad emblem of my childhood sitting on a shelf maybe in my parents' basement

      3.  agate hunting along the shores of Lake Superior

      4.  looking for chunks of unrefined copper in the woods or in the hills of stamp sand along Portage Canal (the canal that cuts off the tip of the Keweenaw Peninsula from Michigan)

          a.  leftovers from processing iron ore

          b.  which very well may be poisoning some Michigan lakes

             i.  and we try not to think too much about this

      5.  making homemade explosives according to the often-poor instructions from Paladin Press books and other, even less reliable sources

          a.  ceasing only when a good friend of mine lost three fingers

   v.  and in a way, I still am—as it's the central story of the place where I am from, the big goodness and the tragedy

      1.  it is how I imagine the ghost of slavery is to Southern writers

          a.  having this central, public history contributes to there even being such a thing as a "Southern Writer," whereas there aren't as obviously "Northern Writers"

      2.  (the boom and the bust—the makings of story itself)

          a.  and certainly the makings of much of my family

e.  perhaps it's only my desire

   i.  that this, my kind of work

      1.  darkness on light onscreen, then on the page

   ii.  be worth as much as what my family did in the dark for hours

      1.  for days

          a.  for years

f.  and the metaphor of mining one's past or childhood for writing material
  i.  an apt construction, experience as *material*
  ii.  is used a lot, and is something I'm concerned about myself
    1.  the ethics and the economics of the writing act
      a.  and that other pressure that it entails
        i.  so maybe the outline is a kind of architecture I am trying to erect
        ii.  to protect myself against my family, meaninglessness, and the future
          1.  an artifice to get inside the past
          2.  like a cold and unlit hole—what family tragedy is there behind me glittering like a vein
        iii.  perhaps it is a womb
          1.  and this then has to do with my mother's death
          2.  a protective sheath, a comfort zone
        iv.  or it could be a shell
      b.  an attempt for rigor as buffer or protection
      c.  or maybe it is elegance for the sake of it
      d.  an infinite recursion
      e.  some wankery
    2.  then there's always the possibility of being stuck, candle snuffed by a sudden blast
      a.  the candles that my family would have to buy themselves and carry—lit—down into the earth, the candles that were the only protection against the emptiness and isolation
    3.  with no way of lighting up again, and no way
  iii.  back out—

# The Clockwise Detorsion of Snails

A Love Essay in Sectors

KAREN HAYS

One—Pupillae

0°

*Indeed, the circle is a special logarithmic spiral whose rate of growth is zero.*

0.5°

Archaeologists recently announced the discovery of the world's oldest known specimen of figurative art. The artifact, a Venus figurine carved from mammoth ivory, was found in the same German cave that previously yielded one of the world's oldest musical instruments, a five-holed flute made from the wing bone of a Pleistocene vulture.

The Venus sculpture is a pendant endowed with enormous barrel-shaped out-poking breasts. She has one wee flipper arm (its match is still missing), a tumescent belly, two hips that flare from just beneath the elbow, two pinched-off legs (no knees), and a deeply clefted sex. The tiny unthreaded pendant eye peeks like a metaphorical sunrise between her tubular boobs, where I would like a neck to be. By hue and proportion she's a naked chicken roasted golden, a couple of inches only—but exquisite nonetheless. According to lead archaeologist Nicholas Conard (white gloved, eyebrows hopping), she is thirty-five thousand years or more old.

The scientific journal at whose website you can view the Venus in full rotis-
serie refers to her as a *prehistoric pinup*. Is she a palm-full of artifice meant to
arouse, I wonder, or a talisman intended to bestow fecundity on those who
don her? Or does she simply say, in perfect, self-assured mentalese: *Here, this
is what is important. This is all that has ever been or will ever be important.
Second only to a good meal, of course. Yours truly, My Hot Torso.* In any case,
I hear the hearth fire—its embers—still popping.

9°

It's breakfast time, and we're having an argument we've had before about the
nature of Man and the artifice of Fidelity and the morality of Making Babies
in this Day and Age, and I'm denying you the basic concession of eye contact
by staring into what's reflected of me in our shared dishes and flatware. Which
is ironic really—my apparent submissiveness—given that I'm the aggressor,
that I'm always the aggressor and that you, because you're so sporting, just coil
yourself into whatever position is least like my own and go pugnaciously along.
In the end it's all the same—foreplay really, a hormone-letting, something we do
with unacknowledged cyclicity. We're like a pair of chitting squirrels scrabbling
around a tree trunk after one another, throwing off loose bark. Which isn't to
say that real feelings aren't occasionally hurt or a real construct isn't at stake.
In fact lately I've begun allowing for the possibility of a serious trespass. I used
to imagine Point of No Return as something we asymptotically approached in
our arguing, but now I wonder if one day we might cross over and suddenly
find our circling less and less like skipping stones and more and more cyclonic.
I imagine the artifacts of our lives uprooted, spun in a dun-colored centrifugal
whirl, and then abruptly dropped—a jumble of emotionally laden and newly
useless shit for us to track down, junk, or divide between us.

Last summer an F-0 touched down in our urban neighborhood, lacing
gigantic boulevard trees criss-cross up the lolling tongue of Portland Avenue.
This minor maelstrom presented us residents with a handful of helpful-seeming
revelations: (1) tornados do strike cities, (2) even when the weather is cool and
not apparently inclement beyond a gentle, pattering rain; (3) no one need die or
be bodily hurt, even in the middle of the afternoon, (4) even when schoolyard

sirens don't start their pole-top spinning for at least ten, fifteen minutes after the damage is done; and, lastly, when all at once the clouds cleared away, (5) an epiphanic spread of sky.

Oh, how: my metaphors annoy you when we're fighting; imperfect they are; I overextend them to begin with; you're consequently helpless to turn them against me; everything breaks down. You hate the way I pick an argument with an ill-fitting, overly dramatic comparison and then retreat to idiotic dust mote gazing. *Spiraling*, you call it. The longer it goes on, the less retrievable I am. I am the data-free province at the heart of the radar map, looking deceptively like the storm's quiescent eye. A perfect logarithmic spiral, my rate of growth is nil, though all the while I'm churning.[1]

25°

The trick of the logarithmic spiral (why the *spira* is so *mirabilis*) is this paradox: starting at any point along the curve and sliding inward, you can make an infinite number of passes about the eye, or origin, without ever actually coming to it. Looking in it. Knowing what's inside it. Being the beauty beheld by it. Yet there is a finite amount of space in which to orbit, because the shape as a whole is bounded. And though the spiral may grow at its distal end, its curve never changes. Stretch, shrink, involve, or evolve it, it stays the same, turning the same way, at the same geometric rate, angle by axis, about its focus. Some miracle. Space and Time and the inner workings of others will always elude us. We may as well admit that all of our retaliations—our art making and head scratching and eye batting and record breaking—are just unabashed expressions of self-love. How many times can you fold this piece of paper? How many times must its thickness be doubled over before, like a cantilevered staircase, it reaches the moon? (Thirty-nine, I think is the number.) More importantly will there be space enough on its treads for just one of your cells when you're through? Can you send a whole army of material up the risers?

---

1    Thought goes underground. Becomes primitive, associative. Ranges for an analogue that might harbor a solution.

33°

Notes on seeing multiples (polyopia): *pupil* comes from *pupilla*, the Latin for *little girl doll*, or the baby-sized you that's reflected in the black of another's eye. If only you would get close enough. If only you'd look up. Masterpiece, you deserve a wide frame. Perfectly circular and custom cut. Wider. Big enough to escape through, to root a new life into, where your doings are secret from not only, but most especially you. Or better yet lots of these. Like a bunch of little portholes opened up. Teeny tiny opercula.[2]

According to paleoanthropologist Donald Johanson (whose pick freed Lucy to the tune of Sky and Diamonds), *sapiens* were spared the fate of our fellow hominids by one thing in particular—complex culture, the flutes and figures Neanderthals never adopted.

39°

What, in addition to our reflections, was on our plates on the morning of the potentially severing breakfast argument (Seeing Others was what was on the table):

*Rubus*, an aggregate fruit of the family rose, its drupelets arranged like dark lens panes. Ripe, the shade of a sun-burnished raven. Seeds beneath drupelets wore their hard coats over Populous[3], awaiting maws of frugivorous birds and (your ilk) foxes. For scarification by gut acid, razing by fire, flinging of

---

2   *Polka dots are a way to infinity*, said bedotting artist Yayoi Kusama. Her paintings manifest the hallucinations that have maddened her since childhood. Black and red and white circles flock in plague-like proportions, self-replicate in vertiginous whorls, fan out like supernovae that just shat the astral bed, lay their claim like incendiary dye packs. They are at once virally indifferent and obscenely glad.

3   Excess is a winning reproductive strategy. Tucked inside each seed is a set of blueprints waiting for its chance in the sun, each fruit bearing way more seeds than can ever manifest their plans. Nature is a ruthless editor.

insults . . . The myriad ways of getting to the germ, of sinking it in and then mercilessly self repeating.[4]

Staring into the iodine shades of my plate's stain, I began to imagine the rube fruit as a cane-strung compound eye. A big, fat ancestral eye. Cyclops eye. A bigger-than-stomach eye. Each of its facets flipped me blurred, fixated, and foreshortened. Dozens double-chinned and turned of hunger. When I snagged their retinas with my fork, they wrinkled and let run the dark vitreous humor.[5] And then, jarred by the new sound of you no longer talking, I made some rude comment about seeds and sowing and future spouses and how I didn't think you should go through with the *procedure* (jesus, god, out loud, said that). Sliced through the optic nerve. Found it gray inside orbit. Doled half berry each into two still-empty waffle squares. Remembered the harvester's warning: blackberries are red when they're still green: a maiden, a mother, a crone.

53°

Dear Peacock,

The hundred eyes of Hera's slain giant are stuck (don't look now) to your tail. It all began when Hera sent that goon, Argus, to guard Io (whom she'd already chained to an olive tree) from Hera's lovelorn philandering husband. Zeus, as you well know, wasn't above turning his mistress into a white heifer, himself into a white cloud, in order to conceal their carrying on right under Hera's nose. A mistake, that. Nothing escapes the olfaction of woman or goddess.

---

4   *There I stumbled on a visual articulation of the tension between sexual interest and boredom that I had been trying to describe,* writes Jennifer Doyle about her experience viewing the "Love Forever: Yayoi Kusama, 1958–1968" exhibit at the MOMA while also thinking about stilted expressions of the erotic in the pre-voyage scenes of *Moby-Dick.*

5   *For obliteration (or self-obliteration) was the term that Kusama gave to a distinctly feminized sensation of unbounding, of somehow being subsumed into the visual environment around one's self, of feeling a loss of boundaries between the self and the world, subject and object, eye and body,* writes Pamela M. Lee about *the phenomenology of the "hysteric,"* a so-called girl problem.

You birds are guided by sight and song, of course, but we mammals also use our noses. That may be because most of us are prudes by design, doing it in the dark without benefit of color. Instead, we broadcast our genotypes (major histocompatibility complexes) with hidden scents and are drawn to partners whose sub-smells are the least like our own. To keep the gene pool heterogeneous: unlike vs. like, ripe vs. unripe, yes vs. no. According to an article in the recent sex-themed issue of *Scientific American Mind*, there are 347 different types of smell receptors in our noses. That's 115 times the number we keep for color in our eyes. Your eyes. (How I love you with my humble ocelli, Peacock!) Because there are so many, it's been suggested that our occult odors, or bouquets as some say, may rival in complexity your hyperchromatic display. That can't really be though, can it, Peacock? That we humans are in possession of a sense so evolved and acute, and are not only not awed by what we perceive, not only not frenzied with recreating it and paying tribute to it, exhausting every limit of our artistic means to better know it, but are instead completely unaware that we perceive at all? Maybe it's like the lyrics of "Art Class," Superchunk's ode to Yayoi Kusama, suggest, and our lives are our real and greatest artworks, our paintings and sculptures and songs mere artifacts.

At any rate, Zeus couldn't give Io up, or wouldn't. He sent Hermes to free her. Hermes lulled Argus's hundred eyes shut with his softest spoken words (a whisper here, a promise) and then stoned him to death. It was jealous Hera who spared his eyes for the green of your tail. Now the stories they tell of you are endless. There's that one from India about how your eye spots, trimmed free and mixed with cane sugar, can cure infertility. And the other one about how ingesting their ashes reverses the course of poisoning. And that one about how your ugly feet, though they carry you well, are the price you pay for your vanity, that whenever you glimpse them, you yelp out obnoxiously. That last bit isn't true though, I know. Your feet were never reflected in me.

As for Io? Io clopped free, but Hera sent a gadfly to chase her to the ends of the earth . . . where Io roams forevermore madly.

Of eyes like hares' and heifers', wrote eighteenth century encyclopedists, Ware and Smellie: *Such animals, doomed to be pursued and devoured by others, are thus, with a very slight motion of the head, enabled to look behind and before. One eye is turned in front and the other in the rear.*

*Cow eyes*, that boy in freshman chemistry used to call me. Like it was some kind of compliment. Like I was demure, or worse, sacred. (His own eyes he hid behind a camera.) *Your pupils*, he said to me once, *are so big*. And then, as though desire were a state to be coveted, a quality of possession and not lack: *I'm so jealous*.

As for how the spotted moth got Io's spooked eyes, I confess ignorance. She has a vestigial mouth, I know that much, but as a moth only mates and never eats (like the way human women, in estrus, temporarily lose their appetites for food). Her prickled green larvae devour the leaves of blackberries (you laugh at how I slice my fruit to fit one half per waffle pocket at breakfast), will sting you righteously if ever you try to pluck one, and bear no resemblance whatsoever to their ruddy, blue-eyed adult forms, or *imagines*.[6]

Another thing: the flight path of a moth toward a light source traces the same logarithmic spiral as the drupelets whorled round a bramble fruit, as the human embryo about its perfect spine, as the centrifugal funnel of nerves from each of our focusing corneas, as a bird of prey after a rabbit, as a map of rabbit progeny from a single pair (the way they procreate—damn), as DNA, and also the horns of rams and rhinos.[7] We admire nature's turns, forgetting that *spira mirabilis* answers first to economy—rules of closest packing, greatest coverage, and least crowding. Not the sumptuousness we crave, the overflowing so redolent of love.

Dear Peacock, forget all of that cautionary nonsense. I don't know why I brought any of it up. (*Do* I look back too much? And at the same time forward? With my one eye short-sighted, the other far-? My strange asymmetry after that burning fever, refusing in first grade, as I did, a pirate's patch? My wonky depth perception ever since?) Ours is a proud love no matter how you see it.

---

6 Entomologists identify sexual maturity as *the imaginal stage* of an insect's life; all of its young guises have been tried on and duly shed, and the animal is, at long last, the spanking image of its kind.

7 Salvador Dalí writes, *The rhinoceros is not content with having one of the most beautiful logarithmic curves on its nose, no, even in its behind it has myriad sunflower-shaped logarithmic curves.*

You are irresistible when you look at me that way—from your tail, unblinking.
Don't stop. Promise?

Your Henny

86°

According to the ancient Greeks, of course, it was lusty Pan and not Cro-Magnon
(nor his African ancestors) who fashioned the first set of pipes. Pan made his
from the hollow river reeds into which the chaste maiden Syrinx turned just
as Pan was set to jump her. With his thwarted goat breath, Pan blew and blew
and blew, and in the end he supposedly felt much better.[8]

89.8°

Dear Syrinx, sorry for all the blowing.

Two—Torted Beginnings

90°

This is how like a dog I am circling my bedding.

90.3°

If a snail's logarithmic spiral grows by the golden ratio (phi) for every quarter
turn it takes in space, and an eight-thousand-word personal essay about the
compulsory nature of metaphor-making and romantic love is made to approxi-
mate that vortex, with the word substituting for the spiral's initial radius, the
essay will take somewhere between 4¼ and 4½ spins before it runs out of

---

8   *It is excessive, redundant, and superfluous in its languid and fervent overachieving,*
    writes Elizabeth Grosz, describing the way that sex (the notion) wicks like dripped
    ink into subjects to which it does not belong. No noun, no verb is immune to its
    contagion.

language. The first revolution will be 9½ words long (*I love you, I love you, I love you, ___*), the second about 65, the third around 445, the fourth 3050, and the less-than-half a spin remaining, 4430. This is roughly the number to which I must count before I will make the basic concession of eye (daggers) contact with you.

94°

Snail expert Ronald Chase suspects the Greeks drew on their knowledge of snails when they outfitted Cupid with his arrows. Many snails are hermaphrodites, and at least to the human eye, their mating rituals verge less on love than battle. (Combative sex occurs in species whose males shoulder no paternal burden.) A pair starts out by orbiting one another with increasingly closer circles, communicating receptivity in their circumscribing slimes. Each of them keeps a harpoon-shaped secretion called a love dart in its mucus quiver. The first to land its dart in the other's fleshy mantle has the upper foot (so to speak) and will play the male. Chase thinks the dart's coating suppresses the enzymatic responses of the struck one so that her immune system will not reject what he has to deliver (which he will do for a period lasting up to six or even ten hours). It is possible for snails to mate even if both darts misfire, but a good hit ensures there will be more eggs—a boon for him, burden for her (their carrier). New snails will hatch with their shells tightly wrapped and nearly colorless. The tiny whorls will remain, each like an umbilicus, lifelong at their shells' eyes, or centers. The nascent snail makes its first meal out of the shell it hatches from. Kind of like an ouroboros, but only just the once.

101°

Captive Helen of Troy, near the Island of Tyre, paces the shore, staring seaward. She squints for sails and rigging. The mutt, her companion, returns to her side (his beach-gritted fur, wide eyes baring white crescents, loyalty) crunching, lapping, wrong- and hurt-looking. The snail he punctured on his eyetooth grinds to coquina in his millstones, tiles his tongue, frescoes his lips and gums: a sea green turns crimson, black, and purple.

Thereafter Helen demands of her suitors (their *eyes on stalks, starry*) robes to match the dog's stained muzzle. Phoenicians harvest the color from the predatory sea snail, spiky murex, whose rasp-lined radula bores telltale circles into the shells of its prey—holes through which the murex chemically dissolves and then drinks them. Though the snail's mucus spills milky clear in the Mediterranean, alkali, air, and sunlight cook it into a dark, regal dye. The fadeless dark dye, it is said, of a phoenix tail and blood coagulating. The color is so deep and venous, Homer uses *purple* and *blood* interchangeably, and Nero orders killed those who violate sumptuary laws by donning Tyrian purple undeservingly.

Excess: beaches made of murex slag; snails' coin-shaped opercula, burned as incense; opercula found among wreckage of Phoenician ships alongside ceramic casks (amphorae!—legless, stopper-headed ants balanced emphatically upright, hands on hips, armies) still full of the world's most ancient, unspilled wine. Missing: the soft parts, the stink and the colorful integument.

On display in abandoned dye-works near Lebanon: geologic heaps of spiky murex, ten thousand per toga, three thousand years sibilant. Each whistles through the ghost of a hole carefully tapped (through which, claimed the ancients, the live snail's vein had to be meticulously threaded) the tale of a fallen metropolis so wretched smelling: simmer of discarded stomach feet, *Murex brandaris* fished to near extinction, the ink season waxing like most things—in summer, under Dog Star Sirius.

A Rubens painting portraying the discovery of Tyrian dye shows not Helen but bearded Hercules kneeling, a pouch of arrows on his back. The pup looking up at him holds a snail the size of a dinner plate beneath her paws, her muzzle stained though her mouth is uninjured. Mingling in the caress Hercules gives her—his hand heavy on her spaniel skull—are the first sparks of his epiphany and the last dregs of his concern. Triumph by surf and by starfish.

113°

What makes a snail a snail and not some other kind of shelled mollusk is something cryptic indeed—the larval-stage twisting of its guts. This coiling is distinct from the trademark spiral of its shell. It takes place early in a snail's development, when the visceral mass and mantle undergo a two-stage 180°

counterclockwise torsion relative to its fixed head and foot. The nerve cords pretzel into Forever's figure 8 shape, and the organs on the right side begin to atrophy and disappear.

Torsion helps snails avoid being eaten by allowing them to suck their tentacular heads and undular feet up into their chambers. In some gilled species, escape has been further aided by the development of opercula—calcareous or corneous discs attached to the top of the snails' feet that can be brought to seal, in some cases completely, the shells' apertures.[9]

The primary disadvantage of the counterclockwise torsion of snails is the continual self-fouling of the organism's mouth and other sense organs, as the anus and renal vent have been brought to position directly over the animal's head. (It's like frequent, involuntary, relief-driven, dust mote gazing. It's like the cornball love song of yore, "Smoke Gets in Your Eyes." Or the prelibation toast: *Here's mud in your eye!*) Myriad shell innovations, mostly involving holes, slits, and siphons, evolved to counter this problem.

Asymmetry brings challenges for snails when it comes to mating. Most of their shells coil to the right because the genes that favor that condition are dominant. There are, however, some recessive left-coiling snails. Sinistral / left-coiling snails have difficulty mating with dextral / right-coiling snails because sinistral snails circle clockwise and dextral snails circle anticlockwise and hardly the twain shall meet.[10] This handedness, or chirality, is determined at the third division (way before torsion), when the embryonic snail swells from four to eight cells. After this, exponential division continues by a process called spiral

---

9   The operculum is also the name for the fold in the front of the brain where our capacity for speech, reading, and writing dwell. According to the American Institute of Physics, an examination of Einstein's pickled brain conducted forty-four years postmortem revealed this portion missing from the matter of Albert's peculiarly grasping mind (he was late in learning to speak), shoring up the idea that genius is just a lucky overcorrection.

10  Nature loves diversity. Though not necessarily advantageous at the level of the individual, apparently useless genetic anomalies, such as left-handedness in humans, may actually be beneficial to the species as a whole, a kind of insurance policy guaranteeing that novel bodies are around to confront novel challenges in the event that the dominant plan fails.

cleavage, whereby new cells stack up on the interstices of underlying cells in a clockwise or anticlockwise pattern, resulting in a 128-celled snail blastula that bears uncanny resemblance to a microscopic blackberry.[11]

Asymmetry is a strategy not often employed in nature. Bisect most animals length-wise with a mirror and the reflection will give a pretty good estimate of what's concealed. In the human body plan, left-right differences are pretty well hidden from view.[12] And yet asymmetry gets things done. Taking sides.[13] The cells of our bramble fruit beginnings migrate hither and yon in order to form organs.

Molecular biologists at UC Berkeley have shown that the gene sequence which determines the handedness of snails is the exact same one that determines the direction of offset of our innards; falling most often on the left are our hearts.[14]

Over time, some lines of marine snails unwound their viscera and either overgrew or else completely lost their shells. Without the hard parts and telltale spirals, these creatures don't seem much like snails. On the topic of secondary detorsion, wrote sea slug enthusiast Professor W. D. Gunning, not quite a decade after Darwin's *On the Origin of Species*:

11  At the argument's dust-mote stage, only thought capitulates. Metaphors beget metaphors and pass on their traits.

12  Anatomical treatises made by ancient Greeks (not keen on dissection) are fallacy riddled because their authors assumed human bodies to be as symmetrical on the inside as they are on the skin side.

13  Goodness knows our brains are asymmetric. In most of us the left hemisphere, typically responsible for speech and logic, is physically larger and more developed than the right. Since our brains are cross-wired such that the left hemisphere controls the right side of the body, right-handedness, or dextrality, is the more common condition. Some believe that prior to the evolution of speech, long before sinistrality was deemed sinister, fully half of our ancestors were left-handed. Now only about 10 percent of us are southpaws, a trait that confers an unequivocal edge in hand-to-hand combat and certain one-on-one sports.

14  So, yeah, camouflaged somewhere among us are some recessive types whose livers hunker left and whose hearts and stomachs thump and swell on the right, the latter organs less sinistral but no more correct.

And as the two cycles, progression and retrogression, are involved in the life-history of the earth, so the two movements may go on simultaneously in the same species. Man himself is such a species. His brain, and its servant, the hand, have attained the utmost development. His digestive system and his foot have been modified but little from a primitive type. Progression above in that which is most distinctively human may involve retrogression below in that which is distinctively animal.

Have our brains grown at the expense of our other systems, like volcanic arcs generating new land out of slabs of seafloor they've overridden and melted? Is nature so parsimonious that she exacts a toll for every adaptation? Are we as embattled on the inside as we are with one another, harm driving advancement, advancement harm, the motives of our bodies and minds irreconcilable? In the zoo scene at the end of *The Catcher in the Rye*, the carousel plays an odd version of "Smoke Gets in Your Eyes" as it wheels the children round and round. If its lyrics are to be believed, it's the smoldering of our hearts that blinds us.

144°

The primary advantage of the clockwise detorsion of snails is self-expression— the parapodia that, when waved, have earned the symmetric slugs and hares such names as *angel, butterfly, shawl,* and *dancer,* the riot of colors that evolved for hiding and (in lieu of spiny shells) deterring predators, along with poison and the other evidence of their alchemical heritage: ink, of course, and flight.

146°

Crouching on the pier, I reached as far as I could over the water. My foot balls rocked on the silken wood of the dock. Thigh tops pressed breast buds hard into their sockets. Careful not to fall, careful not to drop the long-handled fishing net I had taken off the wall hook. Careful of my shadow, mindful where to cast it, in case the sea hare's sightless eyes (circadian clocks) should interpret it as nightfall and start the slug's descent. A sister, a salter. A giant streaming monolith peering into the water. A line of sweat, trawling my dust from knee crease to splatter, sent shivers, like a stream head, from Determined to Remember.[15] The trick: to scoop it from behind and under. To center the net and leverage it. Upward, in a rush. Water bursting through the mesh like sunlight through a prism. Hands walking the pole backwards through the cavern of my armpit. Lord, I did not want to feed its parts like caviar or slumgullion to irreverent seabirds. Or stop its two wings flapping like skirts around a legless pubis. Or thwart its lurching progress after its two stalked noses, which never resembled a deft rabbit's ears and which could not cup sound. Not ever. Nor make it flee (its flimsy shell beneath mantle), which it could never either, nor be more of its own name. No. I only wanted to raise the animal high enough to feel its weight along the bowed rod. To grow frightened of its slippery alien form and of what my curiosity had done, and might do still. To make it ink—*leukos* and baffle—so that I could watch the purple swirl and eddy and disappear, like a warning against love. And then restore its mystery to the ocean.

In spite of countless afternoons spent kneeling on the dock scanning the water, I never witnessed the frenzy my grandparents, whose net I daily borrowed, described: the water alive with sea hares. Dozens of them. The animals strung together on a single vanishing cord. Like prayer flags anchored between the firmament and the sea floor. Where did they all come from, and where did they all go? I imagined some gyre conveyed the animals through a crack in the lithosphere. A belt looping through the bedrock and reaching up, invisibly, to give net-wielding huntresses a shove. The topmost hare, the most recent girl to fall in.[16]

15  It turns out that sea hares have a lot to do with memory. In 2000, Eric Kandel won a Nobel Prize for discoveries he made observing neurons in the sea slug *Aplysia californica*. Kandel was the first to actually witness what happens in the brain when learning occurs. Using electroshock, he trained sea slugs to retract their gills when he touched their siphons, and then he watched as the synapses between their sensory and motor neurons developed chemically entrenched connections. Examining a single pair of *Aplysia* neurons, Kandel went on to discover CREB, a molecule found in neuron nuclei, which has the power to engrave permanent memories.

16  Even in the nacre towers of academia, conga lines of randy sea hares are known as *daisy chains*. With all but the one bookend slug making use of their female organs, the quantity of eggs produced is staggering, the aftermath of their bacchanal resembling the scene of a food fight where great vats of linguini have been flung.

163°

Recently a team of researchers reported the results of a decade-long study of snail reproduction. Their findings support the Parasite, or Red Queen, hypothesis for the origin of sex. Sex the verb. Sex the gender. Sex.

If the primary objective of life is to perpetuate itself, cloning would seem the advantageous strategy, since every member of a clonal population can produce offspring. By comparison, sex is a costlier, riskier method. Since nature favors parsimonious solutions, the investigators sought to understand the evolutionary benefits sex confers.

What better way to approach this problem than to look at an animal capable of both styles of reproduction? The scientists observed New Zealand lakes colonized by sexual and asexual varieties of the same snail species. In those habitats where sexual reproduction dominated, the snails were under attack by parasitic worms. But in the habitats where clonal reproduction dominated, there was no such existential threat. This suggests that cloning is the preferred reproductive strategy of snails when life is easy and their number one goal can be, simply, to make more of themselves. Under immunological duress, however, everything changes and sexual reproduction becomes the winning MO. Though more of a hassle, sex confers the genetic variability that evolution needs in order to continually MacGyver new defense mechanisms. Clones simply do not have as much in their molecular toolbox to fight the parasites with. If one clone falls, they all do.

As the sexually reproducing snails mutate and evolve, survivors begetting survivors and so on, so too do their parasites mutate and evolve. Prey and predator lock like spinning cogs into an ever-escalating, never-ending arms race. Sex and battle are inextricably linked and mating is a defense mechanism. It is as the Red Queen says to the panting Alice: *It takes all the running you can do to keep in the same place.*

172°

Bedding my circling am I dog a like how is this        ?

173°

Notes on human sex and temporal asymmetries: in 2007 a trio of Italian sci-entists compared women's color vision at three points along their menstrual cycle and found that they were better at discerning color around the time of ovulation. The researchers suggest this may have more to do with rhythmic variations in creativity and attention span than any kind of heightened visual acuity. On the whole the women were unaware of their heightened awareness. Similar studies have produced similar results with respect to olfaction.

In 2004 a paper reviewed how women's views of other women vary over a lunar month. Investigator M. L. Fisher found that women in estrus rated photographs of other women as less attractive than they did at other times of their cycle. This may be because women are a bit fuller of themselves when they are fertile, perceiving themselves as better looking than normal. And why shouldn't they be a little high and blinded and maybe a tad more com-petitive when what's reflected is (this gleaned from a handful of studies): the soft tissues of their breasts and faces rearranged so that both are at their most symmetric, the tides of their color and lips and voices all subtly risen, their waist to hip ratios at their lunar lowest, skin at its lunar smoothest, eyes at their lunar darkest (pupils dilated) and therefore most flirtatious, their gaits also somewhat amped?

Wrote Gunning, *Even the heart moves askance.*

Three—Ink and Flight

180°

What estrual college girl hasn't cut class to stand in the clicking marble hall and gaze up at El Greco's Magdalene, not caring who the maiden is meant to be or getting the point of penitence anyway (the twin arms of the relative humidity recorder giving stale testimony on the floor below, telling it straight, in a continuous unending cord: time is not cyclic like our clocks convince us), and fancy to herself that they share the same wet over-big eyes (if not golden curls) and long fingers (if not other shadow-cast proportions) and jagged moon-rent clouds overhead (if invisible to most), misinterpreted longing, indigo shift, skull for companion, the portraitist's subject—

170°

17

169°

—looking up so that there are whole crescents (whole crescents!) of tear-bulged moon reflected in Magdalene's big, over-dark eyes, and wonder, will they overflow when she looks away (the tension finally broken) or drain out through the puncta in her perforate lower lids, down through the nostrils of her alabaster nose, to gather salty in her downy philtrum (*philtron*: to love, to kiss) from which some tiny sacred obelisk was just seconds ago plucked (they say that your philtrum is the indent God's finger made when he shushed you against telling his secrets, but I can tell from its shape that something was stolen from that divot) and then spill over and onto her lips, the very color the ancients coveted—

158°

18

157°

—and fancy to herself that the pale museum guard, black tied and burgundy vested, stock-still, (or is that a Segal sculpture? even better) is terribly in love with her, suffers a kind of *rigor amorous* mistaken for stoicism, professionalism, allegiance to art, its inviolability (no touching!), a joke—

17  *When a finger points to the moon, the imbecile looks at the finger.*

18  *That which staineth red is nothing so rich as that which giveth the deepe and sad black-ish colour.*

153°

19

152°

—and then, like, Io, walk away, both tickled and convinced?

151°

20

146°

*Estrus* hales from the Latin *oestrus* for *frenzy*, or *gadfly*. As dogged Io and bit Pegasus. (Bellerophon was blinded by the thorns of the *rubus* bush after shearing away from bucking fly-stung Pegasus, after the pair stupidly attempted Mount Olympus.)

143°

21

140°

Since our nearest genetic neighbors still advertise their heat by purpling up their asses, scientists have long questioned why we humans hide our estrus.

19  *Sight is a species of touching.*

20  *The moon got loose last night, and slid down and fell out of the scheme—a very great loss; it breaks my heart to think of it. There isn't another thing among the ornaments and decorations that is comparable to it for beauty and finish. It should have been fastened better. If we can only get it back again.*

21  *All the kids kept trying to grab for the gold ring, and so was old Phoebe, and I was sort of afraid she'd fall off the goddam horse, but I didn't say anything or do anything.*

Possible advantages of concealed fertility are manifold and may have led to the emergence of (still questionable) hominid monogamy. They include: reduction of competition in males / more cooperative group dynamic, enhanced paternal behavior, stability of maternal diet (supplied by hopeful male), and reduced infanticide due to rival patronage.

133°

22

131°

Recent studies suggest that outward signs of human estrus have not really been lost but instead become exceedingly subtle, so that even we are unaware of the ways in which we pick up invitations and put them (scented, folded, furtive, art guard . . .) down.

127°

23

126°

(. . . footnote, greenback, down low . . .)

One investigator had a distinct leg up (pardon slutty double entendre) when it came to detecting estrus: he paid his way through college by managing a strip club and noticed the inverse correlation between tips reported and tampons retrieved. Dancers earned about $75 more per five-hour shift when they were

22  *But of course there is no telling where it went to. And besides, whoever gets it will hide it; I know it because I would do it myself.*

23  *Ovulatory Cycle Effects on Tip Earnings by Lap Dancers: Economic Evidence for Human Estrus?*

in estrus rather than in the luteal (postovulation) phase, and about \$150 more than when the women were menstruating.

118°

24

114°

Overall, women on the pill made less than those cycling naturally and displayed no mid-cycle peak.

112°

25

108°

Another possible advantage of concealed estrus is that it facilitates cuckoldry. There is less mate-guarding by males in species whose females do not advertise their fertility (in humans, a man's piqued jealousy may be a good proxy for his partner's stealthy estrus); a female who finds a genetically more desirable sire may pursue him without too much interference from her bonded provider. Other studies suggest that males combat this physiological subterfuge with the special brew of their seminal fluid; the non-sperm part contains hormones that promote ovulation, aid ovum implantation, and help maintain pregnancy. Members of the opposite sex are like snails and worms locked in a coevolutionary

---

24  *Doe they but see themselves in a looking glasse, the cleare brightnesse therof turneth into dimnesse, upon their very sight. Look they upon a sword, knife, or any edged toole, be it never so bright, it waxeth duskish, so doth also the lively hue of yvorie. The very bees in the hive die.*

25  *I could give up a moon that I found in the daytime, because I should be afraid some one was looking; but if I found it in the dark, I am sure I should find some kind of an excuse for not saying anything about it.*

arms race, males continually adapting to detect estrus, females continually adapting to hide it. Some researchers argue that women have evolved a blind eye to their own estrus (only 60% of them guessing correctly, in spite of a 50:50 chance of getting it right, in one study) simply because having babies is as painful as rearing them is hard, and no early hominid would ever knowingly repeat those experiences. Allowing the mind this kind of shush power over her urges—well, that's a maladaptive brand of wisdom, a danger to her own species. Or? Wait a minute.

90.4°

26

Four—The Stink and the Colorful Integument

90°

Dear Peacock,

When I sliced the blackberry, one of the drupelets (looking more red than raven) stuck to my cutlery in just the right place (toward tip, over teeth) to make my knife look like an angry-eyed shark, with the perfectly funny menace of a child's drawing, tearing into my waffle, both gill- and fin-less. I didn't show you this because it was how, in the middle of our fighting, I was getting even.

All the best,
Sweetheart

85°

Here is the argument the *progressed* brain makes against the *retrogressed* gut-foot.
Our infradian rhythms are at odds with the species: too short—a lunar month, the same rate neurons replace in the spectacularly receptive nose.

26 Syrinx, baby, is that you?

Microsaccades are some of our muscles' fastest rhythms. If they were sound waves, we could hear them, but barely: the microscopic oscillations of our eyes sweeping constantly back and forth, our gazes fixed. Thirty a second, seventy. These are hertz to refresh the luminance, to hold the picture, to do so boldly, staring. It takes all the racing you can do to stay in the same place.

Know my pitch by now.

$$78°$$

Tyre's purple trade was abandoned by Turkish conquerors who favored royal red and fertile green to Helen's murex. The snail's color was supplanted by carmine of the Incas' and Aztecs' crushed scale insect (cactus lovers, those). Sets of scales (the balancing kind, not cochineal) and hanks of yarn are carved into the gravestones of former dye merchants called *purpurarii*. Lean in for lost recipe—

The three shades we painted the bedroom when we conceived our last
   king, all of them chipping: *Amethyst, Thistle, Wisteria*.
Lilac: as it flowered this morning.
Breakfast: as we ate it.
Neko Case's *Middle Cyclone* album playing like an ouroboros: on repeat
   in the kitchen.
Disloyal: the circuitous scent of violets, like Josephine, teasing.
*Ultra*-violets: the privilege of birds, bees, Monet, and mantis shrimp.
Heliotrope: the hue of Victorians half-mourning.
Mauve: the mallow of Linnaeus's floral clock.
Murex: the foils of Cleopatra sailing.
Plum: the color of a newborn's marrow, blooming in spicular circadian
   locks, throughout his entire skeleton.
*Puerpera*: the Latin word for a woman birthing.
Purple: our crepuscular starts and stop,[27]

---

27  *He was looking under the hood of Henry's brain, and how beautiful it was beneath the
    cortical coral reef, in the brain's interior capsules, where pyramidal cells are shaped like
    hyacinth, in complex cones, where neurons are tiny but dense.*

What beats in the best of us, the wounded, our love dubs.

Moment: the overlay of all of these frequencies:

A maiden, a mother, a crone.


Method: Know my pitch by now. Know everything violet-scenting and color-sounding in me by now. Hear everything light-driven and night-fasted in me now—rods, cones, caverns of nose, loins, ears, belly—begging dumbly against its own blindness: *refresh yourself, re-*

59°


Some researchers argue the climate of the African savannah was conducive to advertising hominid estrus via smell; the purple anogenital puffery displayed by members of our cousin genus, *Pan*, was simply misspent energy for us sapiens.

56°


Other *rubus*-stains: aureoles and the line that quickens below an umbilicus, for our babies whose eyes are born color blind and color ambiguous—like a map. Or directions.[28]

47°


When our first king in the middle of the night came: after three hours of floating beneath the pier, looking up from the shaggy green side, between the salt-pickled boards through to the UV-bright side, and waiting, he came. A

---

28  A writer worth her salt does not mix metaphors. She is mindful of her tenses. Respects the bounds of her reader's patience, his desire for clarity and through it, connection. Words and not analogues offer the proper scale for multivalence. Synapses fire in four dimensions. Guitars propagate in three (not counting whatever sound is). But paper confines us to two. If thought is a wave that piles its foam against the unscratchable side of your skin, what undertow pulls the eyes up and back? What do major histocompatibility complexes smell like when you turn up the volume? What architecture do they make when you paint them by the number? Begin.

gentle lapping, a quiet wake of tides and boats, rocked me left to right where I was hiding, when he came. Body, a meniscus: splinters under my nails, my toes bracing. My silver glanced back, scale-glanced, eyes came, lifted back. And then this news from the TV at the nurse's station: a shiver of sharks with fins shredding to ribbons the half moon on some (tourist destination) bay. Soup. Dozens and dozens of them, the autumn so warm, the water so, between my legs, sheets. Came our king at 1:23 a.m. on a Monday, soaked of my own and stork bitten (a strawberry, no, rasp). Salts and silt and plankton rang high in the coils of our ears and noses. Their cilia like sea grasses. A celebration. To change the luminance. To hold the scene. By surf and by pulley.

35°

*Look up, speak nicely, and don't twiddle your fingers all of the time,* said the Red Queen to Alice.

Barren Josephine with two children of her own said this nicer at her divorce ceremony than I did in regard to your potential future spouse(s) at breakfast:

> With the permission of our august and dear husband, I must declare that, having no hope of bearing children who would fulfill the needs of his [substitute applicable nouns here], I am pleased to offer him the greatest proof of attachment and devotion ever offered on this earth.

Now I sometimes wonder what became of the violet petals Napoleon kept in his remembrance locket. He culled them from Josephine's garden after she died and his second wife had provided the requisite heir. And I wonder to what end (every trick has one) is the ebb and flow of that particular scent?[29] You liked how the cuckold begged Josephine not to bathe the fortnight he was away battling. Repeated it. Did you know he also threatened to cover her *with a million hot kisses, burning like the equator,* and sent her, *a kiss on your heart and one much lower down, much lower!*

---

29 *Short-term memories, perhaps, are a little like crushes, with a single surge of chemistry that fades fast; long-term memories are more like marriages, bound together, even trapped together, so you cannot get a new point of view.*

Did you hear that Italian physicists found forty times the modern ambient level of arsenic in saved hanks of his hair? Researchers suspect its provenance is wallpaper dye. Freed from copper by primordial microbes, the poisonous element atomized and was beguiled by him. Incorporated: shared his incarceration island and the stomach cancer that ate in him. On the verdant volcano of his exile. The walls' color over time turning black, née green, from the moisture and fungi that grew on them. Née emerald, not absinthe. Not jealous, this green. No rasp of corundum, cochineal, or fox in between. Unlike the preparation of Tyrian dye and the ripening of blackberries, there was no red intermediate for the wallpaper dye that poisoned Napoleon, and no maternity for his beloved Josephine.

Before breakfast, a cat-sized, cat-legged crow alighted on the top branch of the denuded tree across the street and stayed there, rocking against the sky like a ticking metronome, its plumage blown against the grain. I found something (a folded paper, ivory arm, alabaster obelisk) wet in the laundry, that fell from your pocket.

$7°$

Dear Peacock,

I hate the way you look at the odalisque. That hyper-vertebral freak. I can't stand the way you lap at her thigh, never fucking blinking. A mated bird with a clutch all his own! So grow up or show some decorum whichever I don't care screw it. P.S. I'm thinking of taking a maid and probably also a little black cat (whom I will permit to prance back-arc'd and butt-up all along my new single bed, my slingback shoe on white sheets, slick, slick), even though you're allergic. P.P.S. That ligature mark is healing just fine.

Well and anyway, see you at breakfast.
Olympia (née Venus)

$0°$

## Coda

What if the evolution of a breakfast argument essayed itself turbinate instead of torted? What if its turning was more like the snail's shell than the hare's innards (an eye to the front and an eye to the rear)? Would we start at the spiral's eye together and work our way counterclockwise? Against time, but in the manner of the animal's growth (assuming a dextral, right-coiling snail)? Or would we be wiser to begin at the operculum, the little shut door, and wind our way as the clock turns, like a pair of adventuring pupillae, toward the snail's umbilicus? Nodding to the ridiculousness of scale along the way, gesturing at, without really attempting—accuracy? Letting the tightness of the spiral substitute for the closeness of our focus, choosing some largish species to embody the process, one that fits with nice heft in the holds of our hands—Moon Snail, Shark Eye—like this, in some arbitrary number of revolutions:

Operculum: the condensation of the solar system from its spinning nebula, her arms logarithmically wheeling. Shortly beyond the little lid, where the shell swells and flares a bit (a sign of snail's maturity), would be the accretion of Earth from Sun's leftover matter. And the collision that won Earth its moon.

Now wind far and slowly along that outer coil—a billion years' worth of meteors, heat, and mineral stuttering (asphyxiating consonants).

Then, little protocontinents form and begin shedding their dirt. Volcanoes belch out an atmosphere. UV hones it.

Then comes that particular miracle of primordial soup, electricity, hydrothermal vents, sea ice, and/or maybe clay minerals (who knows) heralding amino acids, proteins, and then bacteria. Photosynthetic stromatolites banded and humped as Van Gogh's *Starry Night* release oxygen from single cells for nearly three billion years.

Then an ocean quickens with big squish beings (clusters of vowels here teeming and fleeing). A supercontinent breaks up for the first time.

A couple hundred million years later sees the advent of hard parts, the rudiments of skeletons. Already a second mass extinction. And soon afterward, gastropods slink along that soft and silted floor (some good, hard words between meaningful spaces—onomatopoeic). The grazing of herbivorous snails nearly eradicates the stromatolites. Carnivorous snails bore holes in the shells of the altogether more successful brachiopods in the *stomach feet* vs. *arm feet* battle.

Close on this arc (one hundred million years or so of rhyming phrases later), find the first land plants and terrestrial animals.

Go two times this length again, past the greatest mass extinction so far, and greet our first birds, mammals, flowering plants, dinosaurs, future peafoul, and blackberry (sentences).

Go one increment more and rest on bipedal hominids. By now continents have many times cleaved and re-accreted. Oceans and ice expanded and retreated. Most of the planet's species arisen and receded. Leaving *Australopithecus* Lucy still an unknowable infinity. See her foot prints in rain-soaked ash, turned to stone. Then come bigger brains from bigger bodies. One-and-a-half million years young is Turkana Boy, *Homo erectus*, whose hunger for meat drives species dispersal: worldwide. Sense the chill of an epoch characterized by glaciation. The heat of *Homo sapiens*.

Artifice. (Read here paragraphs full of sentences all beginning with the letter *I*, vainglorious.) Dexterity. Hold in your palm the precious naked chicken pendant. Spared against the odds. Like humans in some ways. Somewhere before here, know the spark of abstract thinking. Consciousness. Metaphors as defense mechanisms.

Human, now I know your name, you're all I can think of.

Culture debuted as a sex strike. Or so anthropologist Chris Knight posits. Babies with human-sized neocortices need a long time and a lot of food to reach maturity. In order to sustain this big brain aberration, Pleistocene fathers had to be involved in securing provisions. To induce paternal care, females may have traded sex for meat in a somewhat conspiratorial manner, creating an arrangement that favors monogamy and ostracizes (at least among the women) the philanderers.

Did biology beget culture or the opposite? Surely it is no accident that human estrus sneaks while menstruation announces. Bleeding is easy to fake with rust colored ochres (our earliest paints and make-up) but hard to hide (remember the strip club manager) and nearly always augurs fertility. Add to those things the tendency of co-dwelling women to co-ovulate, and you get the basis for a female solidarity. In the time of red, men go out hunting. When they come back with meat, everyone is happy. In his book, *Blood Relations: Menstruation and the Origins of Culture*, Knight suggests the hundred or so found Venus figurines were used during menstrual rites, the missing heads and feet symbolic of women's monthly seclusion. Because they are geographically widespread, but stylistically uniform, the Venus pendants may have been worn to convey a membership in the Ice Age mating game, like a badge that says *Marriage spoken here.*

From here on, hear singing.

Clustered at our snail's center, as if on a pinhead, are Helen, Hercules, Hermes, and Nero. Everything convolving. The Plinys. The ejecta of Vesuvius bombing the stunned Elder. The Phoenicians who brought peacocks to Egypt, thinking its flesh too tough to be edible (and then changing their minds). The Greeks who gave Cupid his arrow. The *purpurarii* who boiled Tyre's coveted purple. Now cochineal. Now Rubens. Now Venetian *bella donnas*, their eyes artificially dilated in the time of El Greco.[30] Now Scheele's green of poisonous wallpaper. Now Napoleon and Josephine and the unearthing of *Bellerophon*, the oldest fossil snail, little curlicue sleeper. Its shell is plani-spiral, but without its guts (soft parts don't keep), paleontologists can't agree on whether the extinct *Bellerophon*'s viscera were torted or not torted. Now Ingre's sinuous-spined Odalisque commissioned by Napoleon's sister. Now Samuel Langhorne Clemens and the book he wrote to eulogize his bride, Olivia. (Eve: *Stars are good, too. I wish I could get some to put in my hair . . . .*) Now Manet's irreverent Olympia

---

30  Symptoms of *belladonna*/atropine poisoning include: increased heart rate; double vision; elevated body temperature, but cessation of sweating; muscle contractions akin to hypnic jerk (the one that jarred you when you were just nearly asleep, eyes not yet rolling, but sensory-steeped—sorry for that) with quivers potentially rhythmic; visual snow; delirium; increased intraocular pressure; persistent pupil dilation; blindness (not love); death (not paralysis). It's thought that Nero's mother used the purple-black berries of belladonna (Naughty Man's Cherries, Devil's Apples) to poison her son's stepfather, Claudius, so that Nero could succeed him, or *wear the purple.* Also, *belladonna* extract was used in the early twentieth century to make Twilight Sleep, an amnestic administered to women in childbirth, who awoke then with no recollection of laboring and, in a way, no proof. Belladonna's green fruits ripen to black (no red in between) in autumn. Its seeds are dispersed by frugivorous animals (heifers and hares) tolerant to its toxins. It is the source of medicinal atropine, such as was administered to dogs who sampled dead sea hares on the beach following a mass slug mortality event along the coast of Australia. Dogs die dogs' deaths anyway.

(her maid, cat, brazen on-looking intimacy). Next the extinction of the tattooed Karankawa (dog-lover) Indians whose discarded shells were buried by the sand of that barrier island I padded with net in hand in southern Texas, long before there came sex-driven spring breakers. Skip to the scrapes of masonry trowels for the construction of the museums and schools we were licked in. (Pliny: *Foxes produce young that are unfinished at birth, and shape them by licking them.*) To J. D. Salinger and Holden Caulfield. (*The thing with kids is,* muses Caulfield, the carousel going round and round, *if they want to grab for the gold ring, you have to let them do it, and not say anything.*) Now hear our parents, their voices soft and susurrant. We can never make them out when they talk about us. Now—some states and some years in between—us. Now my burning fever, spurned pirate patch, and Texas. And estrus. Gadflies, cow eyes. Our introduction like continent reaccretion. Now I'm the apple of my own eye at the Nelson-Atkins museum where I laughed at 2-D nudity as a child, and learned from the scolding I got that sex, hags, and angels are real and deadly serious. Soon I'm the apple of your eye, William Tell. Soon New Mexican lap dancers.

What scientists call the Sixth Extinction—the current one—is probably the fastest one ever. Here, at last, is the falling-out behind our falling-out, the only one I can argue really matters. Will our complex culture continue to screw or once again save us?

Now a diagnosis (one of many) for one of us: the cornea horns, or *keratoconus,* devolving sight into visions of multiples. (Reverse your course to gadflies along the cornucopia's print-like ridges). Swooning *polyopia.* The multiples will waltz in time to the sufferer's heartbeat, the pulse of biology's sick sense of humor.

Now we, married, argue at breakfast. The unknowable eye of the spiral.

Now know your own organism (remember that *Scientific American* article?). It was found in sharks a long time ago, but because Nerve Number Zero shears off with the scalp in autopsies, it was slow to be claimed by humans. NNZ slides up from your nose and taps your two eyeballs, then slinks into your brain and controls (maybe) whom you love and when and how often (that bouquet, the day's length, the moon and its constant pulling), the seasons and sun's rhythms entrained inextricably therein, same as in every other species, secreting love like darts and dizzy *spira mirabilis.* The tireless licking of mother foxes.

So no, this essay is more like the blackberry in the mouth where the drupelets messy pop and mingle. Or escargot (the snails several days fasted and
then fed flour). Or the diagenetically altered shell of something self-fouling,
left like the ones found in the Karankawan middens—evidence for how we
hungered and what we ate. That's all. The only way I know to make sense—
with teeth and eyes and breath and music. Opercula, benders, and excuses.
If sight is a species of touching, so too is this. Come on out now, out of that
dark frame. Baby doll backwards and on home. All Big Banged up and back
where you belong.

## QUOTED WORKS

0°

Maor, Eli. *To Infinity and Beyond: A Cultural History of the Infinite*. Princeton: Princeton
    University Press, 1991.

FOOTNOTE 2

Yoshimoto, Midori. *Into Performance: Japanese Women Artists in New York*. New Bruns-
    wick NJ: Rutgers University Press, 2005.

FOOTNOTE 4

Doyle, Jennifer. *Sex Objects: Art and the Dialectics of Desire*. Minneapolis: University of
    Minnesota Press, 2006.

FOOTNOTE 5

Lee, Pamela M. *Chronophobia: On Time in the Art of the 1960s*. Cambridge: MIT Press,
    2004.

53°

Smellie, William, and John Ware. *The Philosophy of Natural History*. Boston: Brown and
    Taggard, 1860.

FOOTNOTE 7

Descharnes, Robert, and Gilles Neret. *Dalí*. Köln: Taschen, 1998.

FOOTNOTE 8

Grosz, Elizabeth. *Volatile Bodies: Toward a Corporeal Feminism*. Bloomington: Indiana
    University Press, 1994.

113°

Gunning, W. D. "Progression and Retrogression." *The Popular Science Monthly* 8 (1876):
    180–91.

163°

Carroll, Lewis. *Alice's Adventures in Wonderland; and, Through the Looking Glass*. Boston: Lothrop, 1898.

173°

Gunning, W. D. "Progression and Retrogression." *The Popular Science Monthly* 8 (1876): 180–91.

FOOTNOTE 17

Chinese proverb.

FOOTNOTE 18

C. Plinius Secundus. *The Historie of the World, the Ninth Book*. Translated by Philemon Holland. London, 1601.

FOOTNOTE 19

Comte de Buffon. *Histoire Naturelle*. Translated by William Smellie. London, 1781.

FOOTNOTE 20

Twain, Mark. *Eve's Diary*. London: Harper and Brothers, 1906.

FOOTNOTE 21

Salinger, J. D. *The Catcher in the Rye*. New York: Little, Brown, 1945.

FOOTNOTE 22

Twain, Mark. *Eve's Diary*. London: Harper and Brothers, 1906.

FOOTNOTE 23

Miller et al. "Ovulatory Cycle Effects on Tip Earnings by Lap Dancers: Economic Evidence for Human Estrus?" *Evolution and Human Behavior* 28 (2007): 375–81.

FOOTNOTE 24

C. Plinius Secundus. *The Historie of the World, the Seventh Book*. Translated by Philemon Holland. London, 1601.

FOOTNOTE 25

Twain, Mark. *Eve's Diary*. London: Harper and Brothers, 1906.

FOOTNOTE 27

Slater, Lauren. *Opening Skinner's Box: Great Psychological Experiments of the Twentieth Century*. New York: Norton, 2004.

35°

Carroll, Lewis. *Alice's Adventures in Wonderland; and, Through the Looking Glass*. Boston: Lothrop, 1898.

PBS. *Napoleon*. http://www.pbs.org/empires/napoleon/n_josephine/crisis/page_1.html. Accessed July 9, 2017.

PBS. *Napoleon*. http://www.pbs.org/empires/napoleon/n_josephine/emperor/page_1. html. Accessed July 9, 2017.

FOOTNOTE 29

Slater, Lauren. *Opening Skinner's Box: Great Psychological Experiments of the Twentieth Century*. New York: Norton, 2004.

CODA

Twain, Mark. *Eve's Diary*. London: Harper and Brothers, 1906.

C. Plinius Secundus. *The Historie of the World, the Tenth Book*. Translated by Philemon Holland. London: Adam Islip, 1601.

Salinger, J. D. *The Catcher in the Rye*. New York: Little, Brown, 1945.


OTHER CONSULTED WORKS

Barber, Nigel. "Are Fertile Women More Attractive?" *The Human Beast, Psychology Today*. Last modified July 7, 2009. https://www.psychologytoday.com/blog/the-human-beast/200907/are-fertile-women-more-attractive.

Boyko, Ryan H., and Andrew J. Marshall. "The Willing Cuckold: Optimal Paternity Allocation, Infanticide, and Male Reproductive Strategies in Mammals." *Animal Behavior* 77, no. 6 (2009): 1397–407.

Cartlidge, Edwin. "Napoleon Not Murdered, Say Physicists." *Physicsworld.com*. Last modified February 14, 2008. http://physicsworld.com/cws/article/news/2008/feb/14/napoleon-not-murdered-say-physicists.

The Center for History of Physics. "Was Einstein's Brain Different?" http://history.aip.org/exhibits/einstein/einbrain.htm. Accessed July 9, 2017.

Conard, Nicholas J. "A Female Figurine from the Basal Aurignacian of Hohle Fels Cave in Southwestern Germany." *Nature* 459 (2009): 248–52.

Fessler, Daniel M. T. "No Time to Eat: An Adaptationist Account of Periovulatory Changes." *The Quarterly Review of Biology* 78, no.1 (2003): 3–21.

Fields, Douglas R. "Sex and the Secret Nerve." *Scientific American Mind* (Feb/March 2007): 21–27.

Fisher, Maryanne L. "Female Intrasexual Competition Decreases Female Facial Attractiveness." *Proceedings of the Royal Society of London, Biological Sciences (Suppl.)* 271 (2004): s283–s285.

Ghosh, Pallab. "'Oldest Musical Instrument' Found." *BBC News, Science and Environment*. Last modified June 25, 2009. http://news.bbc.co.uk/2/hi/science/nature/8117915.stm.

Giuffre, Giuseppe et al. "Changes in Colour Discrimination during the Menstrual Cycle." *Opthalmologica* 2212, no. 1 (2007): 47–50.

The Institute of Human Origins. www.becominghuman.org.

King, K. C. et al. "The Geographic Mosaic of Sex and the Red Queen," *Current Biology* 19, no. 17 (2009): 1438–41.

Knight, Chris. *Blood Relations: Menstruation and the Origin of Culture.* New Haven CT: Yale University Press, 1995.

Motluk, Alison. "The Secret Life of Semen." *New Scientist.* Last modified August 2, 2006. https://www.newscientist.com/article/mg19125633-500-the-secret-life-of-semen/.

Myers, P. Z. "Spiral Cleavage." *ScienceBlogs, Pharyngula.* Last modified April 6, 2006. http://scienceblogs.com/pharyngula/2006/04/06/spiral-cleavage/.

Pawlowski, Boguslaw. "Loss of Oestrus and Concealed Ovulation in Human Evolution." *Current Anthropology* 40, no. 3 (1999) 257–75.

Popple, Ian. "Are Snails' 'Love Darts' Source of Cupid Lore?" *National Geographic News.* Last modified February 13, 2002. http://news.nationalgeographic.com/news/2002/02/0213_020213_wiresnail.html.

"Prehistoric Pin-up." *Nature.com.* http://www.nature.com/nature/videoarchive/prehistoricpinup/index.html.

Roberts, S. C. et al. "Female Facial Attractiveness Increases during the Fertile Phase of the Menstrual Cycle." *Proceedings of the Royal Society, Biological Sciences (Suppl.)* 271 (2004): s270-s272.

Scott, Philippa. "Millenia of Murex." *Saudia Aramco World* 57, no. 4 (July/August 2006).

Skloot, Rebecca. "Lap-Dance Science." *New York Times Magazine.* Last modified December 9, 2007. http://www.nytimes.com/2007/12/09/magazine/09lapdance.html.

Thornhill, Randy, and Steven W. Gangestad. *The Evolutionary Biology of Human Female Sexuality.* New York: Oxford University Press, 2008.

Thornhill, Randy et al. "Major Histocompatibility Complex Genes, Symmetry, and Body Scent Attractiveness in Men and Women." *Behavioral Ecology* 14, no. 5 (2003): 668–78.

University of California–Berkeley. "Snails and Humans Use Same Genes to Tell Right from Left." *ScienceDaily.* Last modified December 22, 2008. https://www.sciencedaily.com/releases/2008/12/081221210157.htm.

University of Chicago Press Journals. "Female Mammals Follow Their Noses to the Right Mates." *ScienceDaily.* Last modified March 20, 2009. https://www.sciencedaily.com/releases/2009/03/090317153045.htm.

# Postscript

## Forms on the Page

CHEYENNE NIMES

Finder's fee agreement

Int'l shark attack file

Game show transcript

Standardized test

Ticker tape transcript (from TV news)

Rabbinical court ruling

Weed height ordinance

NUFORC (National UFO Reporting Center) report form

Old hotel register

Do-it-yourself exorcism guide

Green card application

Mortuary calendar

Parenthetical remarks

Wanted poster

Hells Angels' code

TV guide

Library overdue notice

Barnum's Animals Crackers

Sundial increments

Road signs across I-80 (rewritten)

Town names explained

Order authorizing wiretap

Genealogy chart

Unassigned genera

Petition to declare a death in absentia

Casino records

Bookies' burn book

Parole officer report

Legal name-change petition

Credit card holder agreement form

Missed connection ad

Bird migration paths charted across globe

Air force command to drop a bomb (World War II or other war)

Joseph Smith's golden plates (rewritten)

Tornado chaser live report

*Consumer Reports* comparison chart

Victim impact statement

Tombstone engravings

Werewolf sightings from Germany, Russia, United States, and France in the 1500s, et cetera

Blueprint of separate parts in a Boeing

Solar/lunar eclipse historical chart

Wild animal tracking

Message in a bottle

Overtime time card

Airport short-term parking announcements

Drawn crime scene dimensions report

Crime scene photo captions

CIA intelligence report

Casualty list

Presidential State of the Union address

Death investigator's handbook

Venn diagram

Chart of the human body

Dissection and autopsy instructions

Anatomy Act of 1832 to stop body snatching

Witness protection and relocation guidelines

Toast to someone or something, as for a wedding or a revolution

Shaman's spell

Codes of conduct

School charter

Playlist

Packing list

Moving list

Photo lineup (with captions)

Recitation of the facts

Criminal sentencing

Motion to dismiss

Charge of depraved indifference

Justification defense

Laws of evidence

Strand of DNA

Ideological line edits

SNAP application

___ by numbers (paint, et cetera)

Natural history museum display captions

List of evidence

Legal motion

Ruling on the admissibility of evidence

Grocery store coupons

Requiem

Ruins of ancient civilization (plaques)

Teamsters' papers

List of things, acts, et cetera, forbidden by international law

War resolution/declaration

Diorama of crime scene

Wound ballistics

Vodou spell

Pledge of allegiance to a flag

Form 1–765, Application for Employment Authorization

Heisenberg's uncertainty principle (rewritten)

Lengthy kibitz

Legal and criminal idioms

Federal, state, and local statutes,
  rules and regulations subject to
  change and open to different
  interpretations

Colloquy

Denunciation

Disquisition

Recantation

Incantation

Quarantine order for animals,
  humans, plants, et cetera

Boarding pass/Amtrak ticket, et
  cetera

Eviction notice

Renter's insurance (itemization)

Palm reading

Day's Inn at Roswell guest book

Constitution

Amendments

Celebrity press conference

Blood oath

Folk wisdom sayings

Capgras delusion psychiatric report

Dramatis personae list

Document of joint understanding

Inscription

Eulogy

Homage

Lament

Roast

Tall tale

Sermon

Joke

Warrant for arrest

Census records

Missing animal flyer

Nondisclosure form

Disclosure form

Serial killer correspondence (to
  newspapers, admirers, et cetera)

Casino house rules

Letters to business establishments (à
  la Joe Wenderoth)

Apocrypha of ____

Table of elements

Cockatiel's running vocabulary

Evacuation order

List of exculpatory evidence

List of exculpatory evidence that's
  been suppressed

Hare Psychopathy Checklist
  (rewritten)

Baby blanket knitting pattern

Cruise ship itinerary

Betty Crocker cake directions

National Weather Service rogue wave
  warning

End of the trail plaque

1960s *Life* magazine article

*New York Times* corrections
  disclaimer

Singer sewing machine pattern
  directions

Morning radio traffic report

Erratum

Postscript

Datum

Honor roll

Doctrine

Chain of evidence report

Articles of faith

Land title

Diminished capacity defense

Dying declaration

Pathology report

Witch hunt trial transcript

Timeline

Interrogation account

Investigative report

Guilty verdict (with counts)

Minutes of the ship's mast

Faculty meeting minutes

Probable cause document

Gaussian distribution

MIA report

Cold case file

Six reports done on a discovered
    corpse (toxicology, pathology,
    entomology, anthropology, geol-
    ogy, odontology)

OSHA occupational hazards list

Death warrant

Coroner report

Child custody clause

Inventory

Tour

Rant

How-to guide

Ellis Island intake forms of names
    and changed names

Playbook

*Farmer's Almanac* entries

Narrated chase scene

Talk show host monologue

Utility shut-off notice

Notice to quit premises

Crime classification manual

Hangman game

Stillborn birth paperwork

How to disappear checklist/guide

Bermuda Triangle missing ship
    report

"Ask your doctor about" ad

Secretive orders of enlightened
    mystics

Law enforcement roadblock order

Sidewalk chalk writing in various
    cities and suburbs and cowtown
    areas and deep remote *Deliverance*
    places

Running joke

New Year's resolution

Esoterica

Continua

Pharmaceutical package insert

Opening credits of a disaster movie

Allegorical narrative of _____

Sightings of the Loch Ness monster
    dating back centuries

Show tune

Directions through a subterranean
    passage

Holiday greeting card sayings

Birth announcement

Notations on the backs of photographs from a bad childhood
Invitation to a shower
Fortune cookie sayings
Miranda rights reading (rewritten)
Slave ship manifest/log of voyage
Paths of migration for various animals (e.g. Giant Sea Turtle)
Public domain footage out of old archives
Elementary school recess rules
*Girl Scout Handbook*
Wilderness survival guide
Propaganda leaflet
Prehistoric cave paintings decoding
Summary of the summaries of the summaries
Epilogue to the epilogue to the epilogue
Psychiatrist's pre-sentencing report
Call and response
Monopoly game instructions (rewritten)
Gossip column
Algebraic notation of chess moves
Bicycle repair book
Coroner's inquest
Tax code and exemptions/write-offs
Blackmail letter
Black Hand letter
Forged document
Waiver of Miranda rights
Horoscope
Yoga sequence

Redacted black bars in a document
Translation of a translation
Phone book
Do-it-yourself hair dye instructions
Funeral card
Subpoena duces tecum
Copyright holder release
List of alibis for various suspects of a crime
Summons to appear in court
Traffic ticket
*Encyclopaedia Britannica* entry
Map—directions
Itinerary
Index
Treatment (as for a movie script)
Tarot deck
Reenactment
Recipe
Reminiscence
Letter to the editor
Crime scene investigation report
Pardon
Warning sign
Will
Paperwork to release a lien
Test results
Contest results
Court proceedings
Employee manual
Editorial (and editorial reply)
Commencement speech
Eulogy
Suicide note

Obituary

Manifesto

Ledger

Preamble

Song lyrics

Handbill, leaflet, circular

Stock market analysis

Mission statement

Hunting permit

Budget

Wedding vows

Adoption papers

Questionnaire

Ten Commandments (rewritten)

Thirteen Ways of Looking at ___

Meeting minutes

Memorandum

Graduate school application personal
    statement

Divorce papers

Grant application

Teaching philosophy

Notes from a stakeout

Surveillance report

Party invite

Thank-you note

Legend to an old or new map

GPS directions

Witches' spell/brew

Contract

Weather report

FAA black box recording transcript

Advice column

Resume

Curriculum vitae

Movie review

Letter of application

Resignation letter

Restaurant review

Grimm's fairy tale (rewritten)

Rubric

Exam

Term paper

CliffsNotes

Compare and contrast essay

Formulaic five-paragraph essay

Cause and effect essay

How-to essay

Process essay

Dissertation

Book report

Fashion blueprint

Classification essay

Feedback form

Registration form

Order form

Convention brochure

In-flight disaster instructions/plan

Press release

Scientific report

Journal entry

Nature show script

List of ingredients

Chemical analysis

Taxicab radio transcript

Menu

Stage directions

Fax cover sheet

Abstract

Case study

Q & A

Jacket copy

Introductory chapter

Plea

Grocery list

Footnotes

Dream/nightmare diary

Photograph captions

Long, long sentence

Puzzle

IQ test

Pocket guide

Collage

Puzzle

Year-end report

Job listing

Almanac

World records

Acknowledgments

Disclaimer

Porno script

Delicatessen board

To-go menu

Poison antidote

Last rites

Origin/creation story

Auditory transcript of a tour (e.g. Alcatraz Island)

Subway or bus schedule

First words

Last words

Final prognosis

eBay ad

Death report

Birth certificate

Safety instructions

Acceptance speech/letter

Credits

Thesaurus entry

Dictionary

Debate

Computer simulation study

Text message

Email

Blog post

Lesson plan

Post-it note reminder

Daily minder

Trial transcript

Alternate route directions

Draft notice

Checklist

Statute of limitations for various things

Evidence allowable in court

Exhibits A, B, C

Manifestos

Statements

Speeches

Maxims

Epistles

Diaristic jottings

Narratives

Natural Histories

Performances

Ramblings

Revelations

Ephemera

Countdown

Yearbook

Group portrait

Table of contents

Mail order catalog

Battle plan

Government files

Corporate memos

Police reports and eyewitness
   statements

Patents

Pawn tickets

# Source Acknowledgments

Grateful acknowledgment is made to all those who gave permission for previously published material to appear in this book.

"Grand Theft Auto," by Joey Franklin, was originally published in *The Normal School* 7 (Fall 2011).

"Genome Tome," by Priscilla Long, was originally published in *The American Scholar* 74, no. 3 (Summer 2005). It appears here in its original, unrevised form by permission of University of Georgia Press. All rights reserved.

"As Is," by Brian Oliu, was originally published in the online journal *Booth* in September 2010.

"Son of Mr. Green Jeans: An Essay on Fatherhood, Alphabetically Arranged," by Dinty W. Moore, was originally published in *Crazyhorse* no. 63 (Spring 2003). It was reprinted in *Between Panic and Desire*, also by Dinty W. Moore (Lincoln: University of Nebraska Press, 2008). Copyright 2008 by Dinty W. Moore. Used by permission of the University of Nebraska Press.

"Snakes & Ladders," by Anushka Jasraj, was originally published in *The Lifted Brow* 34 (June 2017).

"We Regret to Inform You," by Brenda Miller, was originally published in *The Sun*, 445 (November 2013). It was re-printed in *An Earlier Life*, also by Brenda Miller (Port Townsend WA: Ovenbird Books, 2016). Copyright 2016 by Brenda Miller. Used by permission of the author.

"The Six Answers on the Back of a Trivia Card," by Caitlin Horrocks, was originally published in *The Normal School* 4 (Spring 2010) as "The Six Answers on the Back of a Trivial Pursuit Card (Genus Edition, Volume Six)."

"Self-Portrait as a 1970s Cineplex Movie Theatre (an Abecedarian)," by Steve Fellner, was originally published online by *The Normal School* in July 2015.

"Section 404," by Cheyenne Nimes, originally appeared in DIAGRAM 10, no.1 as "Section 404 of the Clean Water Act and the Santa Cruz River Sand Shark, Subtitled 'This Troublesome Regulatory Constraint.'"

"The Body (an Excerpt)" was originally published as part of *The Body: An Essay*, by Jenny Boully (Essay Press, 2007), and is reprinted here by permission of the author.

"Questionnaire for My Grandfather," by Kim Adrian, was originally published in the *Gettysburg Review* 18, no.2 (Summer 2005).

"What Signifies (Three Parables)," by David Shields, is a collage of three previously published essays (or parts thereof), including "A Fable" and "Another Fable" from *Other People: Takes and Mistakes*, by David Shields. Copyright 2017 by David Shields. Used by permission of Alfred A. Knopf, an imprint of the Knopf Doubleday Publishing Group, a division of Penguin Random House LLC. All rights reserved. "Information Sickness" was originally published in *Zyzzyva* (Spring 1993); the version used in "What Signifies (Three Parables)" has been excerpted from that essay as it appears in *Remote*, by David Shields. Copyright 2003 by the Board of Regents of the University of Wisconsin System. Reprinted by permission of the University of Wisconsin Press. All rights reserved.

"The Heart as a Torn Muscle," by Randon Billings Noble, was originally published in *Brevity* 48 (Winter 2015).

"'Easy as Pie,' That's a Lie," by Amy Wallen, was originally published in *The Normal School* 10 (Spring 2013).

"Outline toward a Theory of the Mine Versus the Mind and the Harvard Outline," by Ander Monson, was originally published in the *Seneca Review*, 34, no. 1 (Spring 2004). It was re-printed in *Neck-Deep and Other Predicaments: Essays* (Saint Paul: Graywolf, 2007). Copyright © 2007 by Ander Monson. Used by permission of Graywolf Press. All rights reserved.

"The Clockwise Detorsion of Snails: A Love Essay in Sectors," by Karen Hays, was originally published in *The Normal School* 5 (Fall 2010).

# Contributors

**Kim Adrian** (editor) is the author of *The Twenty-Seventh Letter of the Alphabet*, a memoir, and *Sock*, a Bloomsbury "Object Lessons" book. She is a visiting lecturer in the Nonfiction Writing Program at Brown University.

**Judy Bolton-Fasman**'s essays have appeared in the online venues the *Rumpus*, *Brevity*, *Lunch Ticket*, *1966: A Journal of Creative Nonfiction*, *Cognoscenti*, *Split Lip Magazine*, and elsewhere. She has completed a memoir entitled "Asylum Avenue." Judy lives outside of Boston with her family.

**Jenny Boully** is the author of *Betwixt and Between: Essays on the Writing Life*, *The Body: An Essay*, *The Book of Beginnings and Endings: Essays, not merely because of the unknown that was stalking toward them*, and *[one love affair]\**. She teaches creative writing at Columbia College Chicago.

**Laurie Easter**'s work has appeared in *Chautauqua*, the *Rumpus*, *Under the Gum Tree*, *Hippocampus Magazine*, and elsewhere. She holds an MFA from Vermont College of Fine Arts and is a creative nonfiction editor at *Hunger Mountain*.

**Steve Edwards** is the author of the memoir *Breaking into the Backcountry*, the story of his seven months as caretaker of a backcountry homestead along the Rogue River in Oregon. His writing has appeared in *Orion Magazine*, the *Rumpus*, *Electric Literature*, *LitHub*, and elsewhere. He lives in Massachusetts.

**Steve Fellner** lives in western New York.

**Joey Franklin**'s first book, *My Wife Wants You to Know I'm Happily Married*, won the 2015 Association of Mormon Letters book prize for nonfiction and was a finalist for the 2016 Utah Book Award. He teaches literature and creative writing at Brigham Young University in Provo, Utah.

**Karen Hays** received a 2014 Rona Jaffe Foundation Writer's Award for her nonfiction, which can be found in *Conjunctions*, *Passages North*, the *Iowa Review*, the *Georgia Review*, and *The Normal School*.

**Caitlin Horrocks** is the author of the story collection *This Is Not Your City*. Her stories and essays appear in the *New Yorker*, the *Best American Short Stories*, the PEN/O. *Henry Prize Stories*, the *Pushcart Prize*, the *Paris Review*, *Tin House*, and elsewhere. She is fiction editor of the *Kenyon Review* and teaches at Grand Valley State University.

**Anushka Jasraj** was born and brought up in Bombay, India. She holds an MFA in creative writing from the University of Texas–Austin and was a regional winner of the 2012 Commonwealth Short Story Prize. Most recently she was a writing fellow at the Fine Arts Work Center in Provincetown. She is currently writing a thesis on Emily Dickinson.

**Ingrid Jendrzejewski** studied creative writing at the University of Evansville and then physics at the University of Cambridge. Her work has appeared in *Passages North*, the *Los Angeles Review*, the *Conium Review* and the *Mainichi*. She is the recipient of the Bath Flash Fiction Award and the A Room of Her Own Foundation's Orlando Prize.

**Elizabeth Kerlikowske** is president of Friends of Poetry (Kalamazoo, Michigan). Her latest chapbook is *Chain of Lakes* (Kalamazoo Book Arts Center). She is collaborating on a book of poems from paintings with artist Mary Hatch. "Petoskey Catechism" is one of these. The book is due out in spring 2018.

**Kathryn A. Kopple** works in Spanish and English. She is the editor of the Latin American section of The Sunflower Collective and translates for TED. Her original poetry and prose have appeared in the *Threepenny Review*, the *Bellevue Review*, and *Oblong*. She is the author of *Little Velásquez* (Mirth Press).

**Priscilla Long** is the author, most recently, of *Fire and Stone: Where Do We Come From? What Are We? Where Are We Going?* (University of Georgia Press, 2016). Other books include *Crossing Over: Poems*; *The Writer's Portable Mentor: A Guide to Art, Craft, and the Writing Life*; *Minding the Muse: A Handbook for Painters, Composers, Writers, and Other Creators*; and *Where the Sun Never Shines: A History of America's Bloody Coal Industry*.

**Michael Martone** was born in Fort Wayne and grew up there in a foursquare house (the kind that could be ordered from the Sears, Roebuck catalog, the kit delivered in pieces by train car and truck to the lot) on Spring Street in the part of town known as North Highlands or Hungry Hill. It was the highest elevation of "Summit City," Fort Wayne's nickname, derived from the old days when Fort Wayne was the highest point on the canal. Fort Wayne curiously enough is located on a continental divide. Rain that falls on the south side of the city flows south into creeks and rivers and eventually finds its way into the Gulf of Mexico. Rain falling on the north side travels along with the rivers through the Great Lakes into the Atlantic. It is only a matter of a few feet either way. So when the rain does rain, it pools and swamps in the fields and open lots as if it is making up its mind, considering which way to flow. So it floods a lot. One-hundred-year floods arrive, it seems, every other year. Martone was there during the Flood of 1982 when President Ronald Reagan arrived by helicopter to survey the slow disaster. Floods in Fort Wayne are always slow disasters. No rapids, just steady seeping, a gentle swell, the water flat, smooth, and calm like the land it spreads a sheet over. The president's helicopter's rotor wash agitated the water Martone waded in into waves. President Reagan worked his way into the line passing sandbags, building a wall to staunch the St. Mary River near the old canal viaduct. Martone ended up cradling the soggy burlap bag that the president forwarded to him. He has it still. Martone went back to the wreck of the levee after the water receded and retrieved the souvenir of the encounter. Now when he moves, he boxes the bag of sand and transports it from house to house to house, usually displaying it on the fireplace mantle or on the coffee table between the couch and the flat-screen TV. It is always a conversation starter. The president wore a dark blue suit and a tie with a pattern of polka dots. Someone had given him overshoes for the mud, but there still was mud smeared up one pant leg, Martone remembers. They didn't speak. The only sound was the gurgling of the river water on the other side of the saturated levee, the heavy breathing as the hefty sandbags were lifted, and the snap and whir of the cameras taking pictures that, Martone remembers, were keeping a kind of time with the syncopated rhythm of the passing bags. North Highlands, where Martone grew up, had the elevation to survive that flood and all of the others. It got its name Hungry Hill from a time before cars and trucks when the horse drays and wagons stalled on the snow-covered grades, unable to deliver food to the markets there. It is hard for Martone to imagine how his house on Spring Street in the North Highlands neighborhood of Fort Wayne could have been so remote and isolated, the little summit leveled by the more powerful machines that have always been present in his life. Outside his bedroom window each night he would fall asleep watching the strobing lights of the nearby television and radio towers erected to utilize the additional elevation of the topography to boost their signals. There were a dozen of them and more were being built. At night you could not see the steely stitched towers themselves, ribbed with x-ing struts, climbing like articulated zippers, but you could see their navigational beacons. Red. Flashing in different sequences. Some slower. Some with some speed. The blinking lights would not lull Martone to sleep; instead he would wait, wait to see if all the flashing lights, climbing ever higher into the dark sky, would cycle around to the same illuminated moment, synchronize finally into one bright explosion of red light and then go, everywhere and all at once, black.

**Sarah McColl**'s essays have appeared in *McSweeney's Internet Tendency*, *Green Mountains Review*, *South Dakota Review*, and *StoryQuarterly*, where she was second runner-up for the 2016 Nonfiction Prize judged by Meghan Daum. She holds an MFA from Sarah Lawrence College and has received fellowships from the MacDowell Colony and Vermont Studio Center. She lives in Brooklyn, New York.

**Jennifer Metsker** is the writing coordinator at the Stamps School of Art and Design. Her poetry has appeared in the *Cincinnati Review*, the *Southern Review*, *Cimarron Review*, *Gulf Coast*, and many other places. Her art reviews appear in *Arthopper* and *Carbon Culture*, and her audio poetry has been featured on the BBC radio show *Short Cuts*.

**Brenda Miller** is the author of five essay collections, most recently *An Earlier Life* (Ovenbird Books), which received the 2017 Washington State Book Award in memoir. She coauthored *Tell It Slant: Creating, Refining, and Publishing Creative Nonfiction*, and *The Pen and The Bell: Mindful Writing in a Busy World*. Her work has received six Pushcart Prizes. She teaches in the MFA programs at Western Washington University and the Rainier Writing Workshop.

**Ander Monson** is the author of six books of nonfiction, fiction, and poetry, most recently *Letter to a Future Lover* (Graywolf). He directs the MFA program at the University of Arizona and edits the magazine *DIAGRAM*, the New Michigan Press, Essay Daily, and *March Fadness* (the most recent yearly entry in *March Xness*).

**Dinty W. Moore** is author of *The Story Cure: A Book Doctor's Pain-Free Guide to Finishing Your Novel or Memoir*, the memoir *Between Panic and Desire*, and other books. He has published work in *Harpers*, the *New York Times Sunday Magazine*, *The Normal School*, and many other venues. Moore lives in Athens, Ohio, where he grows heirloom tomatoes and edible dandelions.

**Cheyenne Nimes** is a cross-genre writer currently working on poetry/nonfiction hybrids on the nature of evil and Jonestown. She is an NEA recipient in poetry and was a University of Iowa Art Museum resident writer.

**Randon Billings Noble**'s work has appeared in the *New York Times*, the *Georgia Review*, *Fourth Genre*, and elsewhere. Her chapbook, *Devotional*, was published by Red Bird, and her essay collection, *Be With Me Always*, is forthcoming from the University of Nebraska Press in 2019. A Mid Atlantic Arts Foundation Creative Fellow, she has been a resident at the Millay Colony for the Arts and the Virginia Center for the Creative Arts.

**Brian Oliu** is the author of two chapbooks and four full-length collections, *So You Know It's Me* (Tiny Hardcore Press), *Leave Luck to Heaven* (Uncanny Valley Press), *Enter Your Initials For Record Keeping* (Cobalt Press), and *i/o* (Civil Coping Mechanisms). He is at work on a memoir as well as two books on professional wrestling.

**Mary Peelen** writes poetry, fiction, and nonfiction. Her work has appeared in *Alaska Quarterly Review*, *Michigan Quarterly Review*, *New American Writing*, the *Massachusetts Review*, *Antioch Review*, and other journals. She lives in San Francisco.

**David Shields** is the internationally best-selling author of twenty books, including *Reality Hunger, The Thing about Life Is that One Day You'll Be Dead, Black Planet*, and most recently, *Other People: Takes and Mistakes*. He has received Guggenheim and NEA fellowships; his work has been translated into twenty languages.

**Judith Sornberger**'s latest poetry book is *Practicing the World without You* (Cavan Kerry Press, 2018). She's the author of the poetry collection *Open Heart* (Calyx Books) and five chapbooks, including *Wal-Mart Orchid*, winner of the 2012 Helen Kay Chapbook Prize. Her memoir, *The Accidental Pilgrim: Finding God and His Mother in Tuscany*, was published by Shanti Arts Publications in 2015.

**Lee Upton**'s most recent books are *Visitations: Stories* and *Bottle the Bottles the Bottles the Bottles: Poems*. Her first collection of short stories, *The Tao of Humiliation*, won the BOA Short Fiction Award, was a finalist for the Paterson Prize, and was named one of the "best books of 2014" by *Kirkus Reviews*. She is the Francis A. March Professor of English and writer-in-residence at Lafayette College.

**Gwendolyn Wallace** is a high school senior from Connecticut. This is her first publication.

**Amy Wallen**, author of the best-selling novel *MoonPies and Movie Stars*, is associate director at New York State Summer Writers' Institute. Her essays have appeared in the *Gettysburg Review, The Normal School, Country Living*, the *Writers' Chronicle* and elsewhere. Her memoir, *When We Were Ghouls: A Memoir of Ghost Stories*, is part of the American Lives Series published by the University of Nebraska Press (2018).